Decompiling Java

GODFREY NOLAN

Apress®

Decompiling Java
Copyright © 2004 by Godfrey Nolan

Lead Editor: Gary Cornell

Technical Reviewer: John Zukowski

Editorial Board: Steve Anglin, Dan Appleman, Ewan Buckingham, Gary Cornell, Tony Davis, John Franklin, Jason Gilmore, Chris Mills, Steve Rycroft, Dominic Shakeshaft, Jim Sumser, Karen Watterson, Gavin Wray, John Zukowski

Project Manager: Tracy Brown Collins

Copy Edit Manager: Nicole LeClerc

Copy Editor: Rebecca Rider

Production Manager: Kari Brooks

Production Editor: Katie Stence

Proofreader: Linda Seifert

Compositor and Artist: Kinetic Publishing Services, LLC

Indexer: Rebecca Plunkett

Cover Designer: Kurt Krames

Manufacturing Manager: Tom Debolski

Library of Congress Cataloging-in-Publication Data
Nolan, Godfrey.
    Decompiling Java / Godfrey Nolan.
        p. cm.
    Includes index.
    ISBN 1-59059-265-4 (alk. paper)
    1. Java (Computer program language)   I. Title.

    QA76.73.J38N65   2004
    005.13'3—dc22   2004014051

Printed and bound in the United States of America 9 8 7 6 5 4 3 2 1

Distributed to the book trade in the United States by Springer-Verlag New York, Inc., 175 Fifth Avenue, New York, NY 10010 and outside the United States by Springer-Verlag GmbH & Co. KG, Tiergartenstr. 17, 69112 Heidelberg, Germany.

In the United States: phone 1-800-SPRINGER, e-mail orders@springer-ny.com, or visit http://www.springer-ny.com. Outside the United States: fax +49 6221 345229, e-mail orders@springer.de, or visit http://www.springer.de.

For information on translations, please contact Apress directly at 2560 Ninth Street, Suite 219, Berkeley, CA 94710. Phone 510-549-5930, fax 510-549-5939, e-mail info@apress.com, or visit http://www.apress.com.

The source code for this book is available to readers at http://www.apress.com in the Downloads section.

In memory of Hanpeter Van Vliet

Contents at a Glance

About the Author .... *ix*

About the Technical Reviewer .... *xi*

Acknowledgments .... *xiii*

Chapter 1   Introduction *1*

Chapter 2   Ghost in the Machine *17*

Chapter 3   Tools of the Trade *61*

Chapter 4   Protecting Your Source: Strategies for
             Defeating Decompilers *79*

Chapter 5   Decompiler Design *121*

Chapter 6   Decompiler Implementation *159*

Chapter 7   Case Studies *237*

Appendix   Classfile Grammar *247*

Index *255*

Contents

About the Author . . . . *ix*

About the Technical Reviewer . . . . *xi*

Acknowledgments . . . . *xiii*

Chapter 1 Introduction *1*

Compilers and Decompilers *2*
Virtual Machine Decompilers *3*
Why Java? *3*
History: Basic Chronology *6*
Legal Issues *9*
Moral Issues *12*
Protecting Yourself *13*
Book Outline *15*
Conclusion *16*

Chapter 2 Ghost in the Machine *17*

The JVM: An Exploitable Design? *18*
Inside a Classfile *22*
Conclusion *60*

Chapter 3 Tools of the Trade *61*

Employing Hexadecimal Editors *61*
The Problem of Insecure Code *64*
Disassemblers *67*
Decompilers *72*
Obfuscators *75*
Conclusion *76*

Chapter 4 Protecting Your Source: Strategies for Defeating Decompilers 79

Compilation Flags 81
Writing Two Versions of the Applet or Application 86
Employing Obfuscation 88
Web Services and Server-Side Execution 106
Encryption 108
Digital Rights Management 109
Fingerprinting Your Code 110
Selling the Source Code 117
Native Methods 117
Conclusion 119

Chapter 5 Decompiler Design 121

Introduction 122
Defining the Problem 125
(De)Compiler Tools 128
Strategy 141
Parser Design 149
Conclusion 157

Chapter 6 Decompiler Implementation 159

ClassToXML Output: An Overview 159
JLex Specification 165
CUP Specification 170
Test Suite 182
Summarizing Decompiler Implementation 233
Conclusion 236

Chapter 7 Case Studies 237

Case Studies 237
Conclusion 244

Appendix Classfile Grammar 247

Index 255

About the Author

Godfrey Nolan is President of RIIS LLC, where he specializes in web site optimization. He has written numerous articles for different magazines and newspapers in the US, the UK, and Ireland. Godfrey has had a healthy obsession with reverse engineering bytecode ever since he wrote "Decompile Once, Run Anywhere," which first appeared in *Web Techniques* in September 1997.

About the Technical Reviewer

John Zukowski is a freelance writer and strategic Java consultant for JZ Ventures, Inc. His latest endeavor is to create a next-generation mobile phone platform with SavaJe Technologies. Look for the 1.5 edition of his *Definitive Guide to Swing for Java 2* in the fall of 2004 (also published by Apress).

Acknowledgments

THERE ARE COUNTLESS PEOPLE I have to thank in some small way for helping me with this book. Apologies if I've forgotten anyone.

- My wife, Nancy, and also my children, Rory and Dayna, for putting up with all the times I've missed a family outing while writing this book. And we're talking lots and lots of missed outings.

- Jonathon Kade, for all your hard work helping with the decompiler and Chapter 6 in general.

- Gary Cornell, without whom this book would never have seen the light of day.

- Tracy Brown Collins and Rebecca Rider at Apress, for putting up with my countless missed deadlines. Do I need to say lots and lots again?

- John Zukowski, for all the helpful comments. And yes, I'm still ignoring the one about having a comma in Hello World.

- Dave and Michelle Kowalske and all my other in-laws, for knowing when not to ask, "Is that book finished yet?"

- Finally, to my parents, who have always taught me to aim high and who have supported me when, more often than not, I fell flat on my face.

CHAPTER 1

Introduction

WHEN COREL BOUGHT WordPerfect for almost $200 million from the Novell Corporation in the mid 1990s, nobody would have thought that in a matter of months they would have been giving away the source code free. However, when Corel ported WordPerfect to Java and released it as a beta product, a simple program called Mocha[1] could quickly and easily reverse engineer, or decompile, significant portions of Corel's Office for Java back into source code.

Decompilation is the process that transforms machine-readable code into a human readable format. When an executable, a Java class file, or a DLL is decompiled, you don't quite get the original format; instead you get a type of pseudo source code, often incomplete and almost always without the comments. But often what you get is more than enough to understand the original code.

The purpose of this book is to address an unmet need in the programming community. For some reason, the ability to decompile Java has been largely ignored even though it is relatively easy for anyone with the appropriate mindset to do. In this book, I would like to redress the balance by looking at what tools and tricks of the trade are currently being employed by people who are trying to recover source code and those who are trying to protect it using, for example, obfuscation.

This book is for those who want to learn Java by decompilation, those who simply want to learn how to decompile Java into source code, those who want to protect their code, and finally those who want to better understand Java bytecodes and the Java Virtual Machine (JVM) by building a Java decompiler.

This book takes your understanding of decompilers and obfuscators to the next level by

- Exploring Java bytecodes and opcodes in an approachable but detailed manner.

- Using examples that show you what to do when an applet only partially decompiles.

- Providing you with simple strategies you can use to show users how to protect their code.

- Showing you what it takes to build your own decompiler.

---

1. Mocha was one of the early Java decompilers. You'll see more on Mocha later in this chapter.

Compilers and Decompilers

Computer languages were developed because most normal people cannot work in machine code or its nearest equivalent, Assembler. Thankfully, we realized pretty early in computing technology that humans just weren't cut out to program in machine code. Computer languages, such as Fortran, COBOL, C, Visual Basic, and more recently, Java and C#, were developed to allow us to put our ideas in a human-friendly format that can then be converted into a format that a computer chip can understand.

At its most basic, the compiler's job is to translate this textual representation— source code—into a series of 0's and 1's—machine code—which the computer can interpret as actions or steps that you want it to perform. It does this using a series of pattern matching rules. A lexical analyzer tokenizes the source code[2] and any mistakes or words that are not in the compiler's lexicon are rejected immediately. These tokens are then passed to the language parser, which matches one or more tokens to a series of rules and translates these tokens into intermediate code (some early versions of Visual Basic, Pascal, and Java) or sometimes straight into machine code (C and Fortran). Any source code that doesn't match a compiler's rules is rejected and the compilation fails.

So now you know what a compiler does. Well, to be honest, you've only scratched the surface; compiler technology has always been a specialized, and sometimes complicated, area of computing. Modern advances mean things are going to get even more complicated, especially in the virtual machine domain. In part, this drive comes from Java and now .NET. Just in Time (JIT) compilers have tried to close the gap between Java and C++ execution times by optimizing the execution of Java bytecodes. This seems like an impossible task because Java bytecode is, after all, interpreted, whereas C++ is compiled. But JIT compiler technology is making significant advances and is also making Java compilers and virtual machines much more complicated beasts by incorporating these advances.

From your point of view, you need to know that most compilers do a lot of preprocessing and post-processing. The preprocessor readies the source code for the lexical analysis by stripping out all unnecessary information, such as the programmer's comments, and adding in any standard or included header files or packages. A typical post-processor stage is code optimization, where the compiler parses or scans the code, reorders it, and removes any redundancies, which will hopefully increase the efficiency and speed of your code.

Decompilers, no big surprise here, translate the machine code or intermediate code back into source code. In other words, the whole process is reversed. Machine code is tokenized in some way and parsed or translated back into source code. This transformation rarely results in original source code because some information is lost in the pre- and post-processing stages.

---

2. *Lexical* comes from the word lexicon or dictionary.

Take the analogy of idioms in human languages, which are often the most difficult part of a sentence or phrase to translate. My favorite idiom is *L'esprit d'escalier*, which literally translates as *the wit of the staircase*. But what it really means is that perfect witty comment or comeback that pops into your head half an hour too late. Similarly (and I know I'm stretching it a bit here) source code can often be translated into machine code in more than one way. Java source code is designed for humans and not computers, and often some steps may be redundant or can be performed more quickly in a slightly different order. Because of these lost elements, few (if any) decompilations result in the original source.

Virtual Machine Decompilers

Several notable attempts have been made to decompile machine code; Christina Cifuentes' dcc is one of the most recent.[3] However, at the machine code level, the data and instructions are commingled, and it is a much more difficult, but not impossible, to recover the original code.

In a virtual machine, the code has simply passed through a preprocessor and the decompiler's job becomes one of simply reversing the preprocessing stages of compilation. This makes interpreted code much, much easier to decompile. Sure, there are no comments, and worse still, no specification, but then again, there are also no research and development (R&D) costs.

Why Java?

The original JVM was designed to run on a TV cable set-top box. As such, it was a very small stack machine that pushed and popped its instructions on and off a stack using only a limited instruction set. This made the instructions very easy to understand with relatively little practice. Because the compilation process was a two-stage process, the JVM also required the compiler to pass on a lot of information, such as variable and method names, that would not otherwise be available. These names could be almost as helpful as comments when you were trying to understand decompiled source code.

The current design of the JVM is independent of the Java 2 Software Development Kit (SDK). In other words, the language and libraries may change, but the JVM and the opcodes are fixed. This means that if Java is prone to decompilation now, then it is always likely to be prone to decompilation. In many cases, as you shall see, decompiling a Java class is as easy as running a simple DOS or Unix command.

---

3. dcc comes from cc, which used to be the standard command-line command for compiling C programs, and still is, if like me you're IDE impaired.

In the future, the JVM may very well be changed to stop decompilation, but this would break any backward compatibility and all current Java code would have to be recompiled. And although this has happened before in the Microsoft world with different versions of Visual Basic, a lot more companies than Sun develop virtual machines.

JVMs are now available for almost every operating system and web browser. In fact, Java applets and applications can run on any computer or chip from a mainframe right down to a handheld or a smartcard as long as a JVM and appropriate class libraries exists for that platform. So it's no longer as simple as changing one JVM.

What makes this situation even more interesting is that companies that want to Java enable their operating system or browser usually create their own JVMs. Sun is now only really responsible for the JVM specification. It seems that things have now progressed so far that any fundamental changes to the JVM specification would have to be backward compatible. Modifying the JVM to prevent decompilation would require significant surgery, and in all probability, it would break this backward compatibility, thus ensuring that Java classes will decompile for the foreseeable future.

It's true that no such compatibility restrictions exist on the Java SDK, where more and more functionality is added almost daily. And the first crop of decompilers did dramatically fail when inner classes were first introduced in the Java Development Kit (JDK) 1.1. However, this isn't really a surprise because Mocha was already a year out of date when 1.1 was released and other decompilers were quickly modified to recognize inner classes.

Top Ten Reasons Why Java Is More Vulnerable to Decompilation

1. For portability, Java code is partially compiled and then interpreted by the JVM.

2. Java's compiled classes contain a lot of symbolic information for the JVM.

3. Because of backward compatibility issues, the JVM's design is not likely to change.

4. The JVM has very few instructions or opcodes.

5. The JVM is a simple stack machine.

6. Standard applets and applications have no real protection against decompilation.

7. Java applets are typically small and therefore intelligible without comments.

8. Larger Java applications are automatically compiled into smaller modular classes.

9. Java applets are typically downloaded for free.

10. Java hype and cutthroat competition equal plenty of applications and plenty of people willing to decompile them.

So unlike other Java books, I don't expect that this book will go out of date with the next release of the JDK. Sure, some extra features may be added, but the underlying architecture will remain the same. Let's begin with a simple example in Listing 1-1.

Listing 1-1. Simple Java Source Code Example

```java
public class Casting {
    public static void main(String args[]){
        for(char c=0; c < 128; c++) {
                System.out.println("ascii " + (int)c + " character "+ c);
        }
    }
}
```

Listing 1-2 shows the output for a simple class file whose source is shown in Listing 1-1 using javap, Sun's class file disassembler that came with the original versions of Sun's JDK. You can decompile Java so easily because, as you'll see later in the book, the JVM is a simple stack machine with no registers and a limited number of high-level instructions or opcodes.

Listing 1-2. Javap Output

```
Compiled from Casting.java
public synchronized class Casting extends java.lang.Object
    /* ACC_SUPER bit set */
{
    public static void main(java.lang.String[]);
/* Stack=4, Locals=2, Args_size=1 */
    public Casting();
/* Stack=1, Locals=1, Args_size=1 */
}
```

```
Method void main(java.lang.String[])
    0 iconst_0
    1 istore_1
    2 goto 41
    5 getstatic #12 <Field java.io.PrintStream out>
    8 new #6 <Class java.lang.StringBuffer>
   11 dup
   12 ldc #2 <String "ascii ">
   14 invokespecial #9 <Method java.lang.StringBuffer(java.lang.String)>
   17 iload_1
   18 invokevirtual #10 <Method java.lang.StringBuffer append(char)>
   21 ldc #1 <String " character ">
   23 invokevirtual #11 <Method java.lang.StringBuffer append(java.lang.String)>
   26 iload_1
   27 invokevirtual #10 <Method java.lang.StringBuffer append(char)>
   30 invokevirtual #14 <Method java.lang.String toString()>
   33 invokevirtual #13 <Method void println(java.lang.String)>
   36 iload_1
   37 iconst_1
   38 iadd
   39 i2c
   40 istore_1
   41 iload_1
   42 sipush 128
   45 if_icmplt 5
   48 return

Method Casting()
    0 aload_0
    1 invokespecial #8 <Method java.lang.Object()>
    4 return<
```

It should be obvious that a lot of the source code information exists in a class file; my aim is to show you how to take this information and reverse engineer it into source code. However, in many cases, Java classes won't decompile without some extra effort; you'll need to understand the underlying design and architecture of a Java classfile and the JVM itself, which is what I'm going to provide you with in the remainder of this book.

History: Basic Chronology

Since before the dawn of the humble PC . . . . Scratch that. Since before the dawn of COBOL, decompilers have been around in one form or another. In fact, you have to go all the way back to ALGOL to find the earliest example of a decompiler. Donnelly and Englander wrote D-Neliac at the Naval Electronic Labs (NEL) in 1960. Its primary function was to convert non-Neliac compiled programs into Neliac compatible binaries. Neliac was an ALGOL-type language that stood for the Navy Electronics Laboratory International ALGOL Compiler.

Over the years, there have been other decompilers for COBOL, Ada, Fortran, and many other esoteric as well as mainstream languages running on IBM mainframes, PDP/11s, and Univacs, among others. Probably the main reason for these early developments was to translate software or convert binaries to run on different hardware.

More recently, reverse engineering and the Y2K problem have become the acceptable face of decompilation. Converting legacy code to get around the Y2K problem often required disassembly or full decompilation. Reverse engineering is a huge growth area that has not disappeared since the turn of the millennium. Problems caused by the Dow Jones hitting the 10-thousand mark—ah, such fond memories—and the introduction of the Euro have all caused financial programs to fall over.

Even without these developments reverse engineering techniques are being used to analyze old code, which typically has thousands of incremental changes, in order to remove any redundancies and convert these legacy systems into much more efficient animals.

At a much more basic level, hexadecimal dumps of PC machine code have always given programmers extra insight into how something is achieved or into how to break any artificial restrictions placed on the software. Magazine CDs were either time-bombed or had restricted copies of games; these could be patched to change demonstration copies into full versions of the software using primitive disassemblers such as the DOS debug command.

Anyone well versed in Assembler can learn to quickly spot patterns in code and bypass the appropriate source code fragments. Pirate software is a huge problem for the software industry; disassembling the code is just one technique employed by the professional or amateur bootlegger. Hence the downfall of many an arcane copy protection technique.

However, the DOS debug command and Hexidecimal editors are primitive tools and it would probably be quicker to write the code from scratch than to try to re-create the source code from Assembler. For many years now, traditional software companies have also been involved in reverse engineering software. They have studied new techniques, and their competition has copied these techniques all over the world using reverse engineering and decompilation tools. Generally, this is accomplished using in-house decompilers, which are not for public consumption and are definitely not going to be sold over the counter.

It's likely that the first real Java decompiler was actually written in IBM and not by Hanpeter Van Vliet, author of Mocha. Daniel Ford's whitepaper *Jive: A Java Decompiler,* dated May 1996, appears in IBM Research's search engines. This whitepaper just beat Mocha, which wasn't announced until July 1996.

Academic decompilers such as the University of Queensland's dcc are available in the public domain. Fortunately for the likes of Microsoft, decompiling Office using dcc would create so much code that it would be about as user friendly as Debug or a hexadecimal dump. Most modern commercial software's source code is so large that it becomes unintelligible without the design documents and lots of source code comments. Let's face it; many people's C++ code is hard enough to read six months after they wrote it. So how easy would it be for someone else to decipher C code that came from compiled C++ code without any help, even if the library calls aren't traversed?

What does come as a big surprise is the number of decompilers that are currently available but aren't that well publicized. Decompilers or disassemblers are available for Clipper (Valkyrie), FoxPro (ReFox), Pascal, C (dcc and decomp), Ada, and, of course, Java. Even the Newton, loved by *Doonesbury* aficionados everywhere, isn't safe.

Not surprisingly, decompilers are much more common for interpreted languages, such as Visual Basic, Pascal, or Java, because of the larger amounts of information being passed around. Some even have built-in dynamic compilers that regenerate source code on the fly, which is then subsequently recompiled into machine code, depending on the initial decompilation.

Visual Basic Decompilers

Let's take a look at Visual Basic (VB), another interpreted language, as an example of what can happen to interpreted languages. Early versions of VB were interpreted by the vbrun.dll in a somewhat similar fashion to Java and the JVM; and just like a Java classfile, the source code for VB programs is also bundled within the binary. Bizarrely, Visual Basic 3 retains even more information than Java; this time even the programmer's comments are included.

The original versions of VB generated an intermediate pseudocode, called p-code, which was also in Pascal and originates in the P-System.[4] And before you say anything, yes, Pascal and all its derivatives are just as vulnerable; this statement also includes early versions of Microsoft's C compiler, just so that nobody else feels left out. The p-codes are not dissimilar to bytecodes and are essentially VB opcodes that are interpreted by vbrun.dll at run time. Ever wonder why you need to include vbrun.dll with VB executables? Well now you know—you need to include vbrun.dll so that it can interpret the p-code and execute your program.

Doctor (Hans-Peter) Diettrich from Germany is the author of the eponymously titled DoDi—perhaps the most famous Visual Basic decompiler. These days DoDi—also known as Vbis3—is outdated because it only decompiles VB3 binaries, although there were rumors of a version for VB4. But because VB

---

4. http://www.threedee.com/jcm/psystem/

moved to compiled rather than interpreted code, the number of decompilers completely fell away.

At one time, Visual Basic also had its own culture of decompilers and obfuscators, or protection tools as they're called in VB. Doctor Diettrich provides VBGuard for free on his site, and other programs, such as Decompiler Defeater, Protect, Overwrite, Shield, and VBShield, are available from other sources. But they too have all but disappeared with VB5 and VB6.

This was, of course, before .NET. With the arrival of .NET, we've once again come full circle and VB is once again interpreted. Not surprisingly, we're already seeing decompilers and obfuscators such as the Exemplar and Anakrino decompilers as well as Demeanor and Dotfuscator.

Hanpeter Van Vliet

Oddly enough for a technical subject, this book also has a very human element. Hanpeter Van Vliet wrote the first public domain decompiler, Mocha, while recovering from a cancer operation in the Netherlands. He also wrote an obfuscator called Crema that attempted to protect an applet's source code. If Mocha was the Uzi machine gun, then Crema was the bulletproof jacket. In a now classic Internet marketing strategy, Mocha was free, whereas there was a small charge for Crema.

The beta version of Mocha caused a huge controversy when it was first made available on Hanpeter's web site, especially after it was featured in a *c|net* article. Because of the controversy, Hanpeter took the very honorable step of removing Mocha from his web site. He then held a vote about whether or not Mocha should once again be made available. The vote was ten to one in favor of Mocha, and soon after it reappeared on Hanpeter's web site.

However, Mocha never made it out of beta, and while I was conducting some research for a *Web Techniques* article on this very subject, I learned from his wife that Hanpeter's throat cancer finally got him. He died at the age of 34 on New Year's Eve, 1996.

The source code for both Crema and Mocha were sold to Borland shortly before Hanpeter's death, with all proceeds going to Hanpeter's wife, Ingrid. Some early versions of JBuilder shipped with an obfuscator, which was probably Crema. This *attempted* to protect Java code from decompilation by replacing ASCII variable names with control characters.

I'll talk more about the host of other Java decompilers and obfuscators later in the book.

Legal Issues

Before you start building your own decompiler, why don't you take this opportunity to consider the legal implications of decompiling someone else's code for your own enjoyment or benefit? Just because Java has taken decompiling technology out of some very serious propeller head territory and into more mainstream computing doesn't make it any less likely that you or your company will get sued. It may make it more fun, but you really should be careful.

To start with, why don't you try following this small set of ground rules:

- Do not decompile an applet, recompile it, and then pass it off as your own.

- Don't even think of trying to sell a recompiled applet to any third parties.

- Try not to decompile an applet or application that comes with a license agreement that expressly forbids decompiling or reverse engineering the code.

- Don't decompile an applet to remove any protection mechanisms and then recompile it for your own personal use.

Over the past few years, big business has tilted the law firmly in its favor when it comes to decompiling software. Companies can use a number of legal mechanisms to stop you from decompiling their software; these would leave you with little or no legal defense if you ever had to appear in a court of law if someone discovered that you had decompiled their programs. Patent law, copyright law, anti–reverse engineering clauses in shrinkwrap licenses, as well as a number of laws such as the Digital Millennium Copyright Act (DMCA) may all be used against you. Different laws may apply in different countries or states; for example, the "no reverse engineering clause" software license is a null and void clause in the European Union (EU), but the basic concepts are the same—decompile a program for the purpose of cloning the code into another competitive product and you're probably breaking the law.

The secret here is that you shouldn't be standing, kneeling, or pressing down very hard on the legitimate rights—that is, the copyright rights—of the original author. That's not to say that conditions exist in which it is OK to decompile. However, certain limited conditions do exist where the law actually favors decompilation or reverse engineering through a concept known as *fair use*. From almost the dawning of time, and certainly from the beginning of the industrial age, many of humankind's greatest inventions have come from an individual who has created something special while standing on the shoulders of giants. For example, both the invention of the steam train and the common light bulb were relatively modest incremental steps in technology. The underlying concepts were provided by other people, and it was up to Stephenson or Edison to create the final object. You can see an excellent example of the Stephenson's debt to many other inventors such as James Watt in the following timeline of the invention of the Stephenson's Rocket at http://www.usgennet.org/usa/topic/steam/timeline.html. This concept of standing on the shoulders of giants is one of the reasons why patents first appeared—to allow people to build on other creations while still giving the original inventor some compensation for their initial idea for period of, say, 20 years.

In the software arena, trade secrets are typically protected by copyright law rather than through any patents. Sure, patents can protect certain elements of a program, but it is highly unlikely that a complete program will be protected by a patent or a series of patents. Software companies want to protect their investment, so they typically turn to copyright law or software licenses to prevent people from essentially stealing their research and development efforts.

Copyright law is not rock solid; if it was, there would be no inducement to patent an idea and the patent office would quickly go out of business. Copyright protection does not extend to interfaces of computer programs, and a developer can use the fair use defense if they can prove that they decompiled the program to see how they could interoperate with any unpublished application programming interfaces (APIs) in the program.

If you are living in the EU, then more than likely you work under the *EU Directive on Legal Protection of Computer Programs*. This states that you can decompile programs under certain restrictive circumstances—for example, when you are trying to understand the functional requirements you need to create a compatible interface to your own program. Or, to put it another way, if you need access to the internal calls of a third party program and the authors refuse to divulge the APIs at any price. Then, under the EU directive, you could decompile the code to discover the APIs. However, you'd have to make sure that you were only going to use this information to create an interface to your own program rather than create a competitive product. You also cannot reverse engineer any areas that have been protected in any way.

For many years Microsoft's applications have allegedly gained unfair advantage from underlying unpublished APIs calls to Windows 3.1 and Windows 95 that are orders of magnitude quicker than the published APIs. The Electronic Frontier Foundation (EFF) has come up with a useful road map analogy to help explain this. Say you are trying to travel from Detroit to New York, but your map doesn't show any interstate routes. Sure, you'd eventually get there traveling on the back roads, but the trip would be a lot shorter if you had the Microsoft map, complete with interstates. If these conditions were true, the EU directive would be grounds for disassembling Windows 2000 or Microsoft Office (MSOffice), but you better hire a good lawyer before you try it. Personally, I don't buy it as I can't believe MSOffice could possibly be any slower than it currently is, so if there are any hidden APIs, they certainly don't seem to be causing any impact on the speed of any of the MSOffice applications.

There are precedents that allow legal decompilation in the US too. The most famous case to date is *Sega v. Accolade*.[5] In 1992, Accolade won a case against Sega that ruled that their unauthorized disassembly of the Sega object code was not copyright infringement. Accolade reverse engineered Sega's binaries into an intermediate code that allowed them to extract a software key. This key allowed Accolade's games to interact with Sega Genesis video consoles. Obviously Sega

---

5. http://www.eff.org/Legal/Cases/sega_v_accolade_977f2d1510_decision.html

was not going to give Accolade access to APIs, or in this case, code, to unlock the Sega game platform. The court ruled in favor of Accolade judging that the reverse engineering constituted fair-use. But before you think this gives you carte blanche to decompile code, you might like to know that *Atari v. Nintendo*[6] went against Atari under very similar circumstances.

In conclusion—see you can tell this is the legal section—the court cases in the US and the EU directive stress that under certain circumstances reverse engineering can be used to understand the interoperability and create a program interface. It cannot be used to create a copy to sell as a competitive product. Most Java decompilation will not fall into this interoperability category. It is far more likely that the decompiler wants to pirate the code, or at best, understand the underlying ideas and techniques behind the software.

It is not very clear if reverse engineering to discover how an applet was written would constitute fair use. The US Copyright Act of 1976's exclusion of "any idea, procedure, process, system, method of operation, concept, principle or discovery, regardless of the form in which it is described" makes it sound like the beginning of a defense for decompilation, and fear of the fair use clause is one of the reasons why more and more software patents are being issued. Decompilation to pirate or illegally sell the software cannot be defended.

However, from a developer's point of view, the situation looks bleak. The only protection—in the form of a user's license—is about as useful as the laws against copying music CDs or audiocassettes. It won't physically stop anyone from making illegal copies and it doesn't act as any real deterrent for the home user. No legal recourse will protect your code from a hacker, and it sometimes seems that the people trying to create many of today's secure systems must feel like they are standing on the shoulders of morons. You only have to look at the recent investigation into eBook protection schemes[7] and the whole DeCSS fiasco[8] to see how paper-thin a lot of the recent so called secure systems really are.

Moral Issues

Decompiling Java is an excellent way to learning both the Java language and how the JVM works. It helps people climb up the Java learning curve because they learn by seeing other people's programming techniques. The ability to decompile applets or applications can make the difference between a basic understanding of Java and an in-depth knowledge. Learning by example is one of the most powerful tools. It helps even more if you can pick your own examples and modify them to your own needs.

---

6. http://cyber.law.harvard.edu/openlaw/DVD/cases/atarivnintendo.html

7. http://slashdot.org/article.pl?sid=01/07/17/130226

8. http://cyber.law.harvard.edu/openlaw/DVD/resources.html

However, my book on decompiling would not be complete if I didn't discuss the morality issues behind what amounts to stealing someone else's code. In the early days of software, it was not uncommon to receive the source code with the product. But in the last few decades, market economics have taken over and this practice has almost disappeared with some notable open source exceptions such as GNU and Linux. But now, due to a certain set of circumstances, we find that Java comes complete with its source code.

The author, the publisher, the author's agent, and his agent's mother would like to state that we are not advocating that readers of this book decompile programs for anything other than *educational purposes*. The purpose of this book is to show readers how to decompile source code, but we are not encouraging anyone to decompile other programmers' code and then try to use it, sell it, or repackage it as if it was their own. Please be careful that you do not try to reverse engineer any code that has a licensing agreement stating that you should not decompile it. It is not fair, and you'll only get yourself in trouble. Having said that, there are thousands of applets on the Web, which when decompiled, will help you understand good and bad Java programming techniques.

To a certain extent, I'm pleading the "Don't shoot the messenger" defense. I'm not the first to spot this flaw in Java, and I certainly won't be the last person to write about the subject. My reasons for writing this book are, like the early days of the Internet, fundamentally altruistic. Or, in other words, I found this cool trick and I want to tell everyone about it.

Having said this, let me remind you that you can never be sure that the decompiler generated code that was 100 percent accurate. So you're in for a nasty surprise if you intend to use Java decompilation as the basis for your own products.

Protecting Yourself

Pirated software is a big headache for many software companies and big business for others. At the very least, software pirates could use decompilers to remove any licensing restrictions, but imagine the consequences if the technology was available to decompile Office 2000, recompile it, and sell it as a new competitive product. To a certain extent, that could easily have happened when Corel released the beta version of Corel's Office for Java.

Perhaps this realization is starting to dawn on Java software houses. We are beginning to see two price scales on Java components: one for the classes and one for the source code. This is entirely speculative, but it seems that companies such as Sitraka (now Quest) realized that a certain percentage of their users would decompile their classes, and as a result, a few years ago Sitraka chose to sell the source code for JClass as well as other components. This makes any decompilation redundant as the code is provided along with the classes and it also makes some money for the developer by charging a little extra for the source code.

But is all doom and gloom? Should you just resign yourselves to the fact that Java code can be decompiled or is there anything you can do to protect your code? Here are some options:

- License agreements

- Protection schemes within your code

- Code fingerprinting

- Obfuscation

- Intellectual Property Rights (IPR) protection schemes

- Executable applications

- Server-side code

- Encryption

Although you'll look at all these in more detail later, you should know that the first four only act as deterrents and the last four are effective, but have other implications. Let me explain.

License agreements don't offer any real protection from a programmer who wants to decompile your code.

Spreading protection schemes throughout your code, such as by using combinations of getCodeBase and getDocumentBase or server authentication, is useless because they can be simply commented out of the decompiled code.

Code fingerprinting is what happens when spurious code is used to watermark or fingerprint source code, and it can be used in conjunction with license agreements, but it is only really useful in a court of law. Better decompilation tools will profile the code and remove any extra dummy code.

Obfuscation replaces the method names and variable names in a class file with weird and wonderful names. This is an excellent deterrent, but the source code is still visible and in conjunction with obfuscated code when the better decompilers are used, so often this is not much better than compiling without the debug flag. HoseMocha, another obfuscator, works by adding a spurious *pop* bytecode after every return; it does nothing to the code but it does kill the decompiler. However, developers can quickly modify their decompiler once this becomes apparent, assuming they're still around to make the changes.

IPR protection schemes such as IBM's Cryptolope Live!, InterTrust's DigiBox, and Breaker Technologies' SoftSEAL are normally used to sell HTML documents or audio files on some pay-per-view basis or pay-per-group scheme. However, because they typically have built in trusted HTML viewers, they allow Java applets to be seen but not copied. Unfortunately IPR protection schemes are not cheap.

Worse still, some of the clients are written in 100 percent pure Java and can therefore be decompiled.

The safest protection for Java applications is to compile them into executables. This is an option on many Java compilers—SuperCede, for example. Your code will now be as safe as any C or C++ executables—read a lot safer—but it will no longer be portable because it no longer uses the JVM.

The safest protection for applets is to hide all the interesting code on the web server and only use the applet as a thin, front-end graphical user interface (GUI). This has a downside; it may increase your web server load to unacceptable levels.

Several attempts have been made to encrypt a classfile's content and then decrypt it in the classloader. Although at first glance this seems like an excellent approach, sooner or later the classfile's bytecode has to be decrypted in order to be executed by the JVM, at which point it can be intercepted and decompiled.

Book Outline

Decompiling Java is not a normal Java language book. In fact, it is the complete opposite of a standard Java textbook where the author teaches you how to translate ideas and concepts into Java. You're interested in turning the partially compiled Java bytecodes back into source code so that you can see what the original programmer was thinking. I won't be covering the language structure in depth, except where it relates to bytecodes and the JVM. All emphasis will be on Java's low-level design rather than on the language syntax.

In the first part of this book, Chapters 2 through 4, I'll unravel the Java classfile format and show you how your Java code is stored as bytecode and subsequently executed by the JVM. You'll also look at the theory and practice of decompilation and obfuscation. I'll present some of the decompiler's tricks of the trade and explain how to unravel the Java bytecode of even the most awkward class. You'll look at the different ways people try to protect the source code and, when appropriate, learn to expose any flaws or underlying problems with the different techniques so that you'll be suitably informed before you purchase any source code protection tools.

The second part of this book, Chapters 5 and 6, I will primarily focus on how to write your own Java decompiler. You'll build an extendable Java bytecode decompiler. You'll do this for two reasons. First, although the JVM design is fixed, the language is not. Many of the early decompilers cannot handle Java constructs that appeared in the JDK 1.1, such as inner classes. Second, one of my own personal pet peeves is reading a technical computer book that stops when things are just getting interesting. The really difficult problems are then left to the reader as an exercise. For some unknown reason, this seems to be particularly true of Internet-related books. Partly as a reaction against that mentality, I'm going to go into decompilers in some detail with plenty of practical examples in hopefully as approachable a manner as possible.

And while we're on the subject of pet peeves—sorry, I'll try to keep them to a minimum—I won't be covering a potted history of the Internet or indeed Java. This has been covered too many times before. If you want to know about the ARPANET and Oak, then I'm afraid you're going to have to look elsewhere.[9]

Conclusion

Java decompilation is one of *the* best learning tools for new Java programmers. What better way to find out how to write code than by taking an example off the Internet and decompiling it into source code? It's also a necessary tool when some dotcom web developers have gone belly up and the only way to fix their code is to decompile it yourself. But it's also a menace if you're trying to protect the investment of countless hours of design and development.

The aim of this book is to create some dialog about decompilation and source code protection. I also want to separate the fact from fiction and show you how easy it is to decompile code and what measures you can take to protect it. Both Sun and Microsoft will tell you that decompilation isn't an issue and that a developer can always be trained to read a competitor's Assembler, but separate the data from the instructions and this task becomes orders of magnitude easier. Don't believe it? Then read on and decide for yourself.

---

9. Such as *Core Java 2*, 6th edition, by Cay S. Horstmann and Gary Cornell (Prentice Hall PTR, 2002).

CHAPTER 2

Ghost in the Machine

IF YOU'RE TRYING to understand just how good an obfuscator or decompiler really is, then it helps to be able to see what's going on inside a classfile. Otherwise you're relying on the word of a third-party vendor or, at best, a knowledgeable reviewer. For most people, that's not good enough when you're trying to protect mission critical code. At the very least, you should be able to talk intelligently about the area and ask the obvious questions to understand just what's happening.

Pay no attention to the man behind the curtain.

—Wizard of Oz

At this moment, all sorts of noises are coming out of Microsoft in Redmond saying that there really isn't anything to worry about when it comes to decompiling .NET code. Sure, hasn't everyone been doing it for years at the Assembly level? Similar noises were made when Java was in its infancy.

So, in this chapter, you'll be pulling apart a Java classfile to lay the foundation for the following chapters on obfuscation theory and to help you during the design of your decompiler. In order to get to that stage, you need to understand bytecodes, opcodes, classfiles, and how they relate to the Java Virtual Machine (JVM).

Several very good books are on the market about the JVM. The best is Bill Verner's *Inside the Java Virtual Machine* (McGraw-Hill, 1998). Some of the book's chapters are available online at http://www.artima.com/insidejvm/ed2/. If you can't find this book, then check out Verner's equally excellent "Under the Hood" articles in *JavaWorld*. This series of articles was the original material on which the book was based. Sun's *Java Virtual Machine Specification (2nd Edition)*, written by Tim Lindholm and Frank Yellin, is both comprehensive and very informative for would-be decompiler writers. But because it is a specification, it is not what you would call a good read. This book is available online at http://java.sun.com/docs/books/vmspec or you can purchase it (Addison-Wesley, 1999).

Oddly enough, I've yet to see a book that covers how to build a JVM; every book published so far focuses on the abstract JVM rather than how someone would implement one. With the rise of alternative JVMs from IBM and others, I really expected to see at least one JVM book full of C code for converting bytecode to executable native code, but it never came. Perhaps this is because it would have a very limited audience and its sales would be in the hundreds rather than the thousands.

However, my focus is very different from other JVM books. You could say I'm approaching things from the completely opposite direction. Your task is to get from bytecode to source, whereas everyone else wants to know how source is translated into bytecode and ultimately executed. You should be much more interested in how a classfile can be turned into source rather than how a classfile is interpreted.

In this chapter, you'll be looking at how a classfile can be disassembled into bytecodes and how these bytecodes can be turned into source. Of course, you need to know how each bytecode functions, but you should be less interested in what happens to them when they are within the JVM, and my emphasis will differ accordingly.

The JVM: An Exploitable Design?

Java classfiles are designed to be quickly transmitted across a network or via the Internet. As a result, they are compact and are relatively simple to understand. For portability, a classfile is only partially compiled into bytecodes by javac, Sun's Java compiler. This is then interpreted and executed by a JVM, usually on a completely different machine or operating system.

The JVM's classfile interface is strictly defined by Sun's *Java Virtual Machine Specification*. But how a JVM ultimately turns bytecodes into machine code is left up to the developer. However, that really shouldn't concern you, because once again, your interest should stop at the JVM. It may help if you think of classfiles as being analogous to object files in other languages, such as C or C++, waiting to be linked and executed by the JVM only with a lot more symbolic information.

There are many good reasons why a classfile carries around so much information. For many, the Internet is seen as a bit of a modern day Wild West where crooks and criminals are plotting to infect your hard disk with a virus or waiting to grab any credit card details that might pass their way. As a result, the JVM was designed from the bottom up to protect web browsers from any rogue applets. Through a series of checks, the JVM and the class loader make sure that no malicious code can be uploaded onto a web page.

However, all checks have to be performed lightning-quick to cut down on the download time, so it's not really surprising that the original JVM designers opted for a simple stack machine with lots of information available for those crucial security checks. In fact, the design of the JVM is pretty secure even though some of the early browser implementations made a couple or three serious blunders.

Unfortunately for developers, what keeps the code secure also makes it much easier to decompile. The JVM's restricted execution environment and uncomplicated architecture, as well as the high-level nature of many of its instructions, all conspire against the programmer in favor of the decompiler.

At this point, it is probably also worth mentioning the fragile superclass problem. When a new method is added in C++, all classes that reference that class need to be recompiled. Java gets around this by putting all the necessary symbolic information into the classfile. The JVM then takes care of all the linking and final name resolution, loading all the required classes—including any externally referenced fields and methods—on the fly. This delayed linking or dynamic loading, possibly more than anything else, is why Java is so much more prone to decompilation.

By the way, I'm going to ignore native methods in these discussions. *Native methods,* of course, are when some native C or C++ code is incorporated into the application. This spoils Java application portability, and is one surefire way to prevent a Java program from being decompiled.

So without further ado, let's take a brief look at the design of the JVM.

Simple Stack Machine

The JVM is in essence a simple stack machine with a program register to take care of the program flow thrown in for good luck. The Java class loader takes the class and presents it to the JVM.

You can split the JVM into four separate but distinct parts.

- Heap

- Program counter registers

- Method area

- Stack

Every application or applet has its own heap and method area and every thread has its own register or program counter and program stack. Each program stack is then further subdivided into stack frames, with each method having its own stack frame. That's a lot of information for one paragraph, so in Figure 2-1, I illustrate this in a simple diagram.

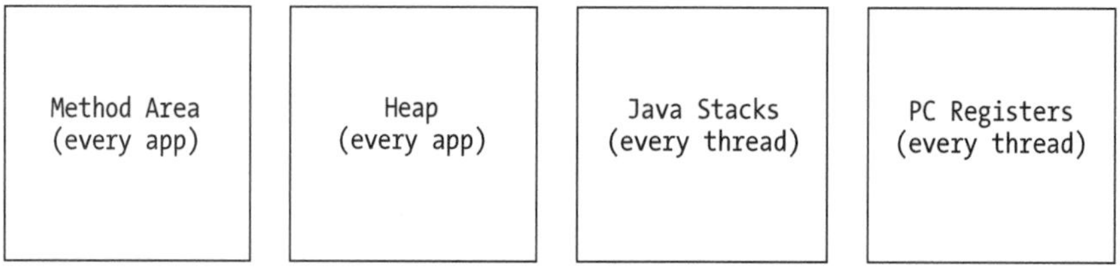

| Method Area (every app) | Heap (every app) | Java Stacks (every thread) | PC Registers (every thread) |

Figure 2-1. The Java Virtual Machine

Heap

I'll deal with the heap first to get it out of the way because it has little or no effect on the Java decompilation process.

Unlike, say, C or C++, Java programmers cannot allocate and deallocate memory; it's all taken care of by the JVM. The new operator allocates objects and memory on the heap, which is automatically freed by the JVM garbage collector when an object is no longer being referenced by the program.

There are several good reasons for this. Security dictates that there are no pointers in Java, so hackers cannot break out of an applet and into the operating system. No pointers mean that someone/thing else—in this case the JVM—has to take care of the allocating and freeing memory. Memory leaks should also become a thing of the past, or so the theory goes. Some applications written in C and C++ are notorious for leaking memory like a sieve because programmers don't pay enough attention to freeing up any unwanted memory at the appropriate point in the program—not that anybody reading this would be guilty of such a sin. Garbage collection should also make programmers more productive with less time spent on debugging memory problems.

However if you do want to know more about what's going on in your heap, try Sun's Heap Analysis Tool (HAT). It uses the hprof file dumps or snapshots of the JVM heap that can be generated by Java 2 SDK, version 1.2 and above. It was designed to, now get this, "debug unnecessary object retention," which translates to memory leaks to you and me. See, garbage collection algorithms, such as reference counting or mark and sweep techniques, aren't 100 percent accurate either. Classfiles can have threads that don't terminate properly, or ActionListeners that fail to deregister, or simply static references to an object that hang around long after the object should have been garbage collected.

HAT has little or no impact on the decompilation process. I only mention it because it's either something interesting to play with or a crucial utility that helps debug your Java code, depending on your mindset or where your boss is standing.

This now leaves us with three areas to focus on: program registers, the stack, and the method area.

Program Counter Registers

For simplicity's sake, the JVM uses very few registers—the program counter that controls the flow of the program and three other registers in the stack. Having said that, every thread has its own program counter register, which holds the address of the current instruction being executed on the stack. Sun chose to use a limited number of registers to cater to architectures that could support very few registers.

Method Area

If you skip ahead to the next section, "Inside the Classfile," where the classfile is broken down into its many constituents, you'll see exactly where the methods can be found. Within every method is its own code attribute, which contains the bytecodes for that particular method.

Although the classfile contains information about where the program counter should point for every instruction, it is the class loader that takes care of where the actual code is placed in the memory area before the code begins to execute.

As the program executes, the program counter keeps track of the current position of the program by moving it to point to the next instruction. The bytecode within the method area goes through its Assembler-like instructions using the stack as a temporary storage area as it manipulates its variables while the program steps through the complete bytecode for that method. A program's execution is not necessarily linear within the method area; jumps and gotos are very common.

Stack

The stack is no more than a temporary storage area for holding temporary variables. All program execution and variable manipulation takes place by pushing and popping the variables off a stack frame. Each thread has its very own stack frame.

The stack consists of three different sections for the local variables: (vars), the execution environment (frame), and the operand stack (optop). The vars, frame, and optop registers point to each different area of the stack. The program method is executed in its own environment and the operand stack is used as the workspace for the bytecode instructions. The optop register points to the top of the operand stack.

As I said, the JVM is a very simple machine that pops and pushes temporary variables onto the operand stack and keeps any local variables in the vars, while continuing to execute the method in the stack frame. The stack is sandwiched between the heap and the registers.

Because the stack is so simple, no complex objects can be stored there. These are farmed out to the heap.

Inside a Classfile

To get an overall view of a classfile, take a look at an applet version of "Hello, World" (see Listing 2-1). Compile it using javac and then make a hexadecimal dump of the binary classfile, shown in Listing 2-2.

Listing 2-1. Hello.java

```java
import java.applet.Applet;
import java.awt.Graphics;
import java.net.InetAddress;
import java.net.UnknownHostException;

public class Hello extends Applet {
        public String getLocalHostName() {
                try {
                        InetAddress address = InetAddress.getLocalHost();
                        return address.getHostName();
                }
                catch (UnknownHostException e) {
                        return "Not known";
                }
        }
        public void paint(Graphics g) {
                g.drawString("Hello " + getLocalHostName() + "!", 50, 25);
        }
}
```

Listing 2-2. Hello.class

```
CAFEBABE0000002E00340A000F001A0A001B001C0A001B001D07001E08001F0700200A0006001A080
0210A000600220A000E00230800240A000600250A002600270700280700290100063C696E69743E01
0003282956010004436F646501000F4C696E654E756D6265725461626C650100106765744C6F63616
C486F73744E616D6501001428294C6A6176612F6C616E672F537472696E673B0100057061696E7401
0016284C6A6176612F6177742F47726170686963733B295601000A536F7572636546696C6501000A4
8656C6C6F2E6A6176610C0010001107002A0C002B002C0C002D001501001D6A6176612F6E65742F55
```

6E6B6E6F776E486F7374457863657074696F6E0100094E6F74206B6E6F776E0100166A6176612F6C6
16E672F537472696E6742756666657201000648656C6C6F200C002E002F0C00140015010001210C00
3000150700310C0032003301000548656C6C6F0100126A6176612F6170706C65742F4170706C65740
100146A6176612F6E65742F496E657441646472657373301000C6765744C6F63616C486F7374010018
28294C6A6176612F6E65742F496E657441646472657373733B01000B676574486F73744E616D65010 00
6617070656E6401002C284C6A6176612F6C616E672F537472696E6742294C6A6176612F6C616E672F
537472696E6742756666665723B010008746F537472696E670100116A6176612F6177742F47726170 6
869637301000A64726177537472696E670100017284C6A6176612F6C616E672F537472696E6742B4949
29560021000E000F0000000000030001001000110001001200000001D0001000100000000052AB70001B
1000000010013000000060001000000060001001400150001001200000035000100020000000DB800
024C2BB60003B04C1205B00001000000090009000400010013000000E0003000000090004000A000
9000D00010016001700010012000000400004000200000024 2BBB000659B700071208B600092AB600
0AB60009120BB60009B6000C10321019B6000DB1000000010013000000A000200000011002300120
0010018000000020019

As you can see, the classfile in Listing 2-2 is small and compact, but it contains all the necessary information for the JVM to execute the "Hello, World" code.

To open up the classfile further, in this chapter, you're going to simulate the actions of a disassembler by breaking down the classfile into its different parts. In the meantime, build your own primitive disassembler called ClassToXML,[1] which takes the classfile and outputs the code into an easy-to-read XML format.

You can break the classfile into the following constituent parts:

- Magic number
- Minor and major version numbers
- Constant pool count
- Constant pool
- Access flags
- This class
- Super class
- Interfaces count
- Interfaces
- Field count

---

1. You can download the ClassToXML code in its entirety from the downloads section of the Apress web site (www.apress.com).

- Fields

- Methods count

- Methods

- Attributes count

- Attributes

Sun's JVM specification uses a struct-like format to show the classfile's different components, as shown in Listing 2-3.

Listing 2-3. Classfile Struct

```
Classfile {
        int                    magic,
        short                  minor_version,
        short                  major_version,
        short                  constant_pool_count,
        cp_info                constant_pool[constant_pool_count-1],
        short                  access_flags,
        short                  this_class,
        short                  super_class,
        short                  interfaces_count,
        short                  interfaces [interfaces_count],
        short                  fields_count,
        field_info             fields [fields_count],
        short                  methods_count,
        method_info            methods [methods_count],
        short                  attributes_count
        attributes_info        attributes[attributes_count]
}
```

However, this always seemed to be a very cumbersome way of displaying the classfile, so you're going to use an XML format because it allows you to traverse in and out of the classfile's inner structures a lot more quickly. It also makes the classfile information a heck of a lot easier to understand as you try to unravel its meaning. You can see the complete classfile structure—with all the XML nodes collapsed—in Listing 2-4.

Listing 2-4. Disassembled Classfile in XML

```xml
<?xml version="1.0" encoding="UTF-8" ?>
- <root>
    <MagicNumber>0xcafebabe</MagicNumber>
    <MajorVersion>46</MajorVersion>
    <MinorVersion>0</MinorVersion>
    <ConstantPool_Count>52</ConstantPool_Count>
  + <ConstantPool>
    <AccessFlags>0x21</AccessFlags>
    <ThisClass>14</ThisClass>
    <SuperClass>15</SuperClass>
    <Interface_Count>0</Interface_Count>
    <Interfaces />
    <Field_Count>0</Field_Count>
    <Fields />
    <Method_Count>3</Method_Count>
  + <Methods>
    <Attributes_Count>1</Attributes_Count>
  + <Attributes>
</root>
```

You'll now look at each of the different nodes and I'll attempt to explain their form and function.

Magic Number

It's pretty easy to find the magic and version numbers because they come at the start of the classfile—you should be able to make them out in Listing 2-2. The magic number in hex is the first four bytes (i.e., 0xCAFEBABE), and it just tells the JVM that it is receiving a classfile. Curiously enough, these are also the first four bytes in multiarchitecture binary (MAB) files on the NeXT platform. I guess some cross-pollination of staff must have occurred between Sun and NeXT during early implementations of Java.

0xCAFEBABE was chosen for a number of reasons. First of all, it is pretty hard to come up with meaningful eight letter words out of the letters A–F. Secondly, rumor has it that it was chosen in honor of some waitresses in a nearby café. It was then only a very small step to choose Java as the new name of the programming language formerly known as Oak. It probably helped that Java was originally designed for kitchen and household appliances.

Mind you, 0xCAFEBABE is also a great lesson in why it isn't a very good idea to choose nerdy names during the prototype stage. More often than not they stay around longer than planned. My first reaction was to think that it's a real pity 0xGETALIFE isn't a legitimate hexadecimal string, but then I couldn't come up with any other meaningful hexadecimal name either.

Microsoft's Common Language Runtime (CLR) files have also got a similar header, BSJB, which was chosen after four of the original developers of the .NET platform, namely Brian Harry, Susan Radke-Sproull, Jason Zander, Bill Evans. OK, maybe 0xCAFEBABE isn't so bad after all.

Minor and Major Versions

The minor and major version numbers are the next four bytes, 0x0000 and 0x002E, or minor version 0 and major version 46 (see Listing 2-2), which means the code was compiled by the JDK 1.4. The JVM uses these major and minor numbers to make sure that it recognizes and fully understands the format of the class file. JVMs will refuse to execute any classfile with a higher major and minor number.

The minor version is for small changes that require an updated JVM; the major number is for wholesale fundamental changes that require a completely different and incompatible JVM, like one designed to stop decompiling.

It is probably worth noting that Sun and Microsoft's JVMs—assuming you can find one of them—are still compatible at the interface level, or, in other words, they use the same bytecodes. It's the different standard classes that cause all the problems, not the underlying JVM.

Constant Pool Count

All class or interface constants are stored in the constant pool. And surprise, surprise—the constant pool count, which takes up the next two bytes, tells you how many variable-length elements follow in the constant pool.

0x0034 or integer 52 is the number in Listing 2-4. The JVM specification tells us that constant_pool[0] is reserved by the JVM. In fact, it doesn't even appear in the classfile, so the constant pool elements are stored in constant_pool[1] to constant_pool[51].

Constant Pool

The next item is the constant pool itself, which is of type cp_info, shown in Listing 2-5.

Listing 2-5. cp_info Structure

```
cp_info {
        byte tag,
        byte info[]
}
```

The constant pool is made up of an array of variable length elements. It's full of symbolic references to other entries in the constant pool with the constant pool count telling you just how many variables are in the constant pool.

Every constant and variable name required by the classfile can be found in the constant pool. These names are typically strings, integers, floats, method names, and so on, all of which remain fixed. Each constant is then referenced by its constant pool index everywhere else in the classfile.

Each element of the constant pool—remember there are 52 in our example—begins with a tag that tells exactly what type of constant is coming next. Table 2-1 shows a list of valid tags and their corresponding value used in the classfile.

Table 2-1. Constant Pool Tags

Constant Pool Tag	Value
CONSTANT_Utf8	1
CONSTANT_Integer	3
CONSTANT_Float	4
CONSTANT_Long	5
CONSTANT_Double	6
CONSTANT_Class	7
CONSTANT_String	8
CONSTANT_Fieldref	9
CONSTANT_Methodref	10
CONSTANT_InterfaceMethodref	11
CONSTANT_NameAndType	12

Many of the tags in the constant pool are symbolic references to other members of the constant pool. For example, each CONSTANT_String_info points at a CONSTANT_Utf8_info tag where the string is ultimately stored. The CONSTANT_Utf8_info has the data structure shown in Listing 2-6.

Listing 2-6. CONSTANT_Utf8_info Structure

```
CONSTANT_Utf8_info {
        byte        tag,
        int         length,
        byte        bytes[length]
}
```

I've collapsed these data structures wherever possible in my XML output of the constant pool, as you can see in Listing 2-7, so that you can read it easily and remove redundant information to save space.

Listing 2-7. Constant Pool for Hello.class

```
<ConstantPool>
<Tag_1>
  <Type>CONSTANT_Methodref</Type>
  <Class_Index>15</Class_Index>
  <NameType_Index>26</NameType_Index>
</Tag_1>
<Tag_2>
  <Type>CONSTANT_Methodref</Type>
  <Class_Index>27</Class_Index>
  <NameType_Index>28</NameType_Index>
</Tag_2>
<Tag_3>
  <Type>CONSTANT_Methodref</Type>
  <Class_Index>27</Class_Index>
  <NameType_Index>29</NameType_Index>
</Tag_3>
<Tag_4>
  <Type>CONSTANT_Class</Type>
  <Value>30</Value>
</Tag_4>
<Tag_5>
  <Type>CONSTANT_String</Type>
  <Value>31</Value>
</Tag_5>
<Tag_6>
  <Type>CONSTANT_Class</Type>
  <Value>32</Value>
</Tag_6>
<Tag_7>
  <Type>CONSTANT_Methodref</Type>
  <Class_Index>6</Class_Index>
  <NameType_Index>26</NameType_Index>
</Tag_7>
<Tag_8>
  <Type>CONSTANT_String</Type>
  <Value>33</Value>
</Tag_8>
```

```
<Tag_9>
  <Type>CONSTANT_Methodref</Type>
  <Class_Index>6</Class_Index>
  <NameType_Index>34</NameType_Index>
</Tag_9>
<Tag_10>
  <Type>CONSTANT_Methodref</Type>
  <Class_Index>14</Class_Index>
  <NameType_Index>35</NameType_Index>
</Tag_10>
<Tag_11>
  <Type>CONSTANT_String</Type>
  <Value>36</Value>
</Tag_11>
<Tag_12>
  <Type>CONSTANT_Methodref</Type>
  <Class_Index>6</Class_Index>
  <NameType_Index>37</NameType_Index>
</Tag_12>
<Tag_13>
  <Type>CONSTANT_Methodref</Type>
  <Class_Index>38</Class_Index>
  <NameType_Index>39</NameType_Index>
</Tag_13>
<Tag_14>
  <Type>CONSTANT_Class</Type>
  <Value>40</Value>
</Tag_14>
<Tag_15>
  <Type>CONSTANT_Class</Type>
  <Value>41</Value>
</Tag_15>
<Tag_16>
  <Type>CONSTANT_Utf8</Type>
  <Value><init></Value>
</Tag_16>
<Tag_17>
  <Type>CONSTANT_Utf8</Type>
  <Value>()V</Value>
</Tag_17>
<Tag_18>
  <Type>CONSTANT_Utf8</Type>
  <Value>Code</Value>
</Tag_18>
```

```
<Tag_19>
  <Type>CONSTANT_Utf8</Type>
  <Value>LineNumberTable</Value>
</Tag_19>
<Tag_20>
  <Type>CONSTANT_Utf8</Type>
  <Value>getLocalHostName</Value>
</Tag_20>
<Tag_21>
  <Type>CONSTANT_Utf8</Type>
  <Value>()Ljava/lang/String;</Value>
</Tag_21>
<Tag_22>
  <Type>CONSTANT_Utf8</Type>
  <Value>paint</Value>
</Tag_22>
<Tag_23>
  <Type>CONSTANT_Utf8</Type>
  <Value>(Ljava/awt/Graphics;)V</Value>
</Tag_23>
<Tag_24>
  <Type>CONSTANT_Utf8</Type>
  <Value>SourceFile</Value>
</Tag_24>
<Tag_25>
  <Type>CONSTANT_Utf8</Type>
  <Value>Hello.java</Value>
</Tag_25>
<Tag_26>
  <Type>CONSTANT_NameAndType</Type>
  <UTF8Name_Index>16</UTF8Name_Index>
  <Utf8Desc_Index>17</Utf8Desc_Index>
</Tag_26>
<Tag_27>
  <Type>CONSTANT_Class</Type>
  <Value>42</Value>
</Tag_27>
<Tag_28>
  <Type>CONSTANT_NameAndType</Type>
  <UTF8Name_Index>43</UTF8Name_Index>
  <Utf8Desc_Index>44</Utf8Desc_Index>
</Tag_28>
```

```
<Tag_29>
  <Type>CONSTANT_NameAndType</Type>
  <UTF8Name_Index>45</UTF8Name_Index>
  <Utf8Desc_Index>21</Utf8Desc_Index>
</Tag_29>
<Tag_30>
  <Type>CONSTANT_Utf8</Type>
  <Value>java/net/UnknownHostException</Value>
</Tag_30>
<Tag_31>
  <Type>CONSTANT_Utf8</Type>
  <Value>Not known</Value>
</Tag_31>
<Tag_32>
  <Type>CONSTANT_Utf8</Type>
  <Value>java/lang/StringBuffer</Value>
</Tag_32>
<Tag_33>
  <Type>CONSTANT_Utf8</Type>
  <Value>Hello</Value>
</Tag_33>
<Tag_34>
  <Type>CONSTANT_NameAndType</Type>
  <UTF8Name_Index>46</UTF8Name_Index>
  <Utf8Desc_Index>47</Utf8Desc_Index>
</Tag_34>
<Tag_35>
  <Type>CONSTANT_NameAndType</Type>
  <UTF8Name_Index>20</UTF8Name_Index>
  <Utf8Desc_Index>21</Utf8Desc_Index>
</Tag_35>
<Tag_36>
  <Type>CONSTANT_Utf8</Type>
  <Value>!</Value>
</Tag_36>
<Tag_37>
  <Type>CONSTANT_NameAndType</Type>
  <UTF8Name_Index>48</UTF8Name_Index>
  <Utf8Desc_Index>21</Utf8Desc_Index>
</Tag_37>
<Tag_38>
  <Type>CONSTANT_Class</Type>
  <Value>49</Value>
</Tag_38>
```

```
<Tag_39>
  <Type>CONSTANT_NameAndType</Type>
  <UTF8Name_Index>50</UTF8Name_Index>
  <Utf8Desc_Index>51</Utf8Desc_Index>
</Tag_39>
<Tag_40>
  <Type>CONSTANT_Utf8</Type>
  <Value>Hello</Value>
</Tag_40>
<Tag_41>
  <Type>CONSTANT_Utf8</Type>
  <Value>java/applet/Applet</Value>
</Tag_41>
<Tag_42>
  <Type>CONSTANT_Utf8</Type>
  <Value>java/net/InetAddress</Value>
</Tag_42>
<Tag_43>
  <Type>CONSTANT_Utf8</Type>
  <Value>getLocalHost</Value>
</Tag_43>
<Tag_44>
  <Type>CONSTANT_Utf8</Type>
  <Value>()Ljava/net/InetAddress;</Value>
</Tag_44>
<Tag_45>
  <Type>CONSTANT_Utf8</Type>
  <Value>getHostName</Value>
</Tag_45>
<Tag_46>
  <Type>CONSTANT_Utf8</Type>
  <Value>append</Value>
</Tag_46>
<Tag_47>
  <Type>CONSTANT_Utf8</Type>
  <Value>(Ljava/lang/String;)Ljava/lang/StringBuffer;</Value>
</Tag_47>
<Tag_48>
  <Type>CONSTANT_Utf8</Type>
  <Value>toString</Value>
</Tag_48>
<Tag_49>
  <Type>CONSTANT_Utf8</Type>
  <Value>java/awt/Graphics</Value>
</Tag_49>
```

```
<Tag_50>
  <Type>CONSTANT_Utf8</Type>
  <Value>drawString</Value>
</Tag_50>
<Tag_51>
  <Type>CONSTANT_Utf8</Type>
  <Value>(Ljava/lang/String;II)V</Value>
</Tag_51>
</ConstantPool>
```

It really is a simple, yet elegant, design when you take the time to examine the output of the class file. Take the first method reference, constant_pool[1], for instance:

```
<Tag_1>
  <Type>CONSTANT_Methodref</Type>
  <Class_Index>15</Class_Index>
  <NameType_Index>26</NameType_Index>
</Tag_1>
```

This tells you that its belongs to the class in constant_pool[15]:

```
<Tag_15>
  <Type>CONSTANT_Class</Type>
  <Value>41</Value>
</Tag_15>
```

which points to constant_pool[41], the applet class:

```
<Tag_41>
  <Type>CONSTANT_Utf8</Type>
  <Value>java/applet/Applet</Value>
</Tag_41>
```

But you also have a NameType_Index to resolve, which will give you the Name and Type of the method.

```
<Tag_26>
  <Type>CONSTANT_NameAndType</Type>
  <UTF8Name_Index>16</UTF8Name_Index>
  <Utf8Desc_Index>17</Utf8Desc_Index>
</Tag_26>
```

Elements 16 and 17 of the constant pool point at the method name and its descriptors. According the JVM specification, method descriptors take the following form:

```
(ParameterDescriptor *) ReturnDescriptor.
```

The return descriptor can be either V for void or one of the field types, shown in Table 2-2.

```
<Tag_16>
  <Type>CONSTANT_Utf8</Type>
  <Value><init></Value>
</Tag_16>
<Tag_17>
  <Type>CONSTANT_Utf8</Type>
  <Value>()V</Value>
</Tag_17>
```

In this case, the name of the method is <init>, an internal JVM method that is in every classfile; its method descriptor is ()V, or void, for the field descriptor mapping (see Table 2-2).

So, you can now re-create the method as follows:

```
void init()
```

Table 2-2. Field Descriptors

Descriptor	Name
B	Byte
C	Char
D	Double
F	Float
I	Int
J	Long
L<classname>	Class
S	Short
Z	Boolean
[	Array

You can try to unravel some other classes too. It may help if you work backward from the target class or method. Some of the strings are pretty unintelligible, but with a little practice, the method signatures become clear.

The earliest types of obfuscators simply renamed these strings to something completely unintelligible, which stopped primitive decompilers, but didn't harm the classfile because the JVM uses a pointer to the string in the constant pool and not the string itself—well, so long as you didn't rename internal methods such as <init> or destroy the references to any Java classes in an external library.

You already know what classes you need for your import statements from the following entries: constant_pool[30,32,41,42,49]. Note that no interfaces or static final classes exist in the earlier simple example (see Listing 2-1). These would come up as field references in the constant pool, but so far, your simple class parser is complete enough to handle any classfile you care to throw at it.

Access Flags

Access flags tell you whether you are dealing with a class or an interface, if it is public or abstract, and assuming it is a class rather than an interface, whether it is final or not. All interfaces are abstract.

```
<AccessFlags>0x21</AccessFlags>
```

At the moment, there are only five access flag types (see Table 2-3), but there may be more in the future. ACC_SUPER was a relatively recent addition; it tells the JVM that the class was compiled with a JDK 1.1 compiler and to treat the superclass methods differently.

Table 2-3. Access Flags

Name	Value	Description
ACC_PUBLIC	0x0001	Class or interface
ACC_FINAL	0x0002	Class
ACC_SUPER	0x0020	JDK1.1 compiler or above
ACC_INTERFACE	0x0200	Interface
ACC_ABSTRACT	0x0400	Class or interface

Access flags are or'd together to come up with a description of the modifier before each variable. This tells you that the Hello class is a public class, which you can verify is true by going all the way back to Listing 2-1.

This and Super

The next two values point at the constant pool index for this class and the super class.

```
<ThisClass>14</ThisClass>
<SuperClass>15</SuperClass>
```

If you follow the XML output in Listing 2-8, constant_pool[14] points at constant_pool[40]. This CONSTANT_Utf8_info structure contains the string Hello, telling us that *this* is the Hello class. The super class is in constant_pool[15] or the applet class as described in constant_pool[41].

Interfaces

The current example doesn't have any interfaces, so you really have to look at a different example to get a better understanding of how interfaces are implemented in the classfile, as shown in Listing 2-8.

Listing 2-8. Human Interfaces

```
interface IProgrammer {
        public void code();
        public void earnmore();
}


interface IWriter {
        public void pullhairout();
        public void earnless();
}


public class Person implements IProgrammer, IWriter {

        public Person() {
                Geek g = new Geek(this);
                Author t = new Author(this);
        }

        public void code() { /* ..... */ }
        public void earnmore() { /* ..... */ }
        public void pullhairout() { /* ..... */ }
        public void earnless() { /* ..... */ }


}
```

```
class Geek {
        IProgrammer iprog = null;

        public Geek(IProgrammer iprog) {
                this.iprog = iprog;
                iprog.code();
                iprog.earnmore();
        }
}

class Author {
        IWriter iwriter = null;

        public Author(IWriter iwriter) {
                this.iwriter = iwriter;
                iwriter.pullhairout();
                iwriter.earnless();
        }
}
```

Listing 2-8 has two interfaces: IProgrammer and IWriter. When you run classtoxml against the class files, you get the following information in the interfaces section.

```
<Interface_Count>2</Interface_Count>
 <Interfaces>
 <Interface>8</Interface>
 <Interface>9</Interface>
</Interfaces>
```

which resolves to the IProgrammer and IWriter strings in the constant pool as follows:

```
<Tag_8>
   <Type>CONSTANT_Class</Type>
   <Value>27</Value>
</Tag_8>
<Tag_9>
   <Type>CONSTANT_Class</Type>
   <Value>28</Value>
</Tag_9>
```

```
<Tag_27>
  <Type>CONSTANT_Utf8</Type>
  <Value>IProgrammer</Value>
</Tag_27>
<Tag_28>
  <Type>CONSTANT_Utf8</Type>
  <Value>IWriter</Value>
</Tag_28>
```

Fields

As it stands, Hello.class has no field information. This is simply because the class-file has no instance variables. As a result, you need to make some simple changes to the original code to declare some variables in the classfile before anything will show up in the classfile fields (see Listing 2-9). In this listing, you also make them static and final to force a ConstantValue field attribute.

Listing 2-9. Hello Localhost with Initializers

```java
import java.applet.Applet;
import java.awt.Graphics;
import java.net.InetAddress;
import java.net.UnknownHostException;

public class Hello extends Applet {
        static final String s = "Hello ";
        static final int w = 50;
        static final int h = 25;

    public String getLocalHostName() {
        try {
            InetAddress address = InetAddress.getLocalHost();
            return address.getHostName();
        }
        catch (UnknownHostException e) {
            return "Not known";
        }
    }
    public void paint(Graphics g) {
        g.drawString(s + getLocalHostName() + "!", w,h);
    }
}
```

If you pull out the relevant section in the XML, you see that there are three fields. The first of these is shown in Listing 2-10.

Listing 2-10. Human Interface's Fields

```
<Field_Count>3</Field_Count>
<Fields>
        <Field>
                <AccessFlags>0x0018</AccessFlags>
                <NameType_Index>16</NameType_Index>
                <Description_Index>17</Description_Index>
                  <Attribute_Count>1</Attribute_Count>
                      <Attributes>
                      <Attribute>
                      <Attribute_Type>ConstantValue</Attribute_Type>
                      <Attribute_Length>2</Attribute_Length>
                      <Attribute_Value_Index>8</Attribute_Value_Index>
                       </Attribute>
                  </Attributes>
        </Field>
        <Field>
                <AccessFlags>0x0018</AccessFlags>
                <NameType_Index>19</NameType_Index>
                <Description_Index>20</Description_Index>
                <Attribute_Count>1</Attribute_Count>
            <Attributes>
                      <Attribute>
                      <Attribute_Type>ConstantValue</Attribute_Type>
                      <Attribute_Length>2</Attribute_Length>
                <Attribute_Value_Index>21</Attribute_Value_Index>
                       </Attribute>
                       </Attributes>
          </Field>
        <Field>
                <AccessFlags>0x0018</AccessFlags>
                <NameType_Index>22</NameType_Index>
                <Description_Index>20</Description_Index>
                  <Attribute_Count>1</Attribute_Count>
                      <Attributes>
                      <Attribute>
```

```
                                    <Attribute_Type>ConstantValue</Attribute_Type>
                                        <Attribute_Length>2</Attribute_Length>
                        <Attribute_Value_Index>23</Attribute_Value_Index>
                                    </Attribute>
                                    </Attributes>
                        </Field>
            </Fields>
```

Field Access flags, as shown in Table 2-4, tell you whether the field is public, private, protected, static, final, volatile, or transient.

Table 2-4. Access Flags

Name	Value	Description
ACC_PUBLIC	0x0001	Class or interface
ACC_PRIVATE	0x0002	Class
ACC_PROTECTED	0x0004	Class
ACC_STATIC	0x0008	Class or interface
ACC_FINAL	0x0010	Class or interface
ACC_VOLATILE	0x0040	Class
ACC_TRANSIENT	0x0080	Class

The first five keywords should be obvious to anyone who has written any Java. However, the volatile keyword tells a thread that the variable may be updated by another thread, and the transient keyword is used in object serialization and was introduced in the JDK 1.1. An Access Flag of 0x0018 denotes a static final field.

You'll need to go back to Table 2-2 to refresh your memory before you unravel the different field descriptors.

```
<Field>
  <AccessFlags>0x0018</AccessFlags>
  <NameType_Index>16</NameType_Index>
  <Description_Index>17</Description_Index>
  <...>
</Field>

<Tag_16>
  <Type>CONSTANT_Utf8</Type>
  <Value>s</Value>
</Tag_16>
```

```
<Tag_17>
  <Type>CONSTANT_Utf8</Type>
  <Value>Ljava/lang/String;</Value>
</Tag_17>
```

The descriptor points back to the field s, which has the field descriptor constant_pool[17] or Ljava/lang/String, which is an instance of a String class.

Field Attributes

Attributes count is, no surprise, the number of attributes, which is immediately followed by the attributes themselves. Several different attribute types are found in the field data structure, the methods data structure, and the attributes data structure itself—the final element of the classfile data structure. However, really only two possible field attributes exist: ConstantValue and Synthetic. ConstantValue is used for constant variables, such as those declared as static and final in the current example. The Synthetic variable was introduced in JDK 1.1 to support inner classes. Users can define their own attribute types, but they're irrelevant to the current discussion.

```
<Attribute_Count>1</Attribute_Count>
<Attributes>
        <Attribute>
                <Attribute_Type>ConstantValue</Attribute_Type>
                <Attribute_Length>2</Attribute_Length>
                <Attribute_Value_Index>8</Attribute_Value_Index>
        </Attribute>
</Attributes>
```

The attribute for the first field is a constant that can be found in constant_pool[8], a string, which, in turn, points at the string Hello.

```
<Tag_8>
   <Type>CONSTANT_String</Type>
   <Value>41</Value>
 </Tag_8>

 <Tag_41>
  <Type>CONSTANT_Utf8</Type>
  <Value>Hello, </Value>
 </Tag_41>
```

You have now decompiled the first field into its original format:

```
static final String s = "Hello, ";
```

Methods

And now, for the most important part of the classfile, the methods. All the source code is converted into bytecode and stored or contained in the method_info area. Well it's actually in the Code attribute within the methods, but you are getting very close. If someone can get at the bytecode, then they can try to convert it back into source. The methods in Listing 2-1's classfile are shown in Listing 2-11.

Listing 2-11. Methods from Hello.class

```
<Methods>
  <Method>
   <AccessFlags>0x0001</AccessFlags>
   <NameType_Index>16</NameType_Index>
   <Description_Index>17</Description_Index>
   <AttributeCount>1</AttributeCount>
   <Attributes>
    <Attribute>
      <Attribute_Type>Code</Attribute_Type>
      <Attribute_Length>29</Attribute_Length>
      <Max_Stack>1</Max_Stack>
      <Max_Locals>1</Max_Locals>
      <Code_Length>5</Code_Length>
      <Code>2ab70001b1</Code>
      <Exception_Table_Length>0</Exception_Table_Length>
      <Exception_Table_Attributes />
      <Code_Attribute_Count>1</Code_Attribute_Count>
      <Code_Attribute_Name_Index>19</Code_Attribute_Name_Index>
      <Code_Attribute_Length>6</Code_Attribute_Length>
      <Code_Attributes>
       <Code_Attribute>start pc: 0 line number 6</Code_Attribute>
      </Code_Attributes>
    </Attribute>
   </Attributes>
  </Method>
  <Method>
   <AccessFlags>0x0001</AccessFlags>
   <NameType_Index>20</NameType_Index>
   <Description_Index>21</Description_Index>
   <AttributeCount>1</AttributeCount>
   <Attributes>
    <Attribute>
      <Attribute_Type>Code</Attribute_Type>
      <Attribute_Length>53</Attribute_Length>
```

```xml
      <Max_Stack>1</Max_Stack>
      <Max_Locals>2</Max_Locals>
      <Code_Length>13</Code_Length>
      <Code>b800024c2bb60003b04c1205b0</Code>
      <Exception_Table_Length>1</Exception_Table_Length>
      <Exception_Table_Attributes>
       <Start_PC>0</Start_PC>
       <End_PC>9</End_PC>
       <Handler_PC>9</Handler_PC>
       <Catch_Type>4</Catch_Type>
      </Exception_Table_Attributes>
      <Code_Attribute_Count>1</Code_Attribute_Count>
      <Code_Attribute_Name_Index>19</Code_Attribute_Name_Index>
      <Code_Attribute_Length>14</Code_Attribute_Length>
      <Code_Attributes>
       <Code_Attribute>start pc: 0 line number 9</Code_Attribute>
       <Code_Attribute>start pc: 4 line number 10</Code_Attribute>
       <Code_Attribute>start pc: 9 line number 13</Code_Attribute>
      </Code_Attributes>
     </Attribute>
    </Attributes>
  </Method>
  <Method>
   <AccessFlags>0x0001</AccessFlags>
   <NameType_Index>22</NameType_Index>
   <Description_Index>23</Description_Index>
   <AttributeCount>1</AttributeCount>
   <Attributes>
    <Attribute>
     <Attribute_Type>Code</Attribute_Type>
     <Attribute_Length>64</Attribute_Length>
     <Max_Stack>4</Max_Stack>
     <Max_Locals>2</Max_Locals>
     <Code_Length>36</Code_Length>
     <Code>2bbb000659b700071208b600092ab6000ab60009120bb60009b
        6000c10321019b6000db1</Code>
     <Exception_Table_Length>0</Exception_Table_Length>
     <Exception_Table_Attributes />
     <Code_Attribute_Count>1</Code_Attribute_Count>
     <Code_Attribute_Name_Index>19</Code_Attribute_Name_Index>
     <Code_Attribute_Length>10</Code_Attribute_Length>
```

```
  <Code_Attributes>
    <Code_Attribute>start pc: 0 line number 17</Code_Attribute>
    <Code_Attribute>start pc: 35 line number 18</Code_Attribute>
  </Code_Attributes>
 </Attribute>
 </Attributes>
</Method>
</Methods>
```

The Methods element is preceded by a method count and the data structure is not dissimilar to the field_info structure in the previous section. This time around, three types of attributes normally appear in method_info: Code, Exceptions, and once again, Synthetic for inner classes.

Different access flags are set for each method depending on what modifiers were used in the original source (see Table 2-5). A number of restrictions exist because some of the access flags are mutually exclusive—in other words, a method cannot be declared as both ACC_PUBLIC and ACC_PRIVATE or even ACC_PROTECTED. However, you won't normally be disassembling illegal byte-codes, so you're unlikely to come across any such eventualities.

```
<AccessFlags>0x0001</AccessFlags>
```

All of the methods in the example are public methods.

Table 2-5. Method Access Flags

Name	Value	Description
ACC_PUBLIC	0x0001	Class or interface
ACC_PRIVATE	0x0002	Class
ACC_PROTECTED	0x0004	Class
ACC_STATIC	0x0008	Class
ACC_FINAL	0x0010	Class
ACC_SYNCHRONIZED	0x0020	Class
ACC_NATIVE	0x0100	Class or interface
ACC_ABSTRACT	0x0400	Abstract
ACC_STRICT	0x0800	Strict

You can now find the name and the method descriptors of the final method.

```
<NameType_Index>22</NameType_Index>
<Description_Index>23</Description_Index>
```

Then you pull out the name and description of the method from constant_pool[22] and constant_pool[23].

```
<Tag_22>
  <Type>CONSTANT_Utf8</Type>
  <Value>paint</Value>
 </Tag_22>
 <Tag_23>
  <Type>CONSTANT_Utf8</Type>
  <Value>(Ljava/awt/Graphics;)V</Value>
 </Tag_23>
```

You can now reassemble the method without any of the underlying code.

```
public void paint(java.awt.Graphics g) {
        /*          */
}
```

Or simply

```
import java.awt.Graphics;
...
public void paint(Graphics g) {
        /*          */
}
```

The remaining methods fall out of the constant pool in a similar fashion.

Method Attributes

Attributes appear in the field, method, and attributes elements of the classfile structure. Each attribute begins with an attribute_name_index that references the constant_pool and an attribute length. But the meat of the classfile is within the method attributes, as shown in Listing 2-12.

Listing 2-12. Paint Method Attributes

```
<AttributeCount>1</AttributeCount>
<Attributes>
 <Attribute>
  <Attribute_Type>Code</Attribute_Type>
```

```
<Attribute_Length>64</Attribute_Length>
<Max_Stack>4</Max_Stack>
<Max_Locals>2</Max_Locals >
<Code_Length>36</Code_Length>
<Code>2bbb000659b700071208b600092ab6000ab6000
            9120bb60009b6000c10321019b6000db1</Code>
<Exception_Table_Length>0</Exception_Table_Length>
<Exception_Table_Attributes />
<Code_Attribute_Count>1</Code_Attribute_Count>
<Code_Attribute_Name_Index>19</Code_Attribute_Name_Index>
<Code_Attribute_Length>10</Code_Attribute_Length>
<Code_Attributes>
  <Code_Attribute>start pc: 0 line number 17</Code_Attribute>
  <Code_Attribute>start pc: 35 line number 18</Code_Attribute>
</Code_Attributes>
</Attribute>
</Attributes>
```

The attribute type above is a *code* attribute. The attribute_length is the length of the code attribute minus the first 6 bytes.[2] The Max stack and Max locals gives the maximum number of variables on the operand stack and local variable sections of the stack frame.

```
<Code_Length>36</Code_Length>
    <Code>2bbb000659b700071208b600092ab6000ab6000
    9120bb60009b6000c10321019b6000db1</Code>
```

<Code_Length></Code_Length> gives the size of the following code array. The code array is simply a series of bytes where each bytecode is a reserved byte value or opcode followed by zero or more operands; or, to put it another way,

```
opcode operand
```

Looking at the output from running classtoxml on Hello.class (see Listing 2-1), you see that there are three methods for the applet, namely getLocalHostName, paint, and the empty constructor that the Java compiler always adds when the developer chooses not to add their own constructor. Each method has its own Code array. Listing 2-12 shows the attributes for the paint method only.

---

2. The attribute type and attribute name take up the first 6 bytes and are not included in the attribute length.

`<init>` Method

Before I explain what bytecode maps onto which opcode, let's look at the simplest method to unravel, the first code segment.

```
<Code>2ab70001b1</Code>
```

When you convert this into opcodes and operands, it becomes

```
2a                 aload 0
b70001       invokespecial #1
b1                 return
```

2a becomes aload 0. This loads the local variable, 0, onto the stack as required by invokespecial. b70001 becomes invokespecial #1, where invokespecial is used to invoke a method in a limited number of cases, such as an instance initialization method or `<init>` to you and me, which is what you have here. #1 is a reference to constant_pool[1], a CONSTANT_Methodref structure. You can collect all the constant pool references for constant_pool[1] as shown here:

```
<Tag_1>
  <Type>CONSTANT_Methodref</Type>
  <Class_Index>15</Class_Index>
  <NameType_Index>26</NameType_Index>
</Tag_1>

<Tag_15>
  <Type>CONSTANT_Class</Type>
  <Value>41</Value>
</Tag_15>

<Tag_26>
  <Type>CONSTANT_NameAndType</Type>
  <UTF8Name_Index>16</UTF8Name_Index>
  <Utf8Desc_Index>17</Utf8Desc_Index>
</Tag_26>

<Tag_16>
  <Type>CONSTANT_Utf8</Type>
  <Value><init></Value>
</Tag_16>
```

```
<Tag_17>
 <Type>CONSTANT_Utf8</Type>
 <Value>()V</Value>
</Tag_17>
```

You can resolve the symbolic references by hand to

```
<Method java.applet.Applet.<init>()V>
```

This is the empty constructor that the javac compiler adds to all classes that don't already have a constructor. The final b1 opcode is a simple return statement. So your first method can be converted straight back into the following code, an empty constructor.

```
public Hello(){
}
```

getLocalHostName() Method

The second code attribute is a much less trivial affair. To get any further, you really need to know what hexadecimal values map onto what opcodes, (see Table 2-6). You will also need to know how each element of the Java language is compiled into bytecode so that you can reverse the process.

Table 2-6. Bytecode to Opcode Mapping

Opcode	Hex Value	Opcode Mnemonic
0	(0x00)	nop
1	(0x01)	aconst_null
2	(0x02)	iconst_m1
3	(0x03)	iconst_0
4	(0x04)	iconst_1
5	(0x05)	iconst_2
6	(0x06)	iconst_3
7	(0x07)	iconst_4
8	(0x08)	iconst_5
9	(0x09)	lconst_0

Table 2-6. Bytecode to Opcode Mapping (continued)

Opcode	Hex Value	Opcode Mnemonic
10	(0x0a)	lconst_1
11	(0x0b)	fconst_0
12	(0x0c)	fconst_1
13	(0x0d)	fconst_2
14	(0x0e)	dconst_0
15	(0x0f)	dconst_1
16	(0x10)	bipush
17	(0x11)	sipush
18	(0x12)	ldc
19	(0x13)	ldc_w
20	(0x14)	ldc2_w
21	(0x15)	iload
22	(0x16)	lload
23	(0x17)	fload
24	(0x18)	dload
25	(0x19)	aload
26	(0x1a)	iload_0
27	(0x1b)	iload_1
28	(0x1c)	iload_2
29	(0x1d)	iload_3
30	(0x1e)	lload_0
31	(0x1f)	lload_1
32	(0x20)	lload_2
33	(0x21)	lload_3
34	(0x22)	fload_0
35	(0x23)	fload_1
36	(0x24)	fload_2
37	(0x25)	fload_3
38	(0x26)	dload_0

Table 2-6. Bytecode to Opcode Mapping (continued)

Opcode	Hex Value	Opcode Mnemonic
39	(0x27)	dload_1
40	(0x28)	dload_2
41	(0x29)	dload_3
42	(0x2a)	aload_0
43	(0x2b)	aload_1
44	(0x2c)	aload_2
45	(0x2d)	aload_3
46	(0x2e)	iaload
47	(0x2f)	laload
48	(0x30)	faload
49	(0x31)	daload
50	(0x32)	aaload
51	(0x33)	baload
52	(0x34)	caload
53	(0x35)	saload
54	(0x36)	istore
55	(0x37)	lstore
56	(0x38)	fstore
57	(0x39)	dstore
58	(0x3a)	astore
59	(0x3b)	istore_0
60	(0x3c)	istore_1
61	(0x3d)	istore_2
62	(0x3e)	istore_3
63	(0x3f)	lstore_0
64	(0x40)	lstore_1
65	(0x41)	lstore_2
66	(0x42)	lstore_3
67	(0x43)	fstore_0

Table 2-6. Bytecode to Opcode Mapping (continued)

Opcode	Hex Value	Opcode Mnemonic
68	(0x44)	fstore_1
69	(0x45)	fstore_2
70	(0x46)	fstore_3
71	(0x47)	dstore_0
72	(0x48)	dstore_1
73	(0x49)	dstore_2
74	(0x4a)	dstore_3
75	(0x4b)	astore_0
76	(0x4c)	astore_1
77	(0x4d)	astore_2
78	(0x4e)	astore_3
79	(0x4f)	iastore
80	(0x50)	lastore
81	(0x51)	fastore
82	(0x52)	dastore
83	(0x53)	aastore
84	(0x54)	bastore
85	(0x55)	castore
86	(0x56)	sastore
87	(0x57)	pop
88	(0x58)	pop2
89	(0x59)	dup
90	(0x5a)	dup_x1
91	(0x5b)	dup_x2
92	(0x5c)	dup2
93	(0x5d)	dup2_x1
94	(0x5e)	dup2_x2
95	(0x5f)	swap
96	(0x60)	iadd

Table 2-6. Bytecode to Opcode Mapping (continued)

Opcode	Hex Value	Opcode Mnemonic
97	(0x61)	ladd
98	(0x62)	fadd
99	(0x63)	dadd
100	(0x64)	isub
101	(0x65)	lsub
102	(0x66)	fsub
103	(0x67)	dsub
104	(0x68)	imul
105	(0x69)	lmul
106	(0x6a)	fmul
107	(0x6b)	dmul
108	(0x6c)	idiv
109	(0x6d)	ldiv
100	(0x6e)	fdiv
111	(0x6f)	ddiv
112	(0x70)	irem
113	(0x71)	lrem
114	(0x72)	frem
115	(0x73)	drem
116	(0x74)	ineg
117	(0x75)	lneg
118	(0x76)	fneg
119	(0x77)	dneg
120	(0x78)	ishl
121	(0x79)	lshl
122	(0x7a)	ishr
123	(0x7b)	lshr
124	(0x7c)	iushr
125	(0x7d)	lushr

Table 2-6. Bytecode to Opcode Mapping (continued)

Opcode	Hex Value	Opcode Mnemonic
126	(0x7e)	iand
127	(0x7f)	land
128	(0x80)	ior
129	(0x81)	lor
130	(0x82)	ixor
131	(0x83)	lxor
132	(0x84)	iinc
133	(0x85)	i2l
134	(0x86)	i2f
135	(0x87)	i2d
136	(0x88)	l2i
137	(0x89)	l2f
138	(0x8a)	l2d
139	(0x8b)	f2i
140	(0x8c)	f2l
141	(0x8d)	f2d
142	(0x8e)	d2i
143	(0x8f)	d2l
144	(0x90)	d2f
145	(0x91)	i2b
146	(0x92)	i2c
147	(0x93)	i2s
148	(0x94)	lcmp
149	(0x95)	fcmpl
150	(0x96)	fcmpg
151	(0x97)	dcmpl
152	(0x98)	dcmpg
153	(0x99)	ifeq
154	(0x9a)	ifne

Table 2-6. Bytecode to Opcode Mapping (continued)

Opcode	Hex Value	Opcode Mnemonic
155	(0x9b)	iflt
156	(0x9c)	ifge
157	(0x9d)	ifgt
158	(0x9e)	ifle
159	(0x9f)	if_icmpeq
160	(0xa0)	if_icmpne
161	(0xa1)	if_icmplt
162	(0xa2)	if_icmpge
163	(0xa3)	if_icmpgt
164	(0xa4)	if_icmple
165	(0xa5)	if_acmpeq
166	(0xa6)	if_acmpne
167	(0xa7)	goto
168	(0xa8)	jsr
169	(0xa9)	ret
170	(0xaa)	tableswitch
171	(0xab)	lookupswitch
172	(0xac)	ireturn
173	(0xad)	lreturn
174	(0xae)	freturn
175	(0xaf)	dreturn
176	(0xb0)	areturn
177	(0xb1)	return
178	(0xb2)	getstatic
179	(0xb3)	putstatic
180	(0xb4)	getfield
181	(0xb5)	putfield
182	(0xb6)	invokevirtual
183	(0xb7)	invokespecial

Table 2-6. Bytecode to Opcode Mapping (continued)

Opcode	Hex Value	Opcode Mnemonic
184	(0xb8)	invokestatic
185	(0xb9)	invokeinterface
186	(0xba)	xxxunusedxxx
187	(0xbb)	new
188	(0xbc)	newarray
189	(0xbd)	anewarray
190	(0xbe)	arraylength
191	(0xbf)	athrow
192	(0xc0)	checkcast
193	(0xc1)	instanceof
194	(0xc2)	monitorenter
195	(0xc3)	monitorexit
196	(0xc4)	wide
197	(0xc5)	multianewarray
198	(0xc6)	ifnull
199	(0xc7)	ifnonnull
200	(0xc8)	goto_w
201	(0xc9)	jsr_w

Let me clarify a few things before I continue. First, this list is shorter than most other opcode lists because we're ignoring any opcodes above 201. These are reserved for future use. True, Sun is already using 203 to 228 for "quick" versions of some existing opcodes. Sun's JVM, for example, will replace any invoke_virtual with an invoke_virtual_quick immediately after resolving the relevant constant_pool entries for the initial invoke_virtual. The _quick version is faster because it uses the stored result of the earlier resolution; as a result, it doesn't need to do any subsequent checking. However, because any JIT or JVM transformations have no effect on the original bytecode in a classfile, you can safely forget about them.

I'm not going to examine how to turn the bytecode into source just yet. However, you can still see how the remaining Code attributes can be turned into opcodes and their operands.

In the second method

```
public String getLocalHostName()
```

you have an exception or a try-catch block.

```
<Exception_Table_Length>1</Exception_Table_Length>
<Exception_Table_Attributes>
 <Start_PC>0</Start_PC>
 <End_PC>9</End_PC>
 <Handler_PC>9</Handler_PC>
 <Catch_Type>4</Catch_Type>
</Exception_Table_Attributes>
```

The exception is thrown when the program counter (pc) equals 0, which is then caught between a pc count of 9 and 11. You can easily calculate what the pc counter is at any stage. Some opcodes take no operands, such as aload_0, some take one, and some even take two operands. The pc is incremented for every byte and each opcode or operand takes a single byte. This helps you judge where to insert the try and catch blocks.

```
<Code>b800024c2bb60003b04c1205b0</Code>
```

The Code attribute can then be broken down as shown in Table 2-7.

Table 2-7. Method 2 Code Attribute Breakdown

PC	Bytecode	Operand	Opcode	Constant Pool Resolution (If Applicable)
0:	b80002	invokestatic	#2	\<Method InetAddress InetAddress.getLocalHost()\>
3:	4c	astore_1		
4:	2b	aload_1		
5:	b60003	invokevirtual	#3	\<Method String InetAddress.getHostName()\>
8	b0	areturn		
9	4c	astore_1		
10	1205	ldc	#5	\<String "Not known"\>
12	b0	return		

invokestatic invokes the static method getLocalHost(). invokestatic invokes a class method directly and doesn't require any local variables to be placed on the stack before the calculation. The result is then stored, astore_1, as a local variable. invokevirtual invokes the getHostName(). Of the four method invocation operands, invokevirtual is the most common. It begins with an aload_1 that pushes the object reference address onto the stack where it can be used by getHostName(). The return value from the method invocation, a String, is then returned from the method, via a return.

If an exception was thrown, say, if the localhost could not be determined, then the ldc operand pushes the Not Known string in constant_pool[5] onto the stack where it is then returned from the method.

If the class is compiled without the -0 option, you can see how the line number attribute shows where the pc matches up with the original code.

```
<Code_Attributes>
  <Code_Attribute>start pc: 0 line number 9</Code_Attribute>
  <Code_Attribute>start pc: 4 line number 10</Code_Attribute>
  <Code_Attribute>start pc: 9 line number 13</Code_Attribute>
</Code_Attributes>
```

This is useful, but not exactly crucial information from a decompilation point of view. Admittedly, you would have to fill in a lot more gaps, but you should be able to see how the code begins to look like the original method.

```
9         public String getLocalHostName() {
10                try {
11                        InetAddress address = InetAddress.getLocalHost();
12                        return address.getHostName();
13                } catch (UnknownHostException e) {
14                        return "Not known";
15                }
16        }
```

Be careful not to place too much faith in the line number attribute because a note in the JVM specification says that the javac in Sun's JDK 1.0.2 can generate LineNumberTable attributes that are not in line number order. Or, to put that another way, sometimes there isn't a one-to-one mapping of the bytecode with the original source, which is a shame. It is also worth mentioning that backward compatibility means that this may not be fixed in future versions.

paint() Method

The final method has the following 36-byte Code attribute.

```
<Code_Length>36</Code_Length>
<Code>2bbb000659b700071208b600092ab6000ab60009120bb6000
    9b6000c10321019b6000db1</Code>
```

You can break this down in a similar fashion to the previous method, as you can see in Table 2-8.

Table 2-8. The Third Method—Code Attribute Breakdown

PC	Bytecode	Operand	Opcode	Constant Pool Resolution (If Applicable)
0	2b	aload_1		
1	bb0006	new	#6	\<Class StringBuffer>
4	59	dup		
5	b70007	invokespecial	#7	\<Method void StringBuffer(String)>
7	1208	ldc1	#8	\<String "Hello">
9	b6009	invokevirtual	#9	\<Method String getLocalHostName()>
12	2a	aload_0		
13	b6000a	invokevirtual	#10	\<Method StringBuffer StringBuffer.append(String)>
16	b6009	invokevirtual	#9	\<Method String getLocalHostName()>
19	120b	ldc1	#11	\<String "!">
21	b6000e	invokevirtual	#14	\<Method StringBuffer StringBuffer.append(String)>
24	b60013	invokevirtual	#19	\<Method String StringBuffer.toString()>
27	1032	bipush	50	
29	1019	bipush	25	
31	b6000d	invokevirtual	#15	\<Method void Graphics.drawString(String, int, int)>
34	b1	return		
35				

new creates a new StringBuffer class object. dup makes a copy of this object reference. The stack now has two copies of an uninitialized StringBuffer. ldc loads a copy of constant_pool[4] string, Hello, onto the stack, which is then turned into a StringBuffer by the static class method StringBuffer(). getLocalHostName() is once again loaded on the stack, popped, and appended using StringBuffer.append(String). The ! string is pushed onto the stack by ldc, where it is once again popped and appended. The StringBuffer is then converted to a string. The two integers are bipush'd onto the stack, and the drawString method is called by popping the two integers and the recently converted string. Finally, the whole result is returned out of the method.

```
<Code_Attributes>
  <Code_Attribute>start pc: 0 line number 17</Code_Attribute>
  <Code_Attribute>start pc: 35 line number 18</Code_Attribute>
 </Code_Attributes>
```

Once again, you can re-create the method using your analysis, and you can add the line numbers using the line number attribute.

```
17        public void paint(Graphics g) {
18                g.drawString(s + getLocalHostName() + "!", w,h);
19        }
```

ClassToXML, available from the downloads area of the Apress web site, will output bytecode like a true disassembler. And now that you've seen just how easy it is to write a disassembler, you can see why so many disassemblers have user interfaces.

The only piece of information I haven't mentioned is which opcodes take zero, one, or more operands; until you know this, you don't know when one command starts and another finishes. I'll return to this in Chapter 6.

Attributes

The final two elements contain the number of classfile attributes and the remaining attributes, which are usually the SourceFile or InnerClasses attributes.

```
<Attributes>
 <Attribute>
  <Attribute_Type>SourceFile</Attribute_Type>
  <Attribute_Length>2</Attribute_Length>
  <Source_File>sourcefile: Hello.java</Source_File>
 </Attribute>
</Attributes>
```

SourceFile is the name of the Java file that was used to originally generate the code. The InnerClasses attribute is a bit more complicated and is ignored by several decompilers that cannot yet handle inner classes.

You're not just limited to the SourceFile and InnerClasses attribute either. You can define new attributes here or indeed in any of the field or methods attribute sections. You may have your own reasons why you want to store information in a custom attribute, perhaps using it for some low-level check or for storing encrypted Code attributes to possibly prevent decompilation. Assuming your new Code attribute follows the format of all other attributes, you can add any attribute you want, which will be ignored by the JVM. Each attribute needs to begin with a two-byte attribute_name_index to resolve the reference to the name of the attribute in the constant pool, and a four-byte attribute_length that gives the length of the remaining bytes in the attribute.

Conclusion

You've finally come to the end of the guts of the classfile and built your own disassembler classtoxml in the process. Hopefully, you can see, or at least begin to see, how it all fits together. Although the design of the classfile is neat and compact, because of the split between the initial and final compilation stages, you have an awful lot of information to help you recover the source. For many years, programmers have been protected by the encryption that compiling to an executable usually offers, but splitting the compilation and carrying around so much information at the intermediate stage is just asking for trouble.

In Chapter 4, you'll take a look at both the theory and practice of the science of obfuscation. Now that you know how a classfile is put together, you will find it a lot easier to see how the different tactics that people employ really protect your code.

CHAPTER 3

Tools of the Trade

In the last chapter, you looked at the very heart of a Java classfile. In the next chapter, you'll perform an in-depth study of all the different ways to protect your code using everything from encryption to obfuscation. After that, you'll move on to build your own simple decompiler.

In this chapter, you're going to look at some of the automated tools as well as some simple techniques that hackers could use to modify your code, or worse, to recover your underlying source code. You'll also take a brief look at all the major obfuscators from third-party vendors, because obfuscation is by far the most popular tool for protecting source code. I'll be covering the theory behind these obfuscators in the next chapter.

But let's begin the chapter by looking at the how someone might crack your applet or application. That way, you can avoid some of the most obvious pitfalls when you're attempting to protect your code. Typically, you might use a key, an applet parameter, or even hard code in the IP address of a server so that only a licensed user can use your program. You'll now look at just some of the ways someone might disable your protection schemes.

Employing Hexadecimal Editors

For many years, hackers have been using hexadecimal editors and other more sophisticated tools such as NuMega's SoftICE and SmartCheck to get around licensing schemes on time-bombed versions of all kinds of software. Cracking demonstration versions of games that came with almost every computer magazine in the late 1980s and 1990s was a rite of passage for many of my fellow programmers.

Typically the programmer tried to protect their game or utility by checking to see if the date was 30 days after the installation date. After 30 days, the evaluation copy would cease to run. Alternatively, if they just couldn't afford to buy the real thing, they'd set the time of their computer so that it would permanently be a couple of days before the evaluation expired. Or, if they were a bit clever, they'd realize that the developer had to store the install date somewhere. If they were lucky, it would be somewhere simple like in the INI file or the registry, and they could permanently set it to some far-off date, such as 1999.

The rite of passage was truly complete when the programmer could just about read Assembler, could set a breakpoint to narrow in on the security functions, could find the piece of code that checked the evaluation date, and could disable it or create a serial number or key that the program would accept so that the evaluation copy became a fully functional version of the software.

There were countless more sophisticated mechanisms for protecting the more expensive programs—the dongle immediately springs to mind, which has to rate as one of the most useless inventions known to man—with varying degrees of success. Usually most protection mechanisms did little more than keep the average person from disabling or cracking them. The tool of choice for this type of attack in the Java world is the Hexadecimal editor.

Far from learning from the past, most programmers are condemned to repeat it. The vast majority of license protection examples out there rely on something as simple as a conditional jump.

```
if condition = true {
    continue;
} else {
print "Evaluation Copy expired";
    System.exit();
}
```

Suppose you come across an applet or application that you'd like to use yourself, but for some reason or other, you decide that you just don't want to pay for it. Let's look at an example of how this might work.

Applets are exceptionally easy to download; these days they mostly come in handy jar files, which make one neat, compact file. However, more often than not, they won't work the first time if you try to serve the applet up on your own web server, because the applet is protected using a copyright parameter or getDocumentBase and getHost to restrict the applet to its original web server. The code sample below will cause the applet to exit before it reaches main() if it is not being served up from the Apress web site.

```
import java.applet.*;

public class Test extends Applet {
        public void init() {
                String host, validDomain;
                boolean isValid = false;

                host = getDocumentBase().getHost();
                validDomain = "www.apress.com";
                isValid = host.equals(validDomain);

                // Continue if the applet is on the licensed domain otherwise exit
                if (isValid == false) {
                        System.exit(1);
                }
```

```
    }
    public void main() {
    // real work happens here
    }


}
```

However, you can edit a hexadecimal version of the file (see Listing 3-1) to change the condition so that it will work on any web server other than the Apress web site.

```
    isValid == true
```

Alternatively, you can edit the string www.apress.com to whatever domain you want to use with your favorite hexadecimal editor such as WinHex.[1]

Listing 3-1. Hex Dump of Test Class

```
00000000   CA FE BA BE 00 03 00 2D   00 27 0A 00 08 00 11 0A   Ê_º3/4...-.'......
00000010   00 08 00 12 0A 00 13 00   14 08 00 15 0A 00 16 00   ...............
00000020   17 0A 00 18 00 19 07 00   1A 07 00 1B 01 00 06 3C   ...............<
00000030   69 6E 69 74 3E 01 00 03   28 29 56 01 00 04 43 6F   init>...()V...Co
00000040   64 65 01 00 0F 4C 69 6E   65 4E 75 6D 62 65 72 54   de...LineNumberT
00000050   61 62 6C 65 01 00 04 69   6E 69 74 01 00 04 6D 61   able...init...ma
00000060   69 6E 01 00 0A 53 6F 75   72 63 65 46 69 6C 65 01   in...SourceFile.
00000070   00 09 54 65 73 74 2E 6A   61 76 61 0C 00 09 00 0A   ..Test.java.....
00000080   0C 00 1C 00 1D 07 00 1E   0C 00 1F 00 20 01 00 0E   ............ ...
00000090   77 77 77 2E 61 70 72 65   73 73 2E 63 6F 6D 07 00   www.apress.com..
000000A0   21 0C 00 22 00 23 07 00   24 0C 00 25 00 26 01 00   !..".#..$..%.&..
000000B0   04 54 65 73 74 01 00 12   6A 61 76 61 2F 61 70 70   .Test...java/app
000000C0   6C 65 74 2F 41 70 70 6C   65 74 01 00 0F 67 65 74   let/Applet...get
000000D0   44 6F 63 75 6D 65 6E 74   42 61 73 65 01 00 10 28   DocumentBase...(
000000E0   29 4C 6A 61 76 61 2F 6E   65 74 2F 55 52 4C 3B 01   )Ljava/net/URL;.
000000F0   00 0C 6A 61 76 61 2F 6E   65 74 2F 55 52 4C 01 00   ..java/net/URL..
00000100   07 67 65 74 48 6F 73 74   01 00 14 28 29 4C 6A 61   .getHost...()Lja
00000110   76 61 2F 6C 61 6E 67 2F   53 74 72 69 6E 67 3B 01   va/lang/String;.
00000120   00 10 6A 61 76 61 2F 6C   61 6E 67 2F 53 74 72 69   ..java/lang/Stri
00000130   6E 67 01 00 06 65 71 75   61 6C 73 01 00 15 28 4C   ng...equals...(L
00000140   6A 61 76 61 2F 6C 61 6E   67 2F 4F 62 6A 65 63 74   java/lang/Object
00000150   3B 29 5A 01 00 10 6A 61   76 61 2F 6C 61 6E 67 2F   ;)Z...java/lang/
00000160   53 79 73 74 65 6D 01 00   04 65 78 69 74 01 00 04   System...exit...
00000170   28 49 29 56 00 21 00 07   00 08 00 00 00 00 00 03   (I)V.!..........
00000180   00 01 00 09 00 0A 00 01   00 0B 00 00 00 1D 00 01   ...............
```

---

1. http://www.sf-soft.de/winhex/index-m.html

```
00000190    00 01 00 00 00 05 2A B7    00 01 B1 00 00 00 01 00    ......*...±.....
000001A0    0C 00 00 00 06 00 01 00    00 00 03 00 01 00 0D 00    ................
000001B0    0A 00 01 00 0B 00 00 00    4C 00 02 00 04 00 00 00    ........L.......
000001C0    1C 03 3E 2A B6 00 02 B6    00 03 4C 12 04 4D 2B 2C    ..>*¶..¶..L..M+,
000001D0    B6 00 05 3E 1D 9A 00 07    04 B8 00 06 B1 00 00 00    ¶..>.š...,..±...
000001E0    01 00 0C 00 00 00 1E 00    07 00 00 00 06 00 02 00    ................
000001F0    08 00 0A 00 09 00 0D 00    0A 00 13 00 0D 00 17 00    ................
00000200    0E 00 1B 00 10 00 01 00    0E 00 0A 00 01 00 0B 00    ................
00000210    00 00 19 00 00 00 01 00    00 00 01 B1 00 00 00 01    ...........±....
00000220    00 0C 00 00 00 06 00 01    00 00 00 13 00 01 00 0F    ................
00000230    00 00 00 02 00 10          ......
```

I'll return to this topic in the next chapter to examine ways around this problem and strategies you might want to employ to properly protect your code.

The Problem of Insecure Code

Even though in many cases no more than a hexadecimal editor is required to disable any protection mechanisms you might employ, nothing will stop a "would be" attacker from employing some lateral thinking. If you want to protect your code, then you should start thinking laterally too because plenty of other possibilities exist that take almost as little work as editing the binary directly.

Let's start with something a little less obvious than a Hexadecimal editor. Instead of disassembling or decompiling an applet, why not take advantage of a classfile's object-oriented nature and just extend it. You can hide static methods or simply override nonstatic methods. Take a look at the insecure code in Listing 3-2, for example.

Listing 3-2. Insecure Code

```
class TestOverride {

    public static void main(String[] args) {
        SecurityCheck sc = new SecurityCheck();
        sc.test();
    }
}

class SecurityCheck {

    SecurityCheck() {
        System.out.println("In Security Check constructor");
        test();
    }
```

```
    void test() {
                // Security checks go in here
        System.out.println("In SecurityCheck.test()");
    }
}
```

You can co-opt this code by writing Listing 3-3.

Listing 3-3. Taking Advantage of Insecure Code

```
class TestOverride {

    public static void main(String[] args) {

        // SecurityCheck sc = new SecurityCheck();
        // sc.test();

        InSecurityCheck   isc = new InSecurityCheck();
        isc.test();

    }
}

class SecurityCheck {

    SecurityCheck() {
        System.out.println("In Security Check constructor");
        test();
    }

    void test() {
        // Security checks go in here
        System.out.println("In SecurityCheck.test()");
    }
}

class InSecurityCheck extends SecurityCheck {

    InSecurityCheck() {
        // Super class constructor is automatically
        // called before subclass constructor is executed
        System.out.println("In InSecurityCheck constructor");
    }
```

```
void test() {
    // overrides test() in Super
    System.out.println("In InSecurityCheck.test()");
}

}
```

In Listing 3-3, you can potentially override the *test* method if it's poorly protected. In a Java classfile, you have access to the public and protected members
with the code. The only things you can't modify are the private members. But
coders are an inherently lazy bunch, and more often than not, the code is not
marked private.

Gary McGraw and Ed Felten laid out just what to avoid in their *JavaWorld*
article "Twelve Rules for Developing More Secure Java Code,"[2] which ultimately
ended up in their book *Securing Java: Getting Down to Business with Mobile
Code* (John Wiley & Sons, 1999). Here are those 12 rules:

1. Don't depend on initialization.

2. Limit access to your classes, methods, and variables.

3. Make everything final (unless there's a good reason not to).

4. Don't depend on package scope.

5. Don't use inner classes.

6. Avoid signing your code.

7. If you must sign your code, put it in one archive file.

8. Make your classes noncloneable.

9. Make your classes nonserializable.

10. Make your classes nondeserializable.

11. Don't compare classes by name.

12. Secrets stored in your code won't protect you.

---

2. http://www.javaworld.com/javaworld/jw-12-1998/jw-12-securityrules.html

There is even an automated tool, JSLint, that rips through static code to determine where someone's code is not following these 12 rules. Unfortunately JSLint—not to be confused with another JSLint, the JavaScript Verifier—is no longer publicly available.

For your purposes, Rule 2 and Rule 3 are the most important. Wherever possible, define your class, method, and variables as private and final unless you have a good reason not to.

If you're interested in studying this subject further, check out the nasty little Java file called `PublicEnemy.java` from Mark LaDue, which is widely available on the Web.[3] This searches for Java files on your hard drive and changes the access flags for a class; by doing this, it doesn't change the classfile's ability to run, but it breaks as many of the rules above as possible.

Disassemblers

If you've spent any time with Java bytecode, you've gradually noticed different patterns and language constructs. With practice and a lot of patience, you will find that bytecode becomes just another language.

So far you've seen two disassemblers: javap, which comes as part of the JDK and ClassfileToXML from Chapter 2, which disassembles the classfile into an XML structure (see the downloads area of the Apress web site for the source code). Let's take a brief look at some other disassemblers to see how they improve on the examples you've seen to date. It's worth noting that most of these disassemblers are now purely of historical or academic interest and are virtually impossible to find, but as you would imagine, they are relatively easy to re-create.

- IceBreaker

- ClassNavigator

- JavaDump

IceBreaker is useful for cracking classfiles that don't fully decompile, ClassNavigator is an easy-to-use interactive graphical user interface (GUI) that helps you make your way around the classfile, and JavaDump[4] gives you an excellent HTML output of any classfile in case you prefer HTML to XML. No current URLs were available for IceBreaker or ClassNavigator at the time of this writing.

---

3. http://www.cigital.com/hostile-applets/

4. http://www.ddj.com/ftp/1998/1998_01/class.txt (requires registration)

Other worthy mentions go to Chuck McManis's "Dumping Java Class Files" code,[5] and Jasmine,[6] a Java assembler or reassembler from Jon Meyer's and Troy Downing's book, the *Java Virtual Machine* (O'Reilly, 1997). I'm sure there are many, many more out there, so I apologize to anyone I've left out.

IceBreaker

Disassemblers can sometimes be much more effective than decompilers, especially when the decompilation process goes wrong. You may have come across your own examples where, under certain conditions, your favorite decompiler cannot recover the source.

Let's take the example of when a decompiled classfile won't recompile because Mocha's control flow analysis wasn't strong enough for the job. The resultant Java source is a mixture of partially decompiled Java code and some of the original Java bytecode commands—typically a number of goto statements that are not part of the Java language.

If this happens, then your options are pretty limited. You could disassemble the code yourself and try and guess what the original source might have been, or you can use IceBreaker, shown in Figure 3-1, to simplify the job.

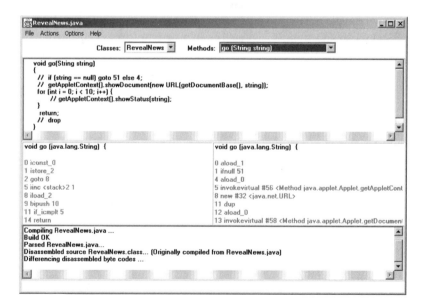

Figure 3-1. Disassembling with IceBreaker

---

5. http://www.javaworld.com/javaworld/jw-08-1997/jw-08-indepth.html

6. http://mrl.nyu.edu/~meyer/jasmin/

IceBreaker's graphical interface consists of four panes. Your attempt at the target source code is in the top section of the GUI, and its corresponding byte-code is in the bottom-left frame. You can see that the target bytecode is in the bottom-right frame. Any differences in the bytecode show up in red. The fourth section at the very bottom of the application displays the output from IceBreaker. Your mission, should you choose to accept it, is to modify your code, rebuild it, and gradually remove any red lines so that your bytecode and the target bytecode are the same. When you reach that stage, you can be pretty sure that your code and the original source are identical, except, of course, for any original programmer comments. You can also conveniently do this method by method, rather than by having to bite off the whole classfile all at once.

> **NOTE** *IceBreaker was written by a friend of mine, Martin Lambert, who is now CTO of SealedMedia. He hails from Surrey, near London, in the UK and he's the only person I've ever known who has an Irish passport issued by the Irish consulate in Tehran. So better ask him to go ahead if you ever meet him in Customs.*

IceBreaker really shines if your decompiled source breaks when you try to run the recompiled code. Because it allows a side-by-side comparison, you're able to see whether the decompiler did its job correctly.

When decompilers were in their infancy, IceBreaker was very useful because none of the early decompilers was 100 percent effective. Difficult problems in the class files could be smoothed out and the source code could be reverse engineered by hand. However, now that the likes of the Java Decompiler (JAD) and SourceAgain are so effective, IceBreaker is probably more useful as a benchmarking tool. IceBreaker makes it very, very easy to tell just how precise a decompiler is because it immediately pinpoints any differences between your bytecode and the target bytecode.

ClassNavigator

Jim Alateras from Comware in Australia is the author of one of my favorite disassemblers, ClassNavigator. To be honest it *is* my favorite disassembler. The interface is all encompassing without being difficult to use, and all the information you need is presented in one neat, intuitive GUI.

ClassNavigator, shown in Figure 3-2, displays a hierarchical map of the methods with the corresponding bytecode for each method as well as context-sensitive constant pool information in the top-right frame.

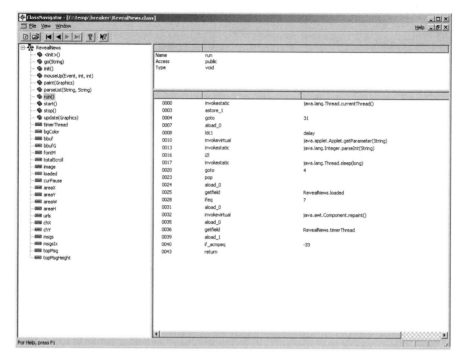

Figure 3-2. The ClassNavigator interface

JavaDump

Many disassemblers are by-products of articles, or as in this case, a book. However, not everyone writes their article while they're in high school. Matt Yourst wrote JavaDump for a *Dr. Dobb's Journal* article called "Inside Java Class Files." This article first appeared in January 1998, the year *before* he made it into MIT.

JavaDump, shown in Figure 3-3, uses a classfile manipulation library called JCF and is perfect if all you want to do is to get an HTML version of the structure of a classfile in a format not too dissimilar from Javadoc.

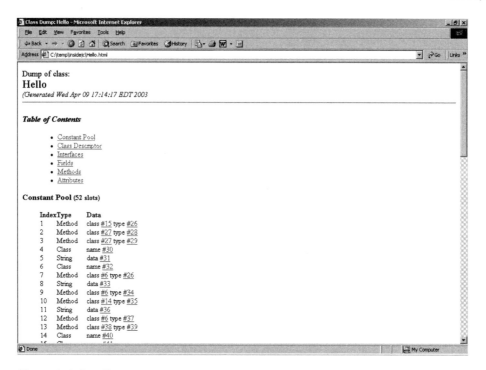

Figure 3-3. JavaDump output

JavaDump breaks the classfile into the following sections:

- Constant pool

- Class descriptor

- Interfaces

- Fields

- Methods

- Attributes

Items in the HTML file are typically hotlinked so that you can bounce around the constant pool, resolving any pointers to their corresponding data very quickly.

JavaDump uses the JDK 1.1 and is invoked using the following command, make sure that jcfutils.zip is in your classpath.

```
java lti.java.javadump.javadump [classfile.class] [-noconstpool]
```

The JCF utilities also include a StripDebug program that removes any debug information, line number attributes, and so on, and rewrites and saves your classfiles.

Decompilers

In 1991, James Gosling lead a team of Sun engineers who wrote the first Java Virtual Machine (JVM), which was known as Oak at the time. They then spent the next three years working on making inroads into the cable and telecommunications market with little or no success. It was early 1995 before the rest of the world began to take a real interest in Java, when HotJava and early beta versions of the JDK hit the developer community with a massive, resounding bang.

And yet it was only a year later when the first decompilers began to appear. It looks like the first public mention of a Java decompiler comes not from Mocha, but in a paper by Daniel Ford, an IBM researcher, in a whitepaper entitled "Jive: A Java Decompiler," which describes a working decompiler.

The first and only beta of Mocha appeared very soon afterward, in June of 1996. Its author, Hanpeter Van Vliet, named Mocha after the place where Dutch colonists stole a coffee plant from the Yemenese, marking the beginning of the Java coffee trade in what was then known as the Dutch East Indies. Nobody paid any real attention to Mocha until the following August when an article appeared in *c|net*.

Since then, we've seen at least a dozen decompilers: Jive, Mocha, WingDis, the Java Optimize and Decompile Environment (JODE), SourceAgain, DejaVu, JAD, HomeBrew, JReveal, Decafe, JReverse, and jAscii. There are also a number of programs—Jasmine and NMI are two examples—that provide a front end to JAD or Mocha for the command-line impaired. Some, like Mocha, are hopelessly out of date, and several others are no longer available.

Let's take a look at some of my favorite decompilers:

- Mocha

- SourceAgain

- JAD

- JODE

Apologies once again if I've missed your favorite decompiler, but many of the early decompilers, such as DejaVu and WingDis, have all but disappeared. I'm covering Mocha because it's the most famous decompiler, SourceAgain because it is a great example of a professional supported decompiler, JAD because it is the best of the free decompilers, and JODE because it is one of only two open source decompilers that I know about—the other is HomeBrew.

Mocha

Many of the earliest decompilers have long since disappeared; in fact, Jive never even saw the light of day. Mocha's life, like its author, Hanpeter Van Vliet, was short-lived. The original beta from June 1996 had a sister program, Crema, which cost $39. This protected classfiles from being decompiled by Mocha using obfuscation.

Because it is one of the earliest decompilers, Mocha is a simple command-line tool with no front-end GUI. It was distributed as a zip file of classes, which were obfuscated by Crema. Mocha is primed to recognize and ignore class files obfuscated by Crema. Not surprisingly jar files are not supported by Mocha; they didn't exist when Mocha was originally written.

Mocha uses the JDK 1.02. If you are going to decompile a file using Mocha, make sure the mocha.zip file is in your classpath, and decompile it using the following command:

```
java mocha.Decompiler [-v] [-o] Hello.class
```

The decompiler was only ever released as a beta, and as I said, its author met with an untimely demise before he could turn it into what I would call production quality. Mocha's flow analysis is incomplete and it fails on a number of Java constructs. Typically something like IceBreaker would have to be used in conjunction with Mocha to decompile anything other than the simplest Java classfiles. Several individuals have tried to patch Mocha, but these have been largely wasted efforts. It makes much more sense to use either JAD or SourceAgain. Like all early decompilers, Mocha could not decompile inner classes, which didn't appear until JDK 1.1

Just before Hanpeter died he sold the code for Mocha and Crema to Borland, and some of the Crema obfuscation code made it into early versions of JBuilder. Just a few weeks after Van Vliet's death, Mark LaDue's HoseMocha appeared; this allowed anyone to protect their files from being decompiled with Mocha without having to pay for Crema.

SourceAgain

Paul Martino, the founder of Ahpah Software, is the brains behind SourceAgain.[7] The original version was released in October 1997. There are actually two versions: a command-line version, and a professional version that can be plugged into several IDEs such as Symantec's Visual Café.

Both SourceAgain and JAD are not written in Java; I suspect either C or C++. The SourceAgain program is distributed as an executable, and its installation is

---

7. http://www.sourceagain.com

straightforward. Ahpah Software claims that SourceAgain decompiles all Java's language constructs, and as yet, I'm not going to disagree with that statement.

For our purposes, SourceAgain helps separate the early decompilers like Mocha and DejaVu from a second generation of decompilers because their capabilities are so different. First-generation decompilers can be defined as decompilers that cannot handle inner classes. SourceAgain is a very good example of a second-generation decompiler and it supports up to JDK 1.3. Not only can it handle inner classes, it also offers variable name massaging for obfuscated code that has mangled variable and method names.

The Java Decompiler (JAD)

JAD is fast, free, and very effective, and it was one of the first decompilers to handle inner classes properly. It's probably the simplest command-line tool to use in this entire chapter. The last available version of JAD is v1.58 from November 2001, and according to the FAQ, the major known bug is that it doesn't handle inline functions very well, which really shouldn't be an issue because most compilers leave it to the JIT engines to perform any inlining.

JAD[8] is the work of Pavel Kouznetsov, a graduate of the Faculty of Applied Mathematics at Moscow State Aviation School, who was living in Cyprus a few years ago.

For most cases, all you need to do to use JAD is type the following:

```
jad target.class
```

For a one-man show, JAD is remarkably complete. Its most interesting feature is that it can annotate source code with the relevant parts of a classfile's bytecode so that you can see just where each part of the decompiled code came from. This is a great tool for understanding bytecode.

There are many, many GUIs that use JAD as the decompiler engine such as NMI[9] (which originally used Mocha) and Front End Plus (no URL available) from the UK.

JODE

Jochen Hoenicke first wrote guavad, which according to his web page, is a Java disassembler not too dissimilar from javap, while working at the University of

---

8. http://kpdus.tripod.com/jad.html

9. http://www.trinnion.com/javacodeviewer

Oldenberg in Germany. Over the past few years, this has gradually turned into a full-scale decompiler and obfuscator package named JODE,[10] which appears in Figure 3-4.

Figure 3-4. The JODE Decompiler

The best way to call JODE is to use the applet window as shown here:

```
java jode.decompiler.Window
```

An applet not too dissimilar to Figure 3-4 appears. Enter the classfile you want to decompile, click start, and assuming it's on your editable classpath, the source will appear in the main frame.

If, after you finish this book, you get the sudden urge to write your own decompiler, then another place to look is at one or the other of the open source decompilers. Jochen's JODE decompiler is a very good place to start.

Obfuscators

Wherever there is a decompiler, you can be pretty sure that you'll find some sort of obfuscator. Java decompilers are so successful because a classfile carries so much information around with it. Even without the programmer's comments, the variable names and method names help anyone reading decompiled source to understand the flow and logic of the Java program.

---

10. http://jode.sourceforge.net

Obfuscators cannot prevent decompilation, but they can scramble the names into unintelligible control characters or Java-like keywords to make it more difficult for humans to understand. However, and you'll see more of this in the next chapter, it's a pretty sad indictment of Java obfuscators that the introduction of Java inner classes in the JDK 1.1 were far more effective at stopping decompilers than most obfuscation techniques currently in use.

In a scene reminiscent of the cold war arms race during the 1960s and 1970s, obfuscators and decompilers will no doubt battle it out to see who can control the source code. But like the arms race, it is the missile or, in this case, the decompiler that almost always wins.

You'll look at obfuscation in much greater detail in the next chapter, but for the moment, the main players in the history of obfuscation are as follows:

- Crema

- SourceGuard

- DashO

- Zelix KlassMaster

There are many others—the Java Obfuscator (JOBE), ShroudIt, JZipper, ObfuscatePro, and Mandate OneClass, to name but a few. By and large, many of the early obfuscators have simply given up the ghost and closed up shop. Crema, like Mocha, is so out of date that even if you did find a copy, you'd probably have to go back to a very early JDK to get it to work. 4thPass software, the creator of SourceGuard, has moved on from obfuscation and now operates primarily in the wireless market. DashO is still being sold by PreEmptive Solutions. In fact, they are also selling .NET versions of their products. Finally Zelix KlassMaster is notable in that it modifies the bytecode flow so that the original source code cannot be recovered from the classfile. However, this type of approach is very susceptible to the Java bytecode verifier, which can refuse to run the code and can potentially make your code much less portable.

I'll cover all these points and more in the next chapter, which hopefully will go some way toward explaining just why Java obfuscation has not exactly been a growth market.

Conclusion

Often books show their age when they review products. It's a form of technological carbon dating that usually makes a book out of date before it hits the presses. However, this book is different because I'm really telling a story of how different people have approached the problem of Java decompilation almost as soon as the language appeared.

   If there is a point that's worth making, it would be that you need to think outside the box because you can be sure your attackers will be using every possible way to get at your code if they really want it. Hopefully I've shown you the types of tools and techniques that are out there—both to protect your code and, just as importantly, to make it easier to get at your code.

Protecting Your Source: Strategies for Defeating Decompilers

Now that we've addressed the problem, you're probably wondering if there is any way you can protect your code. If you're at the point of asking why you should be producing Java applets or applications that can be easily circumvented, then this is the chapter for you.

In the previous chapters, you've seen that, for a number of reasons, Java class-files contain an unusually large amount of symbolic information. Classfiles that haven't been protected in some way return code that is almost identical to the original—except, of course, that it completely lacks any programmer comments. This chapter looks at the steps you can take to limit the amount of information in a classfile and hopefully, make the decompiler's job as difficult as possible.

Decompilation is a nasty problem from a developer's perspective. What is the point of trying to license an applet or even produce demo copies that someone can decompile or disassemble to circumvent all your protections? It seems that it is almost impossible to build in any failsafe protection mechanisms. So in this chapter, I'll introduce you to the current protection schemes as well as touch on what might be coming around the corner.

Readers of this book will probably have a foot in one of two different camps: as programmers, they may be interested in understanding how others achieve interesting effects, but from a business point of view, nobody will want someone else relabeling their code and selling it to third parties as if it was their own. Worse still, under certain circumstances, decompiling Java code can allow someone to attack other parts of your systems. A classic example of this type of problem or method of attack is when database logins and passwords are exposed after some JDBC code is decompiled. Worse still, Trojan horses can be placed in legitimate applets, which are subsequently recompiled and passed off as the original while they collect information such as logins and passwords for possible later use.

> **NOTE**   *As a quick aside, you may have a much simpler reason for wanting to protect your code. Maybe decompilation should be a standard tool for the CTO or even the CEO. When this book was in its infancy, I was in the habit of decompiling everything in sight to see different styles and techniques. However, a number of times I came across code that really should never have seen the light of day. My favorite example was a software company that was about to go public that had a method in their program called* updateS**t();.

What would be ideal would be a black box application that would take a class-file as input, and output an equivalent protected version. Unfortunately, as of yet, nothing out there can offer complete protection. It probably helps if I defined exactly what I am aiming to do when I talk about protecting your source. Perhaps the following quote will help.

> *[We want] to protect the code by making reverse engineering so technically difficult that it becomes impossible or at the very least economically inviable.*
>
> *—Collberg, Thomborson, and Law*[1]

It is difficult to define criteria for evaluating each strategy. I'll try to measure just how effective each tool or technique is using the following three criteria:

- Just how confused is the decompiler (potency)?

- Can it repel all attempts at decompilation (resilience)?

- What is the application overhead (cost)?

You're looking for the potency, or strength, of each technique; you also need to measure how resilient the strategy is against some means of automatically removing the protection; and finally, you need to know what the overhead, or cost, associated with protecting the source is. If the performance of the code is badly degraded, then that's probably going to make the cost too high, or if you convert your code into server-side code using web services, for example, then that's going to incur a much greater ongoing cost than a standalone application.

Let's look at what strategies you can apply to reach your goal—to learn what obfuscators and other tools are available on the market and how effective they are at protecting your code. I'll also talk about how to measure their effectiveness and also touch on what to look out for in the future.

In the first chapter, you already saw the examples of how code can be protected in the judicial system. The following is an *almost* complete list of ways of protecting your Java source code before it gets to that stage.

---

1. "A Taxonomy of Obfuscating Transformations" http://www.cs.arizona.edu/~collberg/ Research/Publications/CollbergThomborsonLow97a/

- Using compilation flags and third-party compilers

- Writing two versions of the applet or application

- Employing obfuscation

- Applying web services and server-side execution

- Using encryption

- Using digital rights management

- Fingerprinting your code

- Selling the source code

- Using native methods

Compilation Flags

Two different types of compilation flags appear to have an impact on the generated bytecode. These are as follows:

```
javac -g:none|{source,lines,vars)
javac -O
```

The -g flag is responsible for generating all debugging information. This tells javac to add line numbers (lines option) and local variable names (vars option), which means that the classfile and constant pool is that much bigger with the added variables and the line number attributes. In Chapter 2, you saw how this allows you to map the bytecode onto the original source code. If you use this option, you can store the name of the original source file in the attributes (source option). Compiling with -g:none will keep lines, vars, and the source file attribute information out of your classfile. You can use HelloWorld.java in Listing 4-1 to see what effect compilation flags have on the bytecode.

Listing 4-1. HelloWorld.java

```
import java.applet.Applet;
import java.awt.Graphics;
import java.net.InetAddress;
import java.net.UnknownHostException;
```

```
public class HelloWorld extends Applet {

    public String getLocalHostName() {
        try {
            InetAddress address = InetAddress.getLocalHost();
            return address.getHostName();
        }
        catch (UnknownHostException e) {
            return "Not known";
        }
    }
    public void paint(Graphics g) {
    public void paint(Graphics g) {
                String s = "Hello ";
                int w = 50;
                int h = 25;

                g.drawString(s + getLocalHostName() + "!", w,h);
    }
}
```

I compiled the HelloWorld.java example in Listing 4-1 using
-g:*source, line, vars* and then output the classfile's information using javap -c -l
in Listing 4-2. If you compile the source using -g with no options, the compiler
drops the local variables section but still includes line number and source file
attributes. Compiling with -g:none flags will further remove the line number and
source file information.

Listing 4-2. HelloWorld.classfile

```
Compiled from HelloWorld.java
public class HelloWorld extends java.applet.Applet {
    public HelloWorld();
    public java.lang.String getLocalHostName();
    public void paint(java.awt.Graphics);
}

Method HelloWorld()
    0 aload_0
    1 invokespecial #1 <Method java.applet.Applet()>
    4 return

Line numbers for method HelloWorld()
    line 6: 0
```

```
Local variables for method HelloWorld()
   HelloWorld this  pc=0, length=5, slot=0


Method java.lang.String getLocalHostName()
    0 invokestatic #2 <Method java.net.InetAddress getLocalHost()>
    3 astore_1
    4 aload_1
    5 invokevirtual #3 <Method java.lang.String getHostName()>
    8 areturn
    9 astore_1
   10 ldc #5 <String "Not known">
   12 areturn
Exception table:
   from   to   target type
      0    9    9    <Class java.net.UnknownHostException>


Line numbers for method java.lang.String getLocalHostName()
   line 10: 0
   line 11: 4
   line 14: 9


Local variables for method java.lang.String getLocalHostName()
   HelloWorld this  pc=0, length=13, slot=0
   java.net.InetAddress address  pc=4, length=5, slot=1
   java.net.UnknownHostException e  pc=10, length=3, slot=1


Method void paint(java.awt.Graphics)
    0 ldc #6 <String "Hello, ">
    2 astore_2
    3 bipush 50
    5 istore_3
    6 bipush 25
    8 istore 4
   10 aload_1
   11 new #7 <Class java.lang.StringBuffer>
   14 dup
   15 invokespecial #8 <Method java.lang.StringBuffer()>
   18 aload_2
   19 invokevirtual #9 <Method java.lang.StringBuffer append(java.lang.String)>
   22 aload_0
   23 invokevirtual #10 <Method java.lang.String getLocalHostName()>
   26 invokevirtual #9 <Method java.lang.StringBuffer append(java.lang.String)>
   29 ldc #11 <String "!">
   31 invokevirtual #9 <Method java.lang.StringBuffer append(java.lang.String)>
```

```
34 invokevirtual #12 <Method java.lang.String toString()>
37 iload_3
38 iload 4
40 invokevirtual #13 <Method void drawString(java.lang.String, int, int)>
43 return

Line numbers for method void paint(java.awt.Graphics)
   line 18: 0
   line 19: 3
   line 20: 6
   line 22: 10
   line 23: 43

Local variables for method void paint(java.awt.Graphics)
   HelloWorld this  pc=0, length=44, slot=0
   java.awt.Graphics g  pc=0, length=44, slot=1
   java.lang.String s  pc=3, length=40, slot=2
   int w  pc=6, length=37, slot=3
   int h  pc=10, length=33, slot=4
```

If you decompile the code using Jad, you can see, in Listing 4-3, that compiling with the -g:none option is about the same as running the classfile through a very primitive renaming obfuscator, but the code is still very much intact.

Listing 4-3. Decompiled Verison of HelloWorld.java

```
// Decompiled by Jad v1.5.8e2. Copyright 2001 Pavel Kouznetsov.
// Jad home page: http://kpdus.tripod.com/jad.html
// Decompiler options: packimports(3)

import java.applet.Applet;
import java.awt.Graphics;
import java.net.InetAddress;
import java.net.UnknownHostException;

public class HelloWorld extends Applet
{

    public HelloWorld()
    {
    }

    public String getLocalHostName()
    {
        try
```

```
    {
        InetAddress inetaddress = InetAddress.getLocalHost();
        return inetaddress.getHostName();
    }
    catch(UnknownHostException unknownhostexception)
    {
        return "Not known";
    }
}

public void paint(Graphics g)
{
    String s = "Hello, ";
    byte byte0 = 50;
    byte byte1 = 25;
    g.drawString(s + getLocalHostName() + "!", byte0, byte1);
}
}
```

Once, the -0, or optimization flag, did perform some rudimentary optimizations, but since Java 2 SDK, version 1.2 was introduced, this flag does not seem to have performed any optimization. In earlier versions of the JDK the optimization flag inlined static, final, and private methods, which meant they executed marginally faster and could handle slightly larger classfiles. One can only suspect that JIT compilers such as Hotspot are much more efficient at optimizing bytecode at runtime, so you don't really need an optimization flag at compile time. The -0 flag now only exists for backward compatibility reasons. No doubt plenty of makefiles and Ant scripts would crash if the -0 option was pulled from the next version of javac.

If you do a lot of debugging and like the -g flag, then it will help protect the code a little if you use -g:none because all the variable name and line number information will be lost. So change the flag before doing a final build, and if you are using a third-party Java IDE, make sure that the default compilation flag is set to -g:none. As you can see from Listings 4-1 and 4-3, I'm not exactly talking about huge impediments to the decompilation process, but why give the decompiler any more information than necessary?

Although other third-party Java compilers may be different, I've found that IBM's Jikes compiler performs almost identically to Sun's javac. So, currently, it looks like the compilation flags are not going to get very far in protecting your source.

Finally, a small word of warning to developers—method names and variables are very visible in Java. The Reflection API will return all the methods in a classfile, so please do not choose embarrassing names for methods or variables in Java. I'm sure vulgar method names are pretty common in other languages, but such names are just so much easier to recover in Java, and therefore, are much more likely to embarrass you or your company in the long run. Enough preaching, but if you do tend to use strange and unusual names, then whatever you do, obfuscate with one of the better obfuscators. Nothing is better at hurting a business proposal or generating adverse publicity before an Initial Public Offering (IPO) than some bad publicity from a badly chosen method or variable name—assuming the days of the software IPO return again someday.

Writing Two Versions of the Applet or Application

Standard marketing practice in the software industry, especially on the Web, is to allow users to download a fully functional evaluation copy of the software that stops working after a certain period of time or number of uses. The theory behind this try-as-you-buy system is that after the allotted time, say 30 days, the user has become so accustomed to your program that they happily pay for a full version.

However, most software developers realize that these fully functional evaluation programs are a double-edged sword. They show the full functionality of the program but are often very difficult to protect no matter what language we're talking about. In Chapter 3, you saw how handy hexadecimal editors are at ripping through licensing schemes whether they are written in C++, Visual Basic, or indeed Java.

Many different types of protection schemes can be employed, but in the world of Java, you only have one very simple protection tool:

```
if boolean = true
        execute
else
        exit
```

These types of schemes have been cracked since the first time they appeared in VB shareware. The protection is simply modified by flipping a portion of code in the hexadecimal editor to the following:

```
if boolean = false
        execute
else
        exit
```

A number of software packages claim to be able to protect and license your software. My advice is to treat this type of program very skeptically unless it is obvious that the software is offering a new angle to this problem. Ask for an example of a protected program and use your favorite decompiler and disassemblers to see if it is truly protected.

The simplest way to steal an applet doesn't even require a decompiler or disassembler. Assuming you've viewed the applet in your browser, open the HTML to find the name of the applet and then copy it from your cache onto your web server. Create a new HTML page and copy everything with the original <applet></applet> tags into your HTML.

When Java was in its infancy—to protect from this dastardly behavior—applets used all sort of getDate(), getDocumentBase(), getCodeBase(), getHost(), and getLocalHost() combinations to try to make sure that your applet was only downloaded from a licensed server, but these are exceptionally simple protection schemes and are trivial to bypass, even without a decompiler.

getDocumentBase() returns the host that served the web page containing the applet, and getCodeBase() returns the address of the applet class files. So you can make sure that the web page is only one server up from your web server by writing some code similar to Listing 4-4.

Listing 4-4. Simple Protection Mechanism

```
public void init() {
        String s = urlencode(getDocumentBase().getHost());
                if((s.compareTo("www.riis.com")) == 0 ){
                        // continue
                }else{
                        System.exit(0);
                }
}
```

You can make the program execute on another web server by changing the ==0 to !=0 using a disassembler, which leaves you in the ironic position where the modified applet now runs on every web server except the original web server. You could also decompile the code, remove the offending check, and recompile it to create an unprotected applet.

Several licensing schemes extended this idea by adding public and private keys to attempt to protect your applet. JTimer from InetSoft Technology Corporation was one such licensing tool. Mark LaDue—author of HoseMocha—took their tool apart in a similar fashion to what I just showed you in Listing 4-4 in his paper "The Maginot License: Failed Approaches to Licensing Java Software Over the Internet." Personally I agree with Mark LaDue's analysis and I don't like the primitive licensing schemes that were so prevalent when Java was mostly used for writing applets.

How much better it would be if you could write a demonstration applet or application that gives the potential customer enough of a flavor of the product without giving away the goods? For instance, you could consider crippling the demo by removing all but the basic functionality while still leaving in the menu options. If that's too much, then consider using a third-party vendor such as WebEx. It allows the potential customer to see your application, but the customer never gets a chance to run it against a decompiler.

Of course, this doesn't stop anyone from decompiling a legitimate copy of the fully functional version after they've bought it, removing any licensing schemes, and then passing it on to other third parties. But they will have to pay to get that far, and often that is enough of an impediment to hackers that they will simply look elsewhere.

> **NOTE** *A not exactly trivial alternative to this licensing approach for applets would be to create an automated robot that searches the web for applets with the same name, size, and fingerprint. The robot could then automatically send an email to the people listed in the DNS record for that domain name to ask them to remove your applet, assuming that the fingerprint matches.*

In the next section, we'll look at what obfuscators are available and what they can do to help you get over this hurdle.

Employing Obfuscation

Maybe a dozen or so different Java obfuscators have seen the light of day. Most of the earlier versions of this type of technology are now pretty difficult to find. You can still find traces of them on the Web if you look hard enough, but apart from one or two notable exceptions, Java obfuscators have mostly faded into obscurity—yet another example of the bottom falling out of the dotcom market.

This leaves you with the interesting problem of how you tell if any of the remaining handful of obfuscators are any good. Or perhaps we've lost something very useful in the original obfuscators that would have protected your code but couldn't hold on long enough when the market took a turn for the worse? You need to understand what obfuscation really means because you have no way of knowing whether one obfuscator is better than another, unless you use market demands as your deciding factor.

When obfuscation is outlawed, only outlaws will sifjdifdm wofiefiemf eifm.

—Paul Tyma, PreEmptive Solutions

In this section, you're going to look at obfuscation theory, and you'll get a little practice. To begin with, it might help if we borrow from Christian Collberg's "Taxonomy of Obfuscating Transformations" to help shed some light on where exactly we stand. In his paper, Christian splits obfuscation into three distinct areas.

- Layout obfuscation

- Control obfuscation

- Data obfuscation

Table 4-1 lists a reasonably complete set of obfuscations that I've separated into these three different types, and in some cases, further classified. You'll take a look at the more important transformations in each section, as this chapter progresses.

Table 4-1. Obfuscation Transformations (with apologies to Christian Collberg)[2]

Obfuscation Type	Classification	Transformation
Layout		Scramble identifiers
Control	Computations	Insert dead or irrelevant code
		Extend loop condition
		Reducible to non-reducible
		Add redundant operands
		Remove programming idioms
		Parallelize code
	Aggregations	Inline and outline methods
		Interleave methods
		Clone methods
		Loop transformations
	Ordering	Reorder statements
		Reorder loops
		Reorder expression
Data	Storage and encoding	Change encoding
		Split variable
		Convert static to procedural data
	Aggregation	Merge scalar variables
		Factor class

---

2. Some transformation types, which are particularly ineffective for Java, are omitted in this table.

Table 4-1. Obfuscation Transformations (with apologies to Christian Collberg) (continued)

Obfuscation Type	Classification	Transformation
		Insert Bogus class
		Refactor class
		Split array
		Merge arrays
		Fold array
		Flatten array
	Ordering	Reorder methods and Instance variables
		Reorder arrays

Most of the Java obfuscators you'll meet only perform layout obfuscation with some limited data and control obfuscation. This is partly due to the Java verification process throwing out any illegal bytecode syntax. The Java Verifier is very important if you write mostly applets because remote code is always verified. These days, where there are fewer and fewer applets, the main reason Java obfuscators don't feature more high-level obfuscation techniques is because the obfuscated code has to work on a variety of Java Virtual Machines (JVMs).

Although the JVM specification is pretty well defined, each JVM has its own slightly different interpretation of the specification, which leads to lots of idiosyncrasies when it comes to how a JVM will handle bytecode that can no longer be represented by Java source. JVM developers don't pay much attention to testing this type of bytecode, and your customers aren't interested in whether or not it's syntactically correct; they just want to know why it won't run on their platform.

As you look into these different areas, please remember that you'll need to employ a certain degree of tightrope walking in advanced forms of obfuscation, what I call *high-mode obfuscation,* so you need to be very careful about what these programs can do to your bytecode. The more vigorous the obfuscation, the more difficult it is to decompile, but the more likely it will fail to pass the Java Verifier or crash some obscure JVM.

The best obfuscators will perform multiple transformations without breaking the Java Verifier or any JVM. Not surprisingly, the obfuscation companies err on the side of caution, which inevitably means less protection for your source code.

Layout Obfuscations

Most obfuscators work by obscuring the variable names or scrambling the iden-tifiers in a classfile to try and make the decompiled source code useless. As you saw in Chapter 2, this doesn't stop the bytecode from getting executed because the classfile uses pointers to the methods names and variables in the constant pool rather than the actual names.

Obfuscated code mangles the source code output by a decompiler by renaming the variables in the constant pool with automatically generated garbage variables while still leaving the code syntactically correct. In effect, it removes all clues that a programmer gives when naming variables (most good programmers will have chosen meaningful variable names). It also means that the decompiled code will require some rework before it can be recompiled.

However, most capable programmers can make their way through obfuscated code with or without the aid of hints from the variable names. With due care and attention—and perhaps the aid of a profiler to understand the program flow and maybe a disassembler to rename the variables—most obfuscated code can be changed back into something easier to handle no matter how significant the obfuscation.

Crema is the original obfuscator and was a complementary program to the oft-mentioned Mocha, written by the late Hanpeter Van Vliet. Mocha was given away free, but Crema cost somewhere around $30. To safeguard against Mocha, you had to buy Crema. It performed some rudimentary obfuscation and had one interesting side effect. It flagged class files so that Mocha refused to decompile any applets or applications that had been previously run through Crema. However, other decompilers soon came onto the market, and they were not so Crema friendly.

Early obfuscators such as JOBE[3] replaced the method names with a,b,c,d ... z(). Crema's identifiers were much more unintelligible, using Java-like keywords to confuse the reader, as shown in Listing 4-5. Several other obfuscators went one step further by using Unicode style names, which had the nice side effect of crashing many of the existing decompilers.

Listing 4-5. Crema-Protected Code

```
private void _mth015E(void 867 % static 931){
        void short + = 867 % static 931.openConnection();
        short +.setUseCaches(true);
        private01200126013D = new DataInputStream(short +.getInputStream());
        if(private01200126013D.readInt() != 0x5daa749)
                throw new Exception("Bad Pixie header");
        void do const throws = private01200126013D.readShort();
```

---

3. http://www-personal.engin.umich.edu/java/unsupported/jobe/doc.html

```
if(do const throws != 300)
        throw new Exception("Bad Pixie version " + do const throws);
_fld015E = _mth012B();
for = _mth012B();
_mth012B();
_mth012B();
_mth012B();
short01200129 = _mth012B();
_mth012B();
_mth012B();
_mth012B();
_mth012B();
void |= = _mth012B();
_fld013D013D0120import = new byte[|=];
void void = |= / 20 + 1;
private = false;
void = = getGraphics();
for(void catch 11 final = 0; catch 11 final < |=;){
        void while if = |= - catch 11 final;
        if(while if > void)
                while if = void;
        private01200126013D.readFully(_fld013D013D0120import,
catch 11 final, while if);
        catch 11 final += while if;
        if(= != null){
                const = (float)catch 11 final / (float)|=;
                =.setColor(getForeground());
                =.fillRect(0, size().height - 4,
(int)(const * size().width), 4);
        }
    }
}
```

JOBE is probably more useful as an unobfuscator than as an obfuscator because of the way it renames methods and variables, getting rid of any Unicode or Java keyword names in the process—nothing wrong with a bit of lateral thinking, especially in the field of reverse engineering. Alternatively you can use something like SourceAgain's automatic variable name generation.

Most of the obfuscators we've met, such as Crema and JOBE, are much better at reducing the size of a classfile rather than protecting the source. However, there is a small twist in the tale, because PreEmptive Solutions holds a patent that breaks the link between the original source and obfuscated code and goes some way toward protecting your code.

All the methods are renamed to a, b, c, d, and so on. But unlike other programs, as many methods as possible are renamed using operator overloading wherever possible. Overloaded methods have the same name but have different numbers of parameters, so more than one method can be renamed a(), as shown here:

```
getPayroll()                            becomes    a()
makeDeposit(float amount)               becomes    a(float a)
sendPayment(String dest)                becomes    a(String a)
```

The classic example from PreEmptive shows the following:

```
// Before Obfuscation

private void calcPayroll(RecordSet rs) {

    while (rs.hasMore()) {
        Employee = rs.getNext(true);
        Employee.updateSalary();
        DistributeCheck(employee);
    }
}

// After Obfuscation

private void a(a rs) {

    while (rs.a()) {
        a = rs.a(true);
        a.a();
        a(a);
    }
}
```

Giving multiple names to the different methods can be very confusing. True, the overloaded methods are difficult to understand, but they are not impossible to comprehend. They too can be renamed into something easier to read. Having said that, operator overloading has proved to be one of the best layout techniques to beat because it does break the link between the original and the obfuscated Java code.

Control Obfuscations

The concept behind control obfuscations is to confuse anyone looking at decompiled source by breaking up the control flow of the source.

Functional blocks that belong together are broken apart and functional blocks that don't belong together are intermingled to make the source much more difficult to understand.

Collberg's paper breaks down control obfuscations further into three different classifications of *computation, aggregation,* and *ordering.* You'll now look at some of the most important of these obfuscations or transformations in a little more detail.

Computation

If you refer back to the computation classification section of Table 4-1, you see that it can be broken down into the following transformations.

Insert Dead or Irrelevant Code

You can insert dead code or dummy code to confuse your attacker; this can include extra methods or simply a few lines of irrelevant code. If you don't want the performance of your original code affected, then add the code so that it never gets executed. But be careful, because many decompilers and even obfuscators remove code that never gets called.

Don't just limit yourself to thinking about inserting Java code; there's no reason why you can't insert irrelevant bytecode. Mark LaDue wrote a small program called HoseMocha that altered a classfile by adding a pop bytecode instruction at the end of every method. As far as most JVMs were concerned, this was an irrelevant instruction and was simply ignored. However Mocha couldn't handle it and crashed. No doubt if Mocha's author had survived, then it could have been easily fixed, but he didn't.

Extend Loop Condition

Obfuscate the code by making the loop conditions much more complicated. You do this by extending the loop condition with a second or third condition that doesn't do anything. It should not affect the number of times the loop is executed or decrease the performance. Try to use the bitshift or ? operator in your extended condition for some added spice.

Reducible to Nonreducible

The Holy Grail of obfuscation is to create obfuscated code that cannot be converted back into its original format. To do this, you need to break the link between the bytecode and the original Java source. The obfuscator transforms bytecode control flow from its original reducible flow to something nonreducible. Because Java bytecode is, in some ways, more expressive than Java, you can use the Java bytecode goto statement to help out.

Let's revisit an old computing adage, which states that using the goto statement is the biggest sin that can be committed by any self-righteous computer programmer. Edsger W. Dijkstra's "Go To Statement Considered Harmful" paper[4] was the beginning of this particular religious fervor. The anti–goto statement camp produced enough anti–goto command sentiment in its heyday to put it right up there with the best Usenet flame wars.[5]

Common sense tells us that it's perfectly acceptable to use the goto statement under certain limited circumstances. For example, you can use the goto statement to replace how Java uses the break and continue statements. The issue is in using goto to break out of a loop or having two goto statements operate within the same scope. You may or may not have seen it in action, but bytecode uses the goto statement extensively as a way to control the code flow. However, the scope of no two goto's ever cross.

The Fortran statement in Listing 4-6 illustrates a goto statement breaking out of a control loop. One of the principal arguments against using this type of coding style is that it can make it almost impossible to model the control flow of a program and introduces an arbitrary nature into a computer program—which, almost by definition, is a recipe for disaster. At this point, we say that the control flow has become irreducible.

Listing 4-6. Breaking Out of a Control Loop Using a goto Statement

```
do 40 i = 2,n
if(dx(i).le.dmax) goto 50
dmax = dabs(dx(i))
40        continue
50        a = 1
```

As a standard programming technique, it's a very bad idea to attempt to have goto statements that cross scope because not only is it likely to introduce unforeseen side effects—because it's no longer possible to reduce the flow into a single flow graph—but it also makes the code unmanageable.

However, some argue that this is the perfect tool for protecting bytecode if you can assume that the person writing the protection tool to produce the illegal gotos knows what they are doing and won't introduce any nasty side effects. It certainly makes it much harder to reverse engineer because the code flow does indeed become irreducible, but it's important that any new constructs added are as similar as possible to the original.

A few of words of warning before I leave this topic: where it is almost without a doubt that a traditionally obfuscated classfile is functionally the same as its

---

4. http://www.acm.org/classics/oct95/

5. It is rumored that the hot air generated in such debates as Vi vs. Emacs, Microsoft vs. Unix, and now .NET vs. Java, would be enough to heat the town of Cwmbran in south Wales until 2010.

original counterpart, the same cannot be said of a rearranged version. A large amount of trust has to be placed in the protection tool, otherwise it will always be blamed for odd intermittent applet or application behavior.

More importantly, although current JVMs are lax about letting bytecodes through, future ones may not be so forgiving. Tools that use encryption or rearrange or generally corrupt the original bytecode might not pass bytecode verification in these stricter JVMs or might simply fail to work. After all, JVM developers were almost certainly not using irreducible bytecode as part of their test suites. There is already one example of a JIT not executing classfiles with irreducible flow modifications. Also, several defunct obfuscators were based on this technique. If possible, always test your transformed code on your target JVMs.

The other downside to this technique is that many reducible to nonreducible transformations can already be easily reversed using an automatic deobfuscator. In the end, I suspect that this Holy Grail is not going to defeat decompilation in the Java world.

Add Redundant Operands

Add extra insignificant terms to some of your basic calculations and round up the result before you use it. For example the following code prints k = 2.

```
import java.io.*;

public class redundantOperands {
        public static void main(String argv[]) {
                int i=1;
                int j=2;
                int k;

                k = i * j;
                System.out.println("k = " + k);
        }
}
```

Add some redundant operands to the code as follows, and the result will be exactly the same because you've cast *k* to an integer before you printed it:

```
import java.io.*;

public class redundantOperands {
```

```
public static void main(String argv[]) {
        int i = 1, j = 2;
        double x = 0.0007, y = 0.0006, k;


        k = (i * j) + (x * y);
        System.out.println(" k = " + (int)k);
    }
}
```

I should stress that using this technique throughout your code has the potential to degrade the performance of your application.

Remove Programming Idioms (or Write Sloppy Code)

Most good programmers will amass a body of knowledge over their careers and will constantly be adding to it.[6] For increased productivity, they will use the same components, methods, modules, and classes over and over again in a slightly different way each time. Like osmosis, a new language gradually evolves until everyone decides to do some things in more or less the same way. Martin Fowler's book *Refactoring: Improving the Design of Existing Code* (Addison-Wesley, 1999) is an excellent collection of how to take some existing code and refactor it into shape. Judging by the sales of this book, this has created a standard way of doing things in Java.

However, this type of language standardization creates a series of idioms that give the hacker way too many helpful hints, even if they can only decompile part of your code. So throw out all your programming knowledge, stop using design patterns or classes that you know have been borrowed by lots of other programmers, and *defactor* your existing code.

Writing sloppy code is easy and a heretical approach that gets under my skin and ultimately affects the performance and long-term maintenance of your code. A more difficult and, from my point of view, better alternative would be to rewrite a common Java class from the SDK and reference the renamed class from your application so that the hacker gets a little more confused and hopefully gives up.

Parallelize Code

Converting your code to threads can significantly increase its complexity. The code does not necessarily have to be thread-compatible as you can see in the HelloThread example in Listing 4-7. The flow of control has sifted from a sequential model to a quasi-parallel model with each thread being responsible for printing a different word.

---

6. Until someone forces them to become a manager.

Listing 4-7. HelloWorld Thread Example

```java
import java.util.*;

public class HelloThread extends Thread
{
    private String theMessage;

    public HelloThread(String message) {
        theMessage = message;
        start();
    }

    public void run() {
        System.out.println(theMessage);
    }

    public static void main(String []args)
    {
        new HelloThread("Hello, ");
        new HelloThread("World");
    }
}
```

The downside of this approach is the programming overhead involved in making sure that the threads are timed correctly and any interprocess communication is working correctly so that the program executes as intended. The upside is that it could take significantly longer to realize that the code can be collapsed into a sequential model.

Aggregations

Aggregations as a form of obfuscation occur when certain elements of the code are folded together to make their structure less obvious. In this section, you will become familiar with aggregating methods and loops.

Inline and Outline Methods

In the "Compilation Flags" section, I mentioned that inlining methods—where every method call is replaced with the actual body of the method—is often used to optimize code because it removes the overhead of the call. In your Java code, this has the side effect of ballooning the code, often making it a much more daunting task to understand. You can also balloon the code by taking some of the inlined methods and outlining them into a dummy method that looks like it's being called but doesn't actually do anything.

Mandate's OneClass obfuscator took this transformation to the extreme by inlining every class in an application into a single Java class. Like all early obfuscation tools, Mandate's OneClass is no longer with us.

Interleave Methods

Although it is a relatively simple task to interleave two methods, it is much more difficult to break them apart.

Listing 4-8 shows two independent methods, and in Listing 4-9, I have interleaved the code together so that it all appears to be connected. This example assumes that you want to show the balance and email the invoice, but there is no reason why it couldn't be interleaved to allow you to only email the invoice.

Listing 4-8. showBalance and emailInvoice

```java
void showBalance(double customerAmount, int daysOld) {
        if(daysOld > 60) {
                printDetails(customerAmount * 1.2);
        } else {
                printDetails(customerAmount);
        }
}
void emailInvoice(int customerNumber) {
        printBanner();
        printItems(customerNumber);
        printFooter();
}
```

Listing 4-9. showBalanceEmailInvoice

```java
void showBalanceEmailInvoice(double customerAmount,
                        int daysOld, int customerNumber) {
        printBanner();
        if(daysOld > 60) {
                printItems(customerNumber);
                printDetails(customerAmount * 1.2);
        } else {
                printItems(customerNumber);
                printDetails(customerAmount);
        }
        printFooter();
}
```

Clone Methods

Clone a method so that the same code but different methods are called under nearly identical circumstances. You could call one method over another based on the time of day to give the appearance that external factors exist when they really do not. Use a different style in the two methods or use it in conjunction with the *Interleave Method* transformation so that the two methods look very different but are really performing the same function.

Loop Transformations

Compiler optimizations often perform a number of loop optimizations. You can perform the same optimizations by hand or code them in your tool to obfuscate the code. Loop unrolling reduces the number of times a loop is called and loop fission converts a single loop into multiple loops. For example, if you know maxNum is divisible by 5, you can unroll the for loop as shown in Listing 4-10.

Listing 4-10. Loop Unrolling

```
// Before
for (int i = 0; i<maxNum; i++){
    sum += val[i];
}
// After
for (int i = 0; i<maxNum; i+=5){
    sum += val[i] + val[i+1] + val[i+2] + val[i+3] + val[i+4];
}
for (x=0; x < maxNum; x++){
    i[x] += j[x] + k[x];
}


for (x=0; x < maxNum; x++) i[x] += j[x];
for (x=0; x < maxNum; x++) i[x] += k[x];
```

Ordering

If you take a look at the Ordering Classification in Table 4-1, you can see that it can be broken down into the following transformations.

Reorder Statements and Expressions

Reordering statements and expressions have a very minor effect on obfuscating the code. However, there is one example where reordering the expressions at a bytecode level can have a much more significant impact—when it once again breaks the link between bytecode and Java source.

PreEmptive Solutions uses a concept known as Transient Variable Caching (TVC) to reorder a bytecode expression. TVC is a straightforward technique that has been implemented in DashO. Say you want to swap two variables, x and y. The easiest way to accomplish this is to use a temporary variable, as shown in Listing 4-11. Otherwise you may end up with both variables containing the same value.

Listing 4-11. Variable Swapping

```
temp = x;
x = y;
y = temp;
```

This produces the bytecode in Listing 4-12 to complete the variable swap.

Listing 4-12. Variable Swapping in Bytecode

```
iload_1
istore_3
iload_2
istore_1
iload_3
istore_2
```

However, the stack behavior of the JVM means that you don't really need a temporary variable. The temporary or transient variable is cached on the stack and the stack now doubles as a memory location. You can quite happily remove the load and store operations for the temporary variable as shown in Listing 4-13.

Listing 4-13. Variable Swapping in Bytecode Using DashO's TVC

```
iload_1
iload_2
istore_1
istore_2
```

The downside to this is that many decompilers know about this trick and can quickly revert to the original code.

Reorder Loops

You can transform a loop, making it go backward (see Listing 4-14). This probably won't do much in the way of optimization, but it is one of the simpler obfuscation techniques.

Listing 4-14. Loop Reversals

```
x = 0;
while (x < maxNum){
        i[x] += j[x];
        x++;
}

x = maxNum;
while (x > 0){
        x--;
        i[x] += j[x];
}
```

Data Obfuscations

Take a look at the Data Obfuscation type in Table 4-1. You can break this down into the classifications discussed in the following sections.

Storage and Encoding

Many of the transformations you have seen so far exploit the fact that programmers write code following some standard conventions. Turn these conventions on their head and you have the basis of a good obfuscation process or tool. The more transformations you employ, the less likely it will be for anyone or any tool to understand the original source. In this section, you will see Data Obfuscations that reshape the data into less natural forms.

Changing Encoding

Collberg's paper shows simple encoding example—an integer variable *int i = 1* is transformed to $i' = x*i + y$. If you choose $x = 8$ and $y = 3$, you get the transformation shown in Listing 4-15.

Listing 4-15. Variable Obfuscations

```
int i = 1;                      int i = 11;
while (i < 1000) {              while (i<8003) {
        val = A[i];                    val = A[(i-3)/8];
        i++;                           i+=8;
}                              }
```

Split Variables

Variables can also be split into two or more parts to create a further level of obfuscation. Collberg suggests a lookup table. For example, if you're trying to define the Boolean value of *a= true*, then you'd split the variable into *a1=0* and *a2=1* and make a lookup table like the one shown in Table 4-2 to convert it back into the Boolean value.

Table 4-2. Boolean Split Lookup Table

a1	a2	a
1	0	false
0	1	true

Convert Static to Procedural Data

An interesting if not very practical transformation is to hide the data by converting it from static data to procedural data. For example, the copyright information in a string could be generated programmatically within your code possibly using a combination of interleave transformation discussed earlier. The method to output the copyright notice could use a lookup table method similar to the one shown in Table 4-2, or it could work by combining the string from several different variables spread throughout the application.

Aggregation

Taking a look at the Aggregation Classification in Table 4-1. You can break this down into the following transformations.

Merge Scalar Variables

Variables can be merged together, or converted to a different base and then merged together. The variables values can be stored in a series of bits and pulled out using a variety of bitmask operators.

Class Transformations

One of my favorite transformations is to use threads to confuse the hacker who is trying to steal code. There is an overhead because threads are harder to understand, harder to get right. If someone is dumb enough to try to decompile code instead of writing their own, then most likely they'll be scared off by lots of threads.

Sometimes, however, it just isn't practical to use threads because the overhead is just too big; the next best obfuscation is to use a series of class transformations. The complexity of a class increases with the depth of a class. Many of the transformations that we've discussed go against the programmer's natural sense of what's good and right in the world; however, if you use inheritance and interfaces to the extreme, then you'll be glad to hear that this will create deep hierarchies that the hacker will need time to understand.

You also don't have to defactor (see "Remove Programming Idioms") if you don't want to; you can refactor instead but with a twist. Normally refactoring simplifies code making it much more maintainable, but we can also refactor two similar classes into a parent class, leaving behind a buggy version of one or more of the refactored classes. You might also want to try refactoring two dissimilar classes into a parent class.

Array Transformations

Like variables, arrays can be split, merged, or interleaved into a single array, folded into multiple dimensions, or flattened into a one- or two-dimensional array. A straightforward approach is to split an array into two separate arrays, one containing even and the other odd indices of the array. A programmer who uses a two-dimensional array does so for a purpose; changing the dimension of the array will create a significant impediment in trying to understand your code.

Ordering Transformations

Ordering the data declarations will remove a lot of the pragmatic information in any decompiled code. Typically data is declared at the beginning of a method or just before it is first referenced. Spread the data declarations throughout your code, while still keeping the data elements in the appropriate scope.

Obfuscation Conclusion

The best obfuscator would use a number of the techniques that you've seen here. Like many of these transformations, you don't need to buy an obfuscator; you can add lots of these transformations yourself. The aim here is to confuse the would-be decompiler as much as possible by removing as much information as possible. You can do this programmatically using your own tools or simply as you write your code. Some of the transformations ask the developer to simulate what happens in an optimization stage of a compiler; others are simply bad coding practice designed to throw the hacker off the scent.

Let me mention a couple of caveats before I leave this section. First, remember that if you're going to obfuscate your code by using the same identifier multiple times in the constant pool, then you might want to talk to PreEmptive Solutions first, because they hold the patent on it. Second, you take your chances with any form of high-mode obfuscation because usually you won't have the luxury of insisting that your code is only run on certain specific JVMs. Finally, writing really bad code will make your code very difficult to read. Be careful that you don't throw the baby out with the bath water. Obfuscated code is hard to maintain and, depending on the transformation, could destroy the performance of your code. Be careful what transformations you apply.

Building Your Own Simple Obfuscator

I couldn't complete the section on obfuscation without showing you how to build your own obfuscator. The design is so simple it's almost primitive and should only be considered a starting point for your own design, but it is an obfuscator.

In Chapter 2, you got a relatively in-depth look inside the classfile structure. It won't hurt to go back to that chapter to remind yourself of the overall structure of a Java classfile. By the end of Chapter 2, you could create an XML dump of any Java classfile.

To obfuscate your target file, first run it through your disassembler—you'll find the ClassToXML code in the downloads area of the Apress web site. Open the XML file using your favorite editor, go to the constant pool section, and scramble some of the identifiers by changing the names to such identifiers as $, !, and =. The constant pool number is used throughout the classfile—that is, the pointer to the string rather than the string itself—so changing the string to something illegal in Java will not affect the functionality of your code.

Now all that remains is to turn the XML file back into a classfile. You'll find the complimentary code to your disassembler, XMLToClass, also available on the Apress web site. This takes the XML file and reassembles the file back into a binary classfile.

Let's take a look at an example of how you hand edit the XML in Listings 4-16 and 4-17 to demonstrate.

Listing 4-16. Before Obfuscation

```
<Tag_40>
  <Type>CONSTANT_Utf8</Type>
  <Value>Hello</Value>
</Tag_40>
<Tag_41>
  <Type>CONSTANT_Utf8</Type>
  <Value>java/applet/Applet</Value>
</Tag_41>
```

```
<Tag_42>
  <Type>CONSTANT_Utf8</Type>
  <Value>java/net/InetAddress</Value>
</Tag_42>
<Tag_43>
  <Type>CONSTANT_Utf8</Type>
  <Value>getLocalHost</Value>
</Tag_43>
```

We'll now take the original strings and convert them to dollar signs ($), as shown in Listing 4-17, but you're free to choose whatever character or series of characters you want. The only restriction is that the original string should be the same size as the obfuscated string. You also need to make sure that any public methods or fields are typically called by outside programs and are not modified.

Listing 4-17. After Obfuscation

```
<Tag_40>
  <Type>CONSTANT_Utf8</Type>
  <Value>Hello</Value>
</Tag_40>
<Tag_41>
  <Type>CONSTANT_Utf8</Type>
  <Value>java/applet/Applet</Value>
</Tag_41>
<Tag_42>
  <Type>CONSTANT_Utf8</Type>
  <Value>java/net/InetAddress</Value>
</Tag_42>
<Tag_43>
  <Type>CONSTANT_Utf8</Type>
  <Value>get$$$$$$$$$</Value>
</Tag_43>
```

Web Services and Server-Side Execution

Sometimes it's the simplest ideas that are the most effective. One of the simpler ideas for protecting code is to split your applet or, indeed, your application, and keep your source code on a remote server away from any prying eyes. The downloaded applet or application is then a straightforward GUI front end without any really interesting code. The server code doesn't even have to be written in Java.

> **CAUTION** *If you're already splitting your applet to access databases, then be careful about using existing two-tier (JDBC) or three-tier (dbAnywhere) architectures for your applets because SQL passwords can be decompiled along with the rest of the code.*

This approach is particularly suited to code that can be reworked as a web service so that not only can you protect your code but you can also register the web service with a third-party web services[7] server, creating another revenue stream in the process. This *might* go toward offsetting the increased server load and any new costs you might incur by taking this approach.

If this appeals to you, then you have several ways you can split the application. For fully functional applications, you might want to look to the Swing classes to create your interface and Java Web Start to get it and the correct JVM out to your customers. Server-side Java servlets can then do the real work behind the scenes. Web Start also makes it easy to sign your code. This helps prevent someone from disassembling your code and trying to hack into your back-end system by sending bogus transmissions in an attempt to uncover what's happening on the server. If you want to create a true web service application, then you'll probably want to put some time into investigating the Simple Object Access Protocol (SOAP).

However, by far the easiest way to split your application is to use XML-RPC where the client applet makes requests via an HTTP POST request in an XML format, as shown in Listing 4-18.

Listing 4-18. XML-RPC Client Method Call

```xml
<?xml version="1.0"?>
<methodCall>
        <methodName>getCube</methodName>
        <params>
                <param>
                        <value><int>3</int></value>
                </param>
        </params>
</methodCall>
```

On the server side, the method for calculating the cube of an integer is safely secured from prying eyes. True, you will need some extra servlet code for handling the XML-RPC wrapper for the responses, but the code is minimal, as you can see in Listing 4-19, which shows an example XML-RPC response.

---

7. Using UDDI, see http://www.uddi.org for more information.

Listing 4-19. XML-RPC Response

```
<?xml version="1.0"?>
<methodResponse>
        <params>
                <param>
                        <value><int>27</int></value>
                </param>
        </params>
</methodResponse>
```

Unfortunately each of these approaches has the same disadvantage of creating or, at the very least, increasing the server load and applet or application execution speed so that it is probably only ideal for you under certain circumstances, like when you want to start charging for your web service.

Encryption

Throughout the ages, mankind has turned to encryption when trying to protect secret transmissions. Not surprisingly, several attempts have been made to prevent decompilation by encrypting classfiles so that nothing can read them except for the target JVM. If the classfile is encrypted until just before it gets executed, then nobody can decompile the code—or so the theory goes, anyway.

The developer first encrypts the classfiles to secure them. When the application is executed, the encrypted classfiles are loaded by a custom ClassLoader, which decrypts the classfiles just before passing them to the JVM. The standard way of encrypting anything in Java is to use the Java Cryptography Extension (JCE).

Now it turns out that creating a custom ClassLoader and decrypting the data is a relatively easy thing to do, as you can see in Listing 4-20.

Listing 4-20. Custom Class Loaders

```
Class CustomClassLoader extends ClassLoader {
        String key;
        CustomClassLoader (String key) {
                this key = key;
        }
        public Class findClass(String name) {
                byte[] b = loadClassData(name);
                return defineClass(name, b, 0, b.length);
```

```
        }
        private byte[] loadClassData(String name) {
                // load class

                //decrypt class

        }
}
```

So does it hold water? Or is it about as safe as an Enigma machine on D-Day? Well it doesn't take long to realize that this approach has a number of holes. At the very least, a compromised JVM can simply output the decrypted classfile to a file for later analysis. But there are also several places where the encrypted file is no longer encrypted and is vulnerable to attack. For example, the custom ClassLoader program can be decompiled, modified so that the decrypted file can be captured as a stream of bytecode, and recompiled so that it dumps the classfile just before it is passed to the JVM.

Other problems are related to key security because the cryptographic key needs to be part of the application so that you can decrypt the classes in the custom class loader. If the hacker can find the key, then they can decrypt your classfiles before they get into the class loader.

But perhaps the biggest problem with this approach is that J2EE application servers, such as IBM's WebSphere or BEA's WebLogic, are fundamentally based on custom class loaders making this an altogether much more difficult approach.

It is more expensive and not that practical, but it might be possible to convert the JVM and the associated encryption routines to a hardware solution. Then nobody could access your decrypted code, because the key would be hard wired into the chip.

However, this approach has two major disadvantages: first, you would destroy Java's portability in the process of creating your encrypted JVM on a chip; and second, you would create a very limited market for your software in the process. Aside from the marketing implications of this decision, the entire security of this solution is also predicated on the hardwired encryption key never falling into the wrong hands. Lots of electronic devices employ similar encryption mechanisms such as DVD players and cable TV set top boxes. And if you've ever heard of DeCSS or cable TV descramblers, you'll realize why this isn't necessarily the best approach.

Digital Rights Management

Perhaps we're approaching the problem from the wrong angle. We know that we need to keep bytecode out of the hands of the end user in order to be able to prevent decompilation. So why not secure the browser and class loader using a trusted browser where the end user cannot access the internals of the browser—the browser cache.

Digital Rights Management (DRM) or Intellectual Property Rights (IPR) software is the future of mainstream computing whether you like it or not. Little by little, the media and the larger software companies are moving to a licensing model. The only way to control this is to use DRM to enforce the licensing restrictions.

The logic behind DRM or IPR protection schemes with respect to Java is that if you can't get at the classfile, then you cannot possibly decompile it, and to do that, you need a secure browser cache. Typically this type of technology uses a trusted browser that carefully controls its own cache and restricts access to any classfiles, HTML, and images.

Trusted browsers are typically used as a mechanism to protect data from being viewed by unauthorized users. This mechanism aims to handle the super distribution model where one user who buys a legitimate copy can pass the data—be it an image, HTML, or text file—to other users. The next user in the chain cannot view the data without contacting the original server to obtain a new key. User's rights, such as printing and the number of times the file can be viewed, can also be strictly controlled. InterTrust and Sealed Media are two examples of companies working in this arena.

It's important to note that the trusted browser should not be written in Java because otherwise it too can be decompiled, allowing access once again to the bytecode, albeit after a lot more work than what you've encountered so far. Be careful too that using a trusted browser to deploy your applet does not drastically limit what platforms you can support. And if you can't use Java, then each trusted browser needs to be ported to different operating systems to support multiple platforms.

To take this one stage further, Bruce Schneier's Cryptogram[8] recently talked about Microsoft's Palladium architecture. This is Microsoft's implementation of the Trusted Computing Platform Alliance (TCPA) specification for a trusted computer where even the administrator does not have full access to the underlying files on a PC.

For the moment, this technology is in its infancy, but expect it to grow. Similar protection schemes in the future are likely to provide the best chance of success in nailing the decompiler issue once and for all. Like the Homeland Security bill, this is a double-edged sword—sure, you protect your code, but in the process, you give up your access to your computer's operating system.

Fingerprinting Your Code

Although it does not actually protect your code, putting a digital fingerprint in your software will allow you to later prove that *you* wrote your code. Ideally, this

---

8. http://www.schneier.com/crypto-gram-0208.html

fingerprint—usually in the form of a copyright notice—will act like a software watermark that you can retrieve at any time, even if your original code has been through a number of changes or manipulations before it made it into someone else's Java application or applet. As I've said several times now, no sure-fire, 100-percent effective way for protecting your code exists, but sometimes that might not matter if you can recover some losses by proving that you wrote the original code.

In case you might be confused, I should point out that digitally fingerprinting your code is completely different than signing your applet or application. Signed applets don't have any effect when it comes to protecting your code. Signing an applet helps the person downloading or installing the software decide whether to trust an applet or not by looking at the digital certificate associated with the software. It is a protection mechanism for someone using your software; it allows them to certify that this application was written by XYZ Widget Corp. The user can then decide whether or not he or she trusts XYZ Widget Corp before continuing to download the applet or launching the application. A digital fingerprint, on the other hand, is typically recovered using a decoding tool that displays the original fingerprint or watermark. It helps protect the copyright of the developer, not the end user's hard drive.

Several attempts at fingerprinting try to protect the entire application using, for example, a defined coding style. More primitive types of fingerprinting encode the fingerprint into a dummy method or variable name. This method name or variable might be made up of a variety of parameters such as the date, the developer's name, the name of the application, and so on. However, this approach can create a Catch-22. If you put a dummy variable in your code and someone just happens to cut and paste the decompiled method complete with the dummy variable into his or her program, how are you going to know it's your code without decompiling their code and probably breaking the law in the process?

Having said that, most decompilers, and even some obfuscators, will strip this information because it does not take an active role as the code is interpreted or executed. So ultimately you need to be able to convince the decompiler or obfuscator that any protected method is part of the original program by invoking the dummy method or by using a fake conditional clause that will never be true so that the method will never get called. Here is an example:

```
if(false) then{
        invoke dummy method
}
```

A smart individual will be able to see a dummy method even if the decompiler cannot see that this clause will never be true, and he or she will come to the conclusion that the dummy method is probably some sort of a fingerprint. So you need to attach the fingerprint information at the method level to make it more robust.

Finally, you don't want the fingerprint to damage the functionality or performance of your application. Because you've seen that the Java Verifier often plays a significant role in determining what protection mechanisms you can apply to your code, you really need to make sure that your fingerprint does not stop your bytecode from making it through the Verifier.

Let's use the points made in the previous discussion to define the criteria for a good digital fingerprinting system.

- No dead-code dummy methods or dummy variables should be used.

- The fingerprint needs to work even if only part of the program is stolen.

- The performance of the applet or application shouldn't be affected. The end user of the program should not notice a difference between the fingerprinted and nonfingerprinted code.

- The fingerprinted code should be functionally equivalent to the original code.

- The fingerprint must be robust enough to survive a decompilation attack as well as any obfuscation tools.

- The bytecode should be syntactically correct to get past the Java Verifier.

- The classfile needs to be able to survive someone else fingerprinting the code with his or her own fingerprint.

- You also need a corresponding decoding tool to recover and view the fingerprint using, preferably, a secret key, because the fingerprint shouldn't be visible to the naked eye or to other hackers.

You shouldn't be too concerned about whether the fingerprint is highly visible or not. On the one hand, if it's both visible and robust then it's likely to scare off the casual hacker. On the other hand, the more seasoned attacker will know exactly where to attack. However, if it isn't visible, the casual hacker doesn't know the application is protected, and then there's no up front deterrent to look elsewhere.

Several fingerprinting systems out there satisfy some of our criteria. Let's take a look at one in particular—jmark from the Nara Institute of Science and Technology in Japan.[9] It seems to meet most of our criteria, except unfortunately you do need to insert a dummy method to make it work. This also means you'll need to insert a dummy method invocation if you're not going to lose the watermark to an obfuscator. This makes it much harder to automate. However, the

---

9. jmark can be found at `http://se.aist-nara.ac.jp/jmark/`

only serious alternative, SandMark, according to it's web site, needs a series of "annotations throughout the source."[10]

jmark uses the structure of the opcodes to encode the fingerprint and it claims to be able to recover a fingerprint when the original classfile is decompiled, subsequently recompiled, and finally run through an obfuscator. Because you're using a dummy method, it really doesn't matter if you replace iadd with isub because the bytecode will remain syntactically correct and still get through the Java Verifier.

It turns out that you can replace iadd with any of the following: isub, imul, idiv, irem, iand, ior, or ixor. And of course this applies to the other seven opcodes too. So you now have 3 bits of information into these opcodes, so let's assign 000_2 to iadd, 001_2 to isub, and continue in this manner all the way up to 111_2 ixor.

Now your fingerprinting tool just has to exploit this bytecode replacement concept by converting your fingerprint or copyright notice into base 2 or a string of bits. And every time you come across one of the eight opcodes in your dummy method, all you have to do is replace it with the next bit of your fingerprint. The decoding tool works by trawling through all the methods looking for the target opcodes, reassembling them into a base 2 string, and then converting it back into readable text.

So assuming that the dummy method is big enough for the copyright notice, then you have yourself a fingerprinting system that will survive both decompilation and obfuscation.

Fingerprinting Example

OK, so much for the theory, let's see if fingerprinting is indeed a practical solution. Listing 4-21 shows another simple example you want to protect.

Listing 4-21. Casting Target Class

```
public class Casting {
    public static void main(String args[]){
                for(char c=0; c < 128; c++) {
                        System.out.println("ascii " + (int)c + " character "+ c);
                }
        }
}
```

You'll begin with a simple class file that prints out a list of ASCII characters from 0 to 127. In Listing 4-22, you insert a dummy method with lots of operators and create a conditional statement that will never be true so that the dummy code doesn't get executed.

---

10. SandMark can be found at http://cgi.cs.arizona.edu/~sandmark/sandmark.html

Listing 4-22. Casting Class with a Dummy Method

```java
public class Casting {
    public static void main(String args[]){
                int i=0;
                char c;
                for(c=0; c < 128; c++) {
                        System.out.println("ascii " + (int)c + " character "+ c);
                }
                if(i==(int)c) {
                        check_std(i);
                }
    }
     // dummy method
    private static void check_std(int k){
        int i, j;
        for(i = 0; i < 10 ; i++)
                for(j = 0; j < 10 ; j++) k+=i*10+j;
                        System.out.println("k = " + k);
        for(i = 0; i < 20 ; i++)
                for(j = 0; j < 30 ; j++) k+=i*3-j;
                        System.out.println("k = " + k);
        for(i = 0; i < 25 ; i++)
                for(j = 0; j < 20 ; j++) k+=i*4-j*3;
                        System.out.println("k = " + k);
    }
}
```

First compile the code using javac. In Listing 4-23, run jmark with no parameters to find its usage.

Listing 4-23. jmark Command-Line Parameters

```
jmark version 1.3.1
Copyright (C) 1997-2002 Akito Monden
Usage: jmark target_file(.class) method_number "watermark" [options]
Options: -k"...." : key phrase
         -a0...2  : algorithm (default = 0)
         -d       : disassemble
```

Remember that there is always a constructor, by default, even if you haven't created one; this means that in this instance, your target method is method_number 3. As a result, you then insert the copyright notice as shown in Listing 4-24.

Listing 4-24. Creating a Fingerprint

```
c:\>jmark Casting.class 3 "(C) RIIS LLC" -k "2secret4me"
#classfile: Casting.class
#method: 3
#watermark: "(C) RIIS LLC"
#key: "2secret4me"
#algorithm: 0 (default)
```

Listing 4-25 shows the format you would use to uncover the fingerprint. You simply run the companion program jdecode against the classfile.

Listing 4-25. Recovering the Fingerprint

```
c:\>jdecode Casting.class -k "2secret4me"
#classfile: Casting.class
#key: "2secret4me"
#algorithm: 0 (default)
#begin{watermark}
1          ""
2          "GQZQ"
3          "(C) RIIS LLC (C) RIIS LLC "
#end{watermark}
```

If you decompile the program using Jad, you can see how the dummy_method has been altered. It's changed pretty dramatically, so make sure you target the dummy method if you don't want to ruin your perfectly good code. The watermark is encoded by changing the bytecodes for imul, isub, and so on so that the original code, although still syntactically correct, is always different from the original dummy method (see Listing 4-26).

Listing 4-26. Decompiled Fingerprinted Code

```
// Decompiled by Jad v1.5.8e2. Copyright 2001 Pavel Kouznetsov.
// Jad home page: http://kpdus.tripod.com/jad.html
// Decompiler options: packimports(3)
// Source File Name:   Casting.java

import java.io.PrintStream;
```

```java
public class Casting
{
    public Casting()
    {
    }

    public static void main(String args[])
    {
        int i = 0;
        char c;
        for(c = '\0'; c < 128; c++)
            System.out.println("ascii " + (int)c + " character " + c);
        if(i == c)
            check_std(i);
    }

    private static void check_std(int i)
    {
        for(int j = 0; j < 10; j++)
        {
            for(int i1 = 0; i1 < 10; i1++)
                i += j * 10 + i1;
        }
        System.out.println("k = " + i);
        for(int k = 0; k < 20; k++)
        {
            for(int j1 = 0; j1 < 30; j1++)
                i += k * 3 - j1;
        }
        System.out.println("k = " + i);
        for(int l = 0; l < 25; l++)
        {
            for(int k1 = 0; k1 < 20; k1++)
                i += l * 4 - k1 * 3;
        }
        System.out.println("k = " + i);
    }
}
```

Because Casting.java is such a simple program, it is pretty obvious that the functionality of the new classfile didn't change because of the fingerprint or watermark, because our dummy method never gets called. However, it's not good enough to assume that is the case when you're fingerprinting real applications.

If you don't have a test suite to test the functionality of your code, then you're probably going to need to create one.

jmark or any other system isn't going to be 100-percent secure because a smart hacker or developer will be able remove the dummy methods, especially if they take the time to run the application through a debugger. Putting different dummy methods in different classes is a good strategy to increase your odds of at least one fingerprint surviving, and doing so will certainly catch the casual hacker.

Selling the Source Code

If source code is so readily accessible, then why not just sell it at a higher price? If your asking price is not too high, you could convince a would-be decompiler to pay for the code, as programmer's comments are usually very informative. The intent is to convince someone that it just doesn't make any sense to decompile, given the time and energy that it sometimes requires.

This won't be for everyone, but why not make some money on the fact that some people will decompile your code to copy it? In the process, you might gain some extra revenue by helping to discourage these otherwise illegal activities by selling the code at a marginally higher price.

Native Methods

If Java really is that difficult to protect, then why not protect your code by writing it in C++ or C? Java allows you to do this by using native methods through the Java Native Interface (JNI). This may not be to everyone's liking because of the portability issues, but it does safeguard the code within the imported object. Now there may be an argument that, for example, the compiled C++ isn't that much safer than Java, but in my opinion, if you want to protect your algorithms, then the safest place to put them is in a native method that can then be called by the rest of your Java application.

There are several versions native methods APIs. The original JDK 1.0.2 version used the Native Method Interface (NMI) that was cumbersome at best. NMI was replaced by the JNI in JDK 1.1, which was subsequently enhanced in the JDK 1.2.[11]

You can incorporate a native method into your code by declaring it as shown in Listing 4-27 in the appropriate method.

---

11. Microsoft also had another flavor called JDirect many moons ago for those interested in pure Java trivia.

Listing 4-27. Native Method Example

```
class JavaHelloWorld {

    // declare the native method
    public native void nativeHelloWorld();


    // load libhello.so or hello.dll
    // depending on your platform
    static {
        System.loadLibrary("hello");
    }


    // invoke the Java class and call
    // the native method Hello World
    public static void main(String[] args) {
        new JavaHelloWorld().nativeHelloWorld();
    }
}
```

Run the following command on your compiled Java classfile:

```
javah -jni JavaHelloWorld
```

This creates the header file for your native method, shown in Listing 4-28.

Listing 4-28. JNI header file

```
/* DO NOT EDIT THIS FILE - it is machine generated */
#include <jni.h>
/* Header for class JavaHelloWorld *

#ifndef _Included_JavaHelloWorld
#define _Included_JavaHelloWorld
#ifdef __cplusplus
extern "C" {
#endif
/*
 * Class:      JavaHelloWorld
 * Method:     nativeHelloWorld
 * Signature: ()V
 */
JNIEXPORT void JNICALL Java_JavaHelloWorld_nativeHelloWorld
  (JNIEnv *, jobject);
```

```
#ifdef __cplusplus
}
#endif
#endif
```

Now create your native method using the same function that was auto-generated in the header file:

```
#include "JavaHelloWorld.h"
#include <stdio.h>

JNIEXPORT void JNICALL Java_JavaHelloWorld_nativeHelloWorld
  (JNIEnv *, jobject);
{
    printf("Hello, Native World!");
}
```

You compile using your favorite C compiler in `libhello.so` if you're on the Solaris platform or use `hello.dll` if you're in Windows. Now you're good to go. The Java classfile loads the native library and prints:

```
Hello, Native World!
```

A word of warning, don't be tempted to just put your protection mechanism in the native code because the hacker will simply comment out the check in the Java code. You'll also need to be careful about connection strings to databases because a good hexdump using a disassembler will recover the login and passwords—native methods or not.

Conclusion

The fact that the Java classfile format contains so much information makes it exceptionally difficult to protect the underlying source. Yet most software developers continue to ignore the consequences, leaving their intellectual property at some risk. What you're looking for in your obfuscator is a process that takes polynomial time to produce and exponential time to reverse.

I hope that the pretty exhaustive list of obfuscation transformations I went over in this chapter helps you approach something nearing that goal. At the very least, check out Christian Collberg's paper, which has enough information to digest for any developer who wants to get started in this area.

It seems that a JVM's bytecode is too open to interpretation to protect with strong obfuscation that will work on he different flavors of the JVM. Table 4-3 summarizes the approaches that you've seen in this chapter.

Although it does seem like an awful lot of trouble to go to when you could just write the application in native code, the portability of Java is very attractive. I believe that there are more than enough obfuscating transformations to make decompilation a very difficult process; I also think that it is possible to make the code so illegible that it will take very close to exponential time to understand the code event if it is completely decompiled. The problem is that you can't achieve that in anything close to a polynomial time frame just yet.

> **NOTE** *Perhaps it is worth noting that many of the original obfuscation tools didn't survive the dotcom implosion and that the companies have either folded or moved into other areas of specialization. So perhaps the market demands aren't even there and people are more than happy to live with the fact that people can recover the source from a classfile.*

Table 4-3. Protection Strategies Overview

Strategy	Potency	Resilience	Cost	Notes
Compilation flags	Low	Low	Low	
Writing two versions of the applet or application	High	High	Medium	
Obfuscation	Medium	Medium	Medium	Can break some JVMs
Web services and server-side execution	High	High	High	
Encryption	Low	Low	Low	
Digital Rights Management	High	High	High	
Fingerprinting your code	Low	Low	Low	Useful for legal protection
Selling the source code	Low	Low	Low	
Native methods	High	High	Low	Breaks code portability

One final word—be very careful about relying on obfuscation as your only method of protection. Remember that disassemblers can also be used to rip apart your classfile and allow someone to edit the bytecode directly. Don't forget that interactive demonstrations over the Web or seriously crippled demonstration versions of your software can also be very effective.

CHAPTER 5

Decompiler Design

FOR THE REMAINDER OF THIS BOOK, I'm going to focus on how you can create your own decompiler, which is, in fact, a cross-compiler that translates bytecode to source code. Although I will be covering the theory behind the relevant design decisions as they arise, my intention is to give you enough background information to get you going rather than to give you a full-blown chapter on compiler theory.

Don't expect your decompiler (ClassToSource in this chapter) to be more comprehensive or better than anything currently on the market; to be honest, it is probably closer to Mocha than JAD or SourceAgain. Like most development, the first 80 to 90 percent of our decompiler is the easiest and the last 10 to 20 percent takes much longer to complete. But ClassToSource will show you the basic steps of how to write a simple Java decompiler that can reverse engineer the majority of code you will come across.

I cover the general design of your ClassToSource decompiler in this chapter and delve into its implementation in Chapter 6. I'll round off the book with a number of case studies and a look at what the future may have in store for Java decompilers, obfuscators, and bytecode rearrangers.

The tone of the next two chapters will be as practical as possible and I'll try not to burden you with too much theory. It is not that I don't want to pad out the book with endless pages of compiler theory, it's just that there are too many other good books on the subject. *Compilers: Principles, Techniques and Tools*, by Aho, Sethi, and Ullman (Pearson Higher Education, 1985), otherwise known as the Dragon book (so called because of its cover design), is just one of the better examples that quickly springs to mind. Appel's *Modern Compiler Implementation in Java* (Cambridge University Press, 2002) is another highly recommended tome. I'm going more for the style of *Crafting a Compiler with C*, by Fischer and LeBlanc (Addison-Wesley, 1991). Having said that, if I think there are some theoretical considerations that you need to know about, then I'll discuss them as necessary.

Introduction

As I mentioned earlier, writing a decompiler is pretty similar to writing a compiler or cross-compiler because both translate data from one format to another. The essential difference between a decompiler and a compiler is that they go in opposite directions. In a standard compiler, source code is converted to tokens and then it is parsed and analyzed to finally produce a binary executable.

As it happens, decompiling is very similar to compiling, only this time, the back end of the compiler is changing the intermediary symbols back into source code rather than into Assembler. Because of the binary format of a Java classfile, you can quickly transform the binary into bytecode and then treat the bytecode as just another language. It might help to think of your decompiler as a cross-compiler or source code translator that transforms bytecode to Java. And remember, with ClassToXML, you've already got a way of converting the binary format of a classfile into XML. You'll be using this XML as the input to your decompiler.

An abundance of other source code translators translate between different languages—for example, you can translate from COBOL to C, or even from Java to Ada or C, which will give you plenty of places to look for ideas.

> **NOTE** *In case you're confused about the difference between opcodes and bytecodes, an opcode is a single instruction, such as* iload, *that may or may not be followed by a data value or operand. Opcodes and operands together are generally referred to as bytecodes.*

Overall, the task of writing a decompiler is simpler; there are several significant reasons for this.

Limited Number of Opcodes

You only need to understand a limited number of possible opcodes. You don't need to worry too much about syntax errors because the Java bytecode language is machine generated. This makes it tightly defined and very predictable. Sure, bytecode rearrangers or optimizers may cause problems, but rearrangers are a very special case. In general, you won't come across them because they have an awful habit of not being able to pass Java Verifiers or, worse still, of not working on some obscure JVM implementation.

No Registers

If James Gosling hadn't turned the hardware clock back 20 years and decided to go for a stack-based architecture, it's very unlikely that this book would ever see the light of day. Most hardware architectures use a minimum of three registers for typical computations, such as the simple equation a + b = c where values a and b are stored in the first two registers, and the result c is stored in a third register or used as part of a much larger computation.

But a Java Virtual Machine (JVM) is a stack-based machine that pushes two operands onto the stack and then adds the top two stack elements by popping the stack twice—performing the addition and then pushing the result back onto the stack. No doubt, any design decisions are made because the virtual stack machine is easy to write and implement on any number of different platforms, from phones to SunFire E15,000's. But this portability is also the JVM's Achilles' heel as it simplifies the design of the JVM tremendously with the JVM designers adopting a Lowest Common Denominator approach to cater for all these diverse architectures.

Data and Instruction Separation

A further reason for the JVM's simple design is Java's security model. The separation of a stack machine's data and instructions allow the JVM to quickly scan the bytecodes and verify that each class file is not going to misbehave.

We know the format of the bytecode at all times on all platforms. In most modern compilers, the original source is translated into several intermediary formats. Typically, a number of transformations are moving from a higher level, such as C or C++, to a much lower level, such as Assembler. Normally these internal languages are rarely if ever published, but as luck would have it, the specification for Java bytecode is published. Thanks to Java's portability and the JVM specification, for the most part, we know what source produces what combinations of opcodes and operands on any number of platforms.

Outside Java, any intermediate languages are much harder to decipher because the specification is rarely published. Decompiler writers have to recognize that sequences of low-level operators represent some high-level functionality by a process of trial and error, with data and instructions scattered everywhere. Even the people behind decompiling early Visual Basic interpreted code have a harder time than their Java counterparts because, unlike Sun, Microsoft didn't publish a specification for VB's intermediate p-code language.

Only a few papers or books cover the whole area of decompilation. One of the best resources is Dr. Cristina Cifuentes' thesis[1] on Reverse Compilation

---

1. http://www.itee.uq.edu.au/~cristina/dcc.html#thesis

Techniques available from the Queensland University of Technology in Australia. Dr. Cifuentes takes the much more arduous task of turning executables, rather than our partly compiled bytecode, back into the original higher-level language. In terms of difficulty, there really is no comparison between converting a class-file back into Java source and converting any executable back into C code. The output isn't defined at all, the data and instructions are not partitioned in any way, and different platforms and even different compilers on the same machine can produce completely different output. For example, a case statement compiled into binary by Visual C++ is a whole lot different than the output produced by a Watcom compiler. And as I suggested earlier, registers exponentially complicate what happens at run time.

JIT Optimization

In compiled or noninterpreted languages, compilers do most of the hard work, such as optimization during the compilation phase. Interpreted languages such as Java do all their work when they are finally executed. The technologies for increasing Java speed—JIT and inlining or hotspot technology being the obvious examples—all focus on speeding up the interpreting phase. They completely ignore the initial compilation in an attempt to overcome the limitations of the stack-based virtual machine design. Interpreters are by and large much easier to decompile as you're always looking at an intermediate format with all the required information still intact in its original form.

Fragile Super Class

The next reason why Java is particularly susceptible to decompilation comes from Java's object-oriented (OO) nature and is called the fragile super class problem. Because of the nature of other OO languages such as C++, it is often necessary to recompile or relink an application when a class in another library is changed. This is true if the implementation of a given method changes or when new methods are added. Java gets around this by adopting a static architecture. All classes are dynamically linked on demand as and when they are needed during execution. Or in English, all classes including the core classes are only linked at runtime.

For this to work, all the symbolic names and types need to be in the classfile. And for simplicity's sake, Java's original designers put all the methods and fields in the class as well as provide pointers to all externally referenced fields and methods in the classfile's constant pool. This separates the data and instructions in any given classfile and gives us a complete map of the program.

Simple Control Structures

Almost as important, from our point of view, is the simplicity of the control structure in Java. Program flow in Java is all based around conditional and non-conditional goto statements, which is one of the reasons why many decompilers find it hard to tell the difference between a while loop and a for loop. But it also means that we don't need to handle complex flows such as any indirect calls. It's also unlikely that this will change in the near future because, thanks to the JVM, design and security restrictions on possible bytecode combinations will only offer very limited scope for any real optimization, especially for any code run through the Java Verifier.

So where do we go from here? I'll begin with a recap of the overall problem domain. Then I'll quickly review what tools are available to help you solve the problem. In addition, I'll show you how to investigate some of the strategies that others before us have used to create a decompiler. Finally I'll outline the design and conclude with some simple decompiler examples.

Defining the Problem

Perhaps now is a good time to recap what you already know about the classfile and the JVM before I get into the design of your decompiler.

Although the main area of focus in this chapter is the bytecode in the class methods where most of the decompilation will take place, you will still need to use much of the other information in the remainder of the classfile, such as the constant pool, to create good decompiled code.

If you quickly review the classfile, you can break it down into the following parts.

- Magic number

- Major and minor versions

- Constant pool

- Access flags

- Interfaces

- Class fields

- Class methods

- Class attributes

If you leave out any attributes for simplicity's sake, you know that the constant pool follows the OxCAFEBABE magic number and the major and minor versions of the compiler. The constant pool contains all the symbolic information and constants used in the rest of the classfile. The symbolic information appears as short character–encoded strings in a Unicode-like format, which detail method signatures as well as parameter and type information for each field and method.

The constant pool is followed by a series of access flags that tell you the type of method, namely class or interface, and whether it's public or private; they also give you a pointer to the name of the superclass in the constant pool.

The remaining three elements of the classfile—interfaces, class fields, and class methods—are all arrays. Interfaces contain the definitions of any interfaces defined in the classfile; class fields contain a series of pointers or indices into the constant pool giving the name and type information for the class; and finally, class methods can be either Java methods or native methods. Note that you cannot decompile native methods because they are essentially C or C++ dynamically linked libraries.

From Chapter 2, you know that the JVM is an abstract stack processor and that each method maintains a unique operand stack, stack pointer, program counter, and an array of local variables that act as general purpose registers. Likewise, in Chapter 2, you also learned the format of the classfile and how to read it in from a file. Figure 5-1 shows a diagram of its architecture.

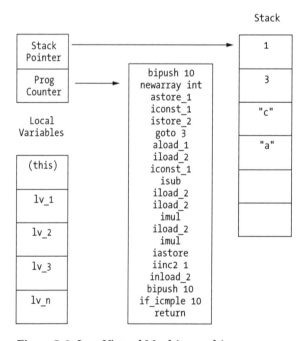

Figure 5-1. Java Virtual Machine architecture

The execution frame uses both a stack and a series of local variables that act like general-purpose registers. Whereas lv_0 is always the address of this, the current method, lv_1, lv_2... lv_n, are the local variables created as the bytecode is interpreted. The stack is used as a temporary storage area and the stack pointer and program counter enable the JVM to know what opcodes need to be executed and where to find their operands on the stack.

The JVM's instruction set of 200 odd opcodes has the usual mathematical, logical, and stack operators as well as a number of high-level opcodes that perform dynamic memory allocation (new), function invocation (invokevirtual), array indexing (aaload), exception processing (throw), type checking (checkcast), and monitors (monitorenter, monitorexit). tableswitch and lookupswitch allow for multiway conditional and unconditional branching as well as the more standard goto and label statements using statements such as ifcmple (goto label if less than or equal).

What you now need is a bytecode grammar that you can use to match the opcodes and convert the data back into Java source. You also need to be able to mirror the control flow and any explicit transfers, such as goto or jsr (jump subroutine) statements, as well as being able to handle any corresponding labels.

From the JVM specification, bytecodes can be broken down into the following types.

- Load and save instructions

- Arithmetic instructions

- Type conversion instructions

- Object creation and manipulation

- Operand stack management instructions

- Control transfer instructions

- Method invocation and return instructions

- Handling exceptions

- Implementing finally

- Synchronization

Each and every opcode has a defined behavior that you use in the parser to re-create the original Java. Both Sun's original JVM specification and the *Java Virtual Machine* (O'Reilly and Associates, 1997) are very good at describing opcodes in what can only be termed Technicolor detail. You can use this information in your decompiler's grammar.

(De)Compiler Tools

All the constraints described in this chapter's introduction enforce a type of computational grammar on your bytecode. The stack-based last in first out (LIFO) architecture is one of the simplest you can encounter. You can codify these actions in a parser so that you can fairly easily reconstruct the source code from these series of opcodes.

You need to make a number of choices before you write your decompiler. You could code the entire decompiler by hand, and several Java decompilers almost certainly take that approach, or you could look at a number of tools that would make your job a whole lot easier.

Flow analysis tools such as Java Tree Builder (JTB)[2] or JJTree[3]—which you won't be using—generate control flow graphs to help you figure out where and why the code branched. You can use compiler-compiler tools such as Lex and Yacc to scan and parse the bytecode; many developers have used them for more complex tasks. Lex and Yacc allow you to codify the grammar into a series of production rules that pattern match the bytecode and whose associated actions generate the source code fragments.

You'll get to look at as many other solutions as possible. I suspect that all high-level code transformations used by Jive, Mocha, and even SourceAgain are hard-coded transformations looking for specific constructs rather than taking a more general approach. It's unlikely that any of these programs tries to interpret rather than predict all combinations of high-level structures.

I will focus on the simpler approach where the high-level structures are hard coded, because it fits in well with your parser methodology. But you will also look at some advanced strategies where the decompiler infers all complicated high-level structures from the series of goto statements in the bytecode.

Compiler-Compiler Tools

Although you will be looking at the different strategies that have been used to decompile Java, your core parser will be a Lex/Yacc parser written in Java using JLex and CUP where the bytecode is recovered from the bottom up rather than the top down. You don't want to reinvent the wheel, and wherever possible, you'll use existing tools like JLex and CUP to implement the functionality you need in

---

2. http://www.cs.purdue.edu/jtb/

3. http://www.j-paine.org/jjtree.html

your language translator. You'll see that decompiling the basic code blocks is straightforward with the exception of a few rather awkward bytcodes.

If you've never come across Lex and Yacc before, they operate on textual input files. The Lex input file defines how the byte stream is to be tokenized using pattern matching. The Yacc input file consists of a series of production rules for the tokens. These define the grammar, and the corresponding actions generate a user-defined output.

After running these input files through Lex and Yacc, the generated output in C or even Java becomes the source code for your decompiler engine. I have two principal reasons for using compiler-compiler tools: firstly, these tools dramatically reduce the number of lines of code, which makes it a whole lot easier for readers to understand concepts; and secondly, it cuts development time in half. JLex and CUP are available on any platform that can support a JVM.

On the negative side, once compiled, the generated code can be a lot slower than what you can achieve by handcrafting a compiler front end. However, making the code easy to follow is a prerequisite of this book. Nobody—especially yours truly—wants to read through reams of code to understand just what is happening, so I'll be sticking to Lex and Yacc.

By a bizarre twist, using compiler-compiler tools such as JLex and CUP is a great way of hiding program logic and defeating decompilers because the rules and logic are at a much higher level. Even if someone decompiles the classfiles associated with ClassToSource, they would need to take another step to recover the original JLex and CUP files from the generated Java. Unfortunately this only has limited applications in the real world.

Now dozens of different compiler-compiler tools exist for different operating systems and target languages. Lex and Yacc are the most commonly known, and they come in Windows as well as the original Unix flavors. There are both free and commercial versions, which output Pascal, C, C++, and Java code. No doubt many other varieties exist that are too numerous to mention (see the comp.compilers FAQ[4] for more information).

Apart from one or two notable exceptions, explanations of Lex and Yacc are always too theoretical and lack that practical dimension of how to put it all together. A number of steps are simple once they are explained, but more often than not, they lead to a great deal of confusion.

> **NOTE** *The first example of Lex and Yacc that I ever came across was a simple calculator. In fact, the second and almost every other example that I've subsequently found were also for calculators of varying degrees of difficulty. You might say that the calculator is the "Hello, World" of the compiler-compiler tool community.*

---

4. http://compilers.iecc.com/faq.txt

A myriad of alternatives are not based on Lex and Yacc. If you take Java as the target language and start with JLex and CUP as the Lex and Yacc variants, you'll also come across ANother Tool for Language Recognition (ANTLR)[5], the compiler-compiler tool formerly known as PCCTS. And, of course, you'll come across Jack (Get it? It rhymes with Yacc.), which became JavaCC.[6]

Lex

Lex uses regular expressions to break up the input stream into tokens, and Yacc tries to take these tokens and match them to a number of production rules using a shift/reduce mechanism. Most production rules are associated with an action, and it's these context-sensitive actions that output, in this case, Java source code.

Tokens are also known as terminals, and production rules are identified by a single non-terminal. Each non-terminal is made up of a series of terminals and other non-terminals. An analogy that most people use explains this as thinking of terminals (tokens) as leaves and non-terminals as the branches.

Yacc

CUP, like Yacc, is a standard, bottom-up LALR(1) parser (LALR stands for lookahead left-right). By bottom-up, I mean that you can construct the parse tree from the leaves, whereas a top-down parser tries to construct the tree from the root. LALR(1) means that the type of parser processes tokens supplied by the scanner Lex from left to right (**L**ALR(1)) using the rightmost derivation (L**A**LR(1)) and can look ahead one token (LA**LR**(**1**)). An LR parser is also known as a predictive parser, and an LALR is the result of merging two LR sets whose items are identical except for the lookahead sets. LALR(1) parsers are very similar to LR(1) parsers, but LALR(1) parsers are typically much smaller because the lookahead token helps reduce the number of possible patterns.

LALR(1) parser generators are the de facto standard in the rest of computing world. However, Java parsers are more likely to fall into the LL(k) category of parsers. LL(k) parsers are top down parsers, scanning from left to right (**LL**(k)) using the leftmost derivation (LL(k))—which is where the top down comes from—and can look ahead k tokens.

Although LL(k) parsers are allegedly easier to write and the user-definable number of lookahead tokens is a major attraction, all my experience is with LALR(1) parsers, so personally, I feel more at home with LALR(1) parsers such as CUP. Many of the standard compiler construction tomes also heavily feature

---

5. http://www.antlr.org/

6. https://javacc.dev.java.net/

Lex and Yacc rather than any other LL(k) alternatives, so there are plenty of examples to get you going. Not surprisingly then, I'm going to use JLex and CUP in ClassToSource.

Hopefully some of you will already familiar with Lex and Yacc, which will help cut any learning curve. Feel free to play around with the other parsers—it comes down to personal preferences and what you feel most comfortable with.[7]

JLex

Eliot Berk originally developed JLex at Princeton University, but now it is maintained by Andrew Appel, also at Princeton, the author of *Modern Compilers in Java/ML/C* (Cambridge University Press, 1997). Like all versions of Lex, JLex allows you to use regular expressions to break up the input stream and turn it into tokens. You'll use it in conjunction with CUP to define your decompiler bytecode grammar, but first I'll show you how to use JLex on its own as a simple scanner (see Listing 5-1 in the "Regular Expression Rules" section).

Lex, whether it's running on Unix or DOS, in C or in Java, is a preprocessing language that transforms the specification or rules into the target language. A C language specification becomes lex.yy.c and a Java specification becomes filename.lex.java after it's run through the Lex program. You then need to compile the code output like any other C or Java program. Lex is normally used in conjunction with Yacc, but you can also use it on its own for simple tasks such as removing comments from source code. However, if you need to attach any logic to the program, then you'll almost certainly need to hook it up to some sort of parser, such as Yacc, or in your case, CUP.

During the introduction to this section, I mentioned how Lex and Yacc have been used for many years by compiler developers in the Unix community. If you're more used to Lex, then JLex does differs in a number of ways. A JLex file is split into three sections:

- User code

- JLex directives

- Regular expression rules

Although the structure (shown in Listing 5-1) is different from the Unix version of Lex—typically compiled using C instead of Java—and the definitions and macros are quite different too, thankfully, the regular expression rules use

---

7. See http://dinosaur.compilertools.net/ for more information and links to some excellent resources.

standard regular expressions. So if you're already familiar with Lex, or even vi or Perl, then it won't seem like you've strayed too far from familiar ground.

User Code

User code is everything that precedes the first %%. It is copied "as-is" into the generated Java file. Typically, this is a series of import statements. And, as you're going to use JLex in conjunction with CUP, your user code will consist of the following:

```
import java_cup.runtime.Symbol;
```

JLex Directives

The directives section is next, beginning after the first %% and ending with another %%. These directives or flags tell JLex how to behave. For example, if you use the %notunix operating system compatibility directive, then JLex will expect a new line to be represented by \r\n and not \n as it is in the Unix world. The remaining directives, listed here, allow you to enter your own code into various parts of the generated file or change the default name of the generated Lex class, function, or type (e.g., from yylex to scanner).

- Internal code

- Init class code

- End of File class

- Macro definitions

- State declarations

- Character counting

- Line counting

- Java CUP compatibility

- Component titles directive

- Default Token Type directive

- End of File directive

- Operating system compatibility

- Character sets

- Format to and from file

- Exceptions code

- End-of-File return value

- Interface to implement

- Making the Generated class public

You are only interested in a few of the directives, such as the %cup or CUP compatibility directive. For your purposes, the directives section will be something as simple as the following:

```
%%

%cup

digit = [0-9]
whitespace  = [\ \t\n\r]
%%
```

Regular Expression Rules

The regular expressions section is where the real scanning takes place. The rules are a collection of regular expressions that break up the incoming stream into tokens so the parser can do its job. If you're familiar with regular expression in Perl or vi, then you really shouldn't have any problems. If you haven't come across regular expressions before, then the JLex manual[8] is a great place to start.

Let's take a simple example to put this all together. Listing 5-1 adds line numbers to any file input from the command line.

Listing 5-1. Num.lex Scanner for Adding Line Numbers to Files

```
// include the import statement in the generated scanner
import java.io.IOException;
```

---

8. http://www.cs.princeton.edu/~appel/modern/java/JLex/

```
// start of the directives
%%

// define the class as public
%public
// rename the class to Num
%class   Num

// Yytoken return type is void
%type   void

// Java code for execution at end-of-file
%eofval{
          return;
%eofval}

// turn line counting on
%line

// internal code added to make it a standalone scanner
%{

public static void main (String args []) {
        Num num = new Num(System.in);
        try {
                num.yylex();          // call the scanner
        } catch (IOException e) { System.err.println(e); }
}
%}

%%
// regular expressions section

\n             {System.out.println(yyline+1);}
.*$            { System.out.println((yyline+1)+"\t"+yytext()); }
```

Install JLex by obtaining a copy of Main.java from the URL provided. Copy it into a directory called JLex and compile it using your favorite Java compiler. Save the Num.lex file (see Listing 5-1), and compile it as follows:

```
java JLex.Main Num.lex
mv Num.yylex.java Num.java
javac Num.java
```

Now you can add line numbers to your file by typing the following:

```
java Num < Num.java > Num_withlineno.java
```

Normally in a scanner/parser combination the scanner operates as parser input. In the first example, you didn't even generate any token, so you have nothing to pass to CUP, your Java parser. You'll see later that JLex and CUP can interoperate with some small modifications. Lex generates a `yylex()` function that eats tokens and passes them on to `yyparse()`, which is generated by Yacc. You'll rename these functions or methods to `scanner()` and `parse()`, but the idea is the same.

I doubt if many commercial compilers are built around Lex and Yacc because they have limited functionality and cannot deal with quirky aspects of some programming languages. Fortran, for example, is a nightmare to tokenize, because it is completely oblivious to whitespace. But for your purposes, Lex and Yacc are excellent utilities, because JVM bytecode is so tightly defined and because they offer a simple and neat way to see how bytecode fits together.

CUP

Yacc, as you may or may not know, stands for "Yet another compiler-compiler" and is essentially a parser generator. Don't worry if up until now you thought Yacc could just as easily have stood for "Yamanashi area communication community" because I'll try to explain in the simplest possible terms exactly what I'm talking about and why it is such a useful tool.

Simply put, Yacc allows you to define grammar rules for parsing incoming lexical tokens, and hopefully, it produces the desired output as defined by your grammar. CUP[9]—also known as JavaCUP—is a public domain Java variant of Yacc, which, because of Java's portability, will compile on any machine that has a JVM and JDK. Like Yacc, CUP is almost certainly a contrived acronym as it comes from mildly cumbersome Construction of Useful Parsers.

Stephen Johnson at the AT&T Bell Laboratories in New Jersey wrote the original version of Yacc. Lex and Yacc as well as sed and awk were almost always included in every Unix implementation since the early days of Berkeley in the 1980s. sed and awk would typically be used for simple command-line parsing tools with Lex and Yacc being reserved for more complicated parsers. Unix system administrators and developers typically use some or all of these tools from time to time in an effort to transform or translate an input file into some other format. These days, Perl has largely taken over from all such utilities, with Lex and Yacc being reserved for only the most difficult of tasks, if at all.

---

9. http://www.cs.princeton.edu/~appel/modern/java/CUP/

Yacc as well as Lex have been copied many times and are available on many platforms. Commercial and public domain variants of Lex and Yacc are available on Windows and DOS, for example, from MKS and from GNU (Flex/Bison). Be warned, however, CUP does not have exactly the same functionality or format as a Yacc grammar written for any C compiler, but it does behave in a somewhat similar fashion. CUP can be compiled on any operating system that supports JDK.

CUP, being a Yacc parser, is closest to an LALR(1) parser and is just one of a number of different Yacc parser generators written for the Java language. Byacc and Jell are two other examples. If you're happier with an LL parser and don't want to use an LALR grammar, then you might want to look at ANTLR or JavaCC from Sun. But for our purposes I'm going to focus primarily on CUP.

To install CUP, copy the source files from the URL provided. An installation script (INSTALL) is provided for Unix along with a makefile for Windows 95/NT (nmake[10]). However, it is very straightforward to compile by typing the following in the CUP root directory:

```
javac java_cup/*java java_cup/runtime/*.java
```

CUP files are made up of the following four sections:

- Preamble or declarations sections

- User routines

- List of symbols or tokens

- Grammar rules

Declarations

The declarations section consists of a series Java package and import statements that vary depending on what other packages or classes you want to import. Assuming that the CUP classes are in your classpath, add the following line of code to include the CUP classes:

```
import java_cup.runtime*;
```

All other imports or package references are optional. A start declaration will tell the parser where to look for the start rule if you want it to start with some other rule. The default is to use the top production rule, so in most grammars, you'll come across the start rule and find that it is redundant information.

---

10. Available with Visual C++

User Routines

Four possible user routines are allowed in CUP (see Listing 5-2): `action` and `parser`, which are used to insert new code and override default scanner code and variables, `init` for any parser initialization, and finally `scan`, which is used by the parser to call the next token. All four possible user routines are optional.

Listing 5-2. User Routines Examples

```
action code {:
        // allows code to be included in the parser class
        public int max_narrow = 10;
        public double narrow_eps = 0.0001;
:};

parser code {:
        // allows methods and variable to be placed
        // into the generated parser class
        public void report_error(String message, Token tok) {
            errorMsg.error(tok.left, message);
        }
:};

// Preliminaries to set up and use the scanner.
init with {: scanner.init(); :};
scan with {: return scanner.yylex(); :};
```

Both `init` and `scan` are commonly used even if it is only to use `scan` to change the name of the scanner/lexer to something more meaningful than `yylex()`. Any routines within `init` are executed before the first token is requested.

Most parsers will have a series of actions defined in the grammar section. CUP puts all these actions in a single class file. The `action` user routine allows you to define variables and add extra code, for example, symbol table manipulation routines that can be referenced in the nonpublic action class. `parser` routines are for adding extra code into the generated parser class—don't expect to use this very often, if at all, except maybe for better error handling.

Symbols

CUP, like the original Yacc, acts like a stack machine. Every time a token is read it is converted into a symbol and placed or shifted onto the stack. These tokens are defined in the "Symbols" section of the parser.

Symbols can be either terminal or non-terminal. Unreduced symbols are called terminal symbols and symbols that have been reduced into some sort of rule or expression are called non-terminal symbols. Or to put it another way, terminal symbols are the symbols/tokens used by the JLex Scanner, and non-terminal symbols are what the terminals become after they satisfy one of the patterns or rules in the "Grammar" section of the parser. Listing 5-3 shows a good example of both terminal and non-terminal tokens.

Symbols can have associated Integer, Float, or String values, which are propagated up the grammar rules until the group of tokens either satisfy a rule and can be reduced or crash the parser if no rule is ever satisfied.

Listing 5-3. Parser.cup

```
mport java_cup.runtime.*;

// Interface to scanner generated by JLex.
parser code {:
        Parser(Scanner s) { super(); scanner = s; }
        private Scanner scanner;
:};
scan with {: return scanner.yylex(); :};

terminal NUMBER, BIPUSH, NEWARRAY, INT, ASTORE_1, ICONST_1;
terminal ISTORE_2, GOTO, ALOAD_1, ILOAD_2, ISUB, IMUL;
terminal IASTORE, IINC, IF_ICMPLE, RETURN, END;

non terminal    function, functions, keyword;
non terminal    number;

functions       ::=    function
                  |         functions function
                  ;

function        ::=    number keyword number number END
                  |         number keyword number END
                  |         number keyword keyword END
                  |         number keyword END
                  |         END
                  ;

keyword         ::=    BIPUSH
                  |         NEWARRAY
                  |         INT
                  |         ASTORE_1
                  |         ICONST_1
```

```
                    |        ISTORE_2
                    |        GOTO
                    |        ALOAD_1
                    |        ILOAD_2
                    |        ISUB
                    |        IMUL
                    |        IASTORE
                    |        IINC
                    |        IF_ICMPLE
                    |        RETURN
                    ;


number          ::=      NUMBER
                    ;
```

A parser's functionality depends on its ability to interpret a stream of input tokens and how it turns these tokens into the desired output as defined by the language's grammar. In order for the parser to have any chance of success, it needs to know every symbol along with its type before any shift/reduce cycles can take place. A symbol table is generated from the list of terminals and non-terminals by CUP and output as a Sym.java file, which needs to be imported into the JLex scanner for JLex and CUP to work together.

Grammar

CUP is an LALR(1) machine, meaning that it can look ahead one token or symbol to try and satisfy a grammar rule. If a production rule is satisfied, then the symbols are popped off the stack and reduced with the production rule. The aim of every parser is to convert these input symbols into a series of reduced symbols right back to the start symbol or token.

In layman's terms, given a string of tokens and a number of rules, the goal is to trace the rightmost derivation in reverse by starting with the input string and working back to the start symbol. You reduce your series of non-terminals to a terminal using bottom-up parsing. All input tokens are terminal symbols that are subsequently combined into non-terminals or other intermediate terminals using this shift/reduce principle. As each group of symbols is matched to production rule, it ultimately kicks off an action that generates some sort of output defined in the production rule action. You'll see how this works in a simple example at the end of this chapter in Listing 5-15.

You'll see that under certain circumstances, it's possible that input tokens or intermediate symbols can satisfy multiple production rules; this is what is known as an *ambiguous grammar*. The precedence keyword mentioned in the "Symbol" section allows the parser to decide which symbol will take a higher precedence. For example, the symbols for multiplication and division might take precedence over the addition or subtraction symbols.

It's worth mentioning that CUP will allow you to dump the shift/reduction table for debugging purposes. Listing 5-4 shows the command that produces a human-readable dump of the symbols and grammar, the parse state machine, the parse tables, and the complete transitions. Some of the output is also shown.

Listing 5-4. Partial Debug Output

```
java java_cup.Main -dump < Parser.cup

# Initializing parser
# Current Symbol is #2
# Shift under term #2 to state #3
# Current token is #3
# Reduce with prod #23 [NT=4, SZ=1]
# Goto state #4
# Shift under term #3 to state #6
# Current token is #2
# Reduce with prod #8 [NT=3, SZ=1]
# Goto state #19
# Shift under term #2 to state #3
# Current token is #18
# Reduce with prod #23 [NT=4, SZ=1]
# Goto state #24
# Shift under term #18 to state #25
# Current token is #2
# Reduce with prod #4 [NT=1, SZ=4]
# Goto state #5
# Reduce with prod #0 [NT=2, SZ=1]
# Goto state #2
# Shift under term #2 to state #3
# Current token is #4
# Reduce with prod #23 [NT=4, SZ=1]
# Goto state #4
```

Now that you've seen what tools you're going to use, you should begin to think about what steps you need to take to create your decompiler. First, you have to find some way to break up the classfile into an appropriate syntax so that it can be tokenized, similar to javap output. ClassToXML will suffice for your purposes. Next you need to write the JLex Scanner to tokenize the output from ClassToXML and finally you'll need to define the CUP grammar and associated actions to convert these tokens back into source.

Strategy

A significant part of the problem with building a decompiler is making it general enough to deal with arbitrary cases. When Mocha comes across an unexpected language idiom, it either aborts or shoots out illegal gotos. Ideally, you should be able to code a general solution decompiler rather than one that is little more than a series of standard routines and an awful lot of exception cases. You don't want ClassToSource to fail on *any* construct, so a general solution is very attractive.

Before you take that approach, though, you need to know if there are any disadvantages to this approach and whether you will gain a better solution at the expense of outputting illegible code that looks nothing like the original source. Or worse still, whether it will take an inordinate amount of time to get there. You could replace all the control structures in a program with a program counter and a single while loop, but that would destroy the mapping and cause you to lose structural or syntactical equivalence, which is definitely not your goal even if it is a general solution.

From our discussions, you know that unlike other languages, such as C++, which doesn't use an interpreter, you don't have the headache of separating data and instructions because all of your data is in the constant pool. In the remainder of this chapter and in the next, you'll also see that recovering source-level expressions is relatively easy. So it seems that your main problem and any corresponding strategy you use is going to mainly concern handling the bytecode's control flow.

After the previous "CUP" section, you may be asking why you need to have a strategy, why can't you just build a grammar in Lex and Yacc and see what comes out the other side? Well unfortunately the parser can recognize only sequential instruction sequences. So you might not be able to parse all JVM instructions in a single bottom-up pass because bytecodes have this awful habit of branching. The stack is used as a temporary storage area, and you need to be able to control what happens to that partial sequence when the code branches. On their own, Lex and Yacc just don't offer that level of functionality, so you need to figure out what approach you need to take to store these partially recognized sequences.

This section looks at a couple of different strategies you can try to help overcome this problem of synthesizing high-level control constructs from goto-like primitives. As I said, the ideal general solution would be where you could decompile every possible if, then, else, or for loop combination without needing any exception cases and while still keeping the source as close as possible to the original. The alternative is to attempt to anticipate all high-level control idioms.

The first choice is to use the techniques based on Cristina Cifuentes' work as described in the paper "A Methodology for Decompilation."[11] This describes dcc, Cifuentes' decompiler for C programs on Intel boxes. Although dcc recovers C and not Java code, a great deal of the discussion and design of Cifuentes' Universal Decompiler is directly applicable to the task at hand.

---

11. www.itee.uq.edu.au/~cristina/clei1.ps

The second choice is the more general approach—where you transform goto statements into equivalent forms. It would be so much simpler if you could just fire off a Lex/Yacc scanner and parser at the classfile and decompile the code in a single pass or, at the very least, dispense with any control flow analysis. Well that's what Todd Proebsting and Scott Watterson attempt to do in their "Krakatoa: Decompilation in Java" paper.[12] Krakatoa, an early decompiler that is now part of the Sumatra/Toba project, uses Ramshaw's algorithm[13] to transform gotos into loops and multilevel breaks. It claims to offer a neat one-pass solution while still keeping the original structure. The Krakatoa approach is tempting, because it is less likely to fail due to any control flow analysis problems.

The third choice comes from Daniel Ford of IBM Research and was part of possibly the very first decompiler, Jive, which I believe never even made it out of IBM Research. Daniel, in his paper "Jive: A Java Decompiler"—which unfortunately is no longer available—puts forward a truly multipass decompiler that "integrates its parse state information with the sequence of machine instructions it is parsing." Jive decompiles by reducing tokens as more and more information becomes available with each successive pass.

Your fourth choice would be to take the truly simple approach. You'd look at a single pass using Lex/Yacc in which you'd use a lot of buffers to maintain the state of each reduction before a branch, and then you'd continue where you left off after the function returns control back to where it was before the jump. Or you could go one step further and use *peephole optimization* as a second pass parser. Peephole optimization is where you hard code combinations of instructions and simply hope you don't come across any new idioms.

Perhaps you could go for something more esoteric, such as some sort of pattern matching AI parser. It's conceivable that a neural network could be trained to output source after it was trained on numerous applets and applications. Strings are passed in at one end of the neural network as tokens push a Java representation of code at the other end. You then train the neural network to turn bytecode phrases into Java phrases similar to your more conventional approaches. Additional code would then take this output information to recover the complete structure. The neural network, like your previous choices, would still be matching patterns because, after all, no matter what tools you use, you are always going to be using pattern matching to some degree. Even if this approach does seem a bit unobtainable, it would have one advantage over other techniques. Due to the fuzzy nature of the solution, it would be better at overcoming any new combinations of bytecodes that might make it possible to handle any bytecode rearranging techniques.

---

12. www.usenix.org/publications/library/proceedings/coots97/full_papers/proebsting2/proebsting2.pdf

13. Lyle Ramshaw's paper "Eliminating go to's While Preserving Program Structure" was written at Digital's System Research Center in Palo Alto in 1985.

Universal Decompiler

First a word of warning from Cristina Cifuentes in "A Methodology for Decompilation." "A naive approach to decompilation attempts to enumerate all valid phrases of an arbitrary attribute grammar and then to perform a reverse match of these phrases to their original source code." Or to put it another way, if you were thinking that you could simply use Lex and Yacc to recover code, then you better think again.

I have already mentioned Cristina Cifuentes' decompiler dcc several times in this book. Essentially dcc is an incomplete decompiler written at the Queensland University of Technology during 1993 and 1994. dcc was different from other earlier decompilers because it recovered source code from binaries rather than from partially compiled objects.

Although it seems that Cifuentes and her colleagues hit a number of roadblocks, they did introduce some interesting concepts that you can take advantage of, especially because you're dealing with bytecode that is more analogous to objects than Intel binaries.

dcc consists of three modules: the front-end loader/parser, the universal decompiling machine (UDM), and the back-end code generator. The front and rear ends are platform dependent, whereas the UDM is machine and language independent. ClassToSource's front end will always be reading in the same stream of Java bytecodes, but there is no reason why the back end couldn't output any language such as Ada, which can already be compiled to bytecode. And, of course, ClassToXML could always be rewritten to handle other input streams such as Visual Basic 3 and 4 or even VB.NET objects.

Front End

The front end simulates an operating system loader, parses the incoming stream, and produces a higher level intermediate code. dcc's front-end parser starts at the entry point determined by the virtual loader and follows every path sequentially, creating a new node at every jump until the final instruction has been mapped. Because of the lack of separation between data and instructions, dcc's loader needs to be a much more complicated module than you need.

The intermediate code generator works closely with the parser, giving each instruction an intermediate code representation as well as associating any used or defined registers. An optimization phase eliminates any redundant instructions by finding obvious combinations or language idioms. This is one of the reasons why the front end cannot be used for more than one language—different languages have different idioms. After this optimization phase, the condensed tokenized version of the input is passed onto the UDM.

Universal Decompiler Machine (UDM)

The UDM performs the flow analysis of the program constructing a control flow graph (CFG) (not to be confused with a context free grammar) and splitting the high-level program into a series of basic blocks.

Cifuentes defines a basic block as being "a sequence of instructions that has a single point of entry and single point of exit." The UDM builds a linked list, or tree, of these basic blocks for every branch, whether it's a loop, a procedure call, or an end of program.

This is followed by a control flow analysis phase, which reduces the CFG into likely control structures, if-then-else, while, and for loops as well as case statements. Irreducible graphs are also converted into reducible versions at this stage, or in extreme circumstances, labeled and output as Assembler.

A structuring algorithm interprets this information and outputs a high-level version of the code, and a data flow analysis module analyzes the defined and used data information to understand the type and scope of the variables.

Back-End Processing

The back end takes the high-level language and maps it onto the target language. Not surprisingly in the case of *dcc*, the target language is C. Global variables are declared, and then code is generated on a procedure-by-procedure basis from the blocks defined in the UDM, with local variables being declared as necessary.

Ramshaw's Algorithm

The full title of Lyle Ramshaw's paper is "Eliminating go to's While Preserving Program Structure".[14] The paper originally came out of some work that Ramshaw was doing during the early 1980s while he was trying to convert Donald E. Knuth's TeX source from Pascal to a programming language called Mesa. You're looking at the algorithm because it can and has been used to convert goto-laden bytecode into goto-free Java source code.

Ramshaw's idea is straightforward; replace all goto statements and their corresponding labels with an exit statement and appropriately labeled repeat-endloop pairs. Listing 5-5 shows a pseudocode example of putting the theory into practice.

---

14. http://gatekeeper.dec.com/pub/DEC/SRC/research-reports/SRC-004.pdf

Listing 5-5. Replacing goto Statements

```
source
-------
action1
if test2 then goto L
action2
L:action3

target
-------
action1
repeat
  if test2 then exit L
  action2
  exit L
endloop:L
```

Control flow in Java bytecode is largely dependent on the simple goto statement. You can use Ramshaw's ideas to replace the goto bytecode statements with
the equivalent for(;;), do-while loops, and break commands.

Ramshaw went to a great deal of trouble to keep the Mesa and Pascal code
structurally equivalent, which is exactly what you are trying to accomplish.
However, your problem is that although the code is syntactically equivalent, it is
the bytecode that will remain syntactically equivalent and not the original source.
Ramshaw's algorithm changes the order of the bytecode and makes it more difficult for you to recover the original source.

For this reason, Ramshaw's work is not going to be of much use in your quest
for a good general decompiler. It may be very useful to an optimizing compiler
where the source is not as important and finding a good general solution becomes
the main criteria. However, there may be a single case where the algorithm is very
useful.

Normally in bytecode you don't have to worry about gotos with crossing
scope, but you may come across some obfuscators that can introduce this sort
of problem. Ramshaw deals with several categories of this irreducible graph
problem in his paper.

Although a Pascal to Mesa translator already existed, Ramshaw found that he
needed to extend the translator to compensate for the fact that Mesa had only
a limited version of the goto statement.

Listing 5-6 shows a classic example of a how not to write goto statements.
The scope of the gotos cross and create an irreducible graph that cannot be
recovered unless the code is rewritten. Ramshaw describes a mechanism called
stretching loops where he uses goto graphs to get around the simplest irreducible
flow problems.

Listing 5-6. Poor Choice of goto Statements

```
goto M
action1
Label L
action2
Label M
action3
goto L
```

Mesa's author was influenced by Knuth's article "Structured Programming with go to Statements"[15] where Knuth recommended not using goto statements that passed control into the center of a loop. So it is mildly ironic that almost a decade later, Ramshaw finds himself converting those very goto statements that Knuth and many others so vehemently opposed in code written by none other than Donald E. Knuth. Having said that, Ramshaw does say that there were little or no occurrences of the offending goto statements and that they were quickly removed from later versions of TeX.

Jive

Jive was probably the first Java decompiler. It was written by Daniel Ford, a manager in the Web Technologies department at the IBM Almaden Research Center, in San Jose, California. The original paper is not available online, but you might be lucky if you request a paper copy by going to http://www.research.ibm.com/.

In this approach to decompilation, you use a multipass scanner. After each successive pass, the bytecode is gradually transformed into something that resembles the original Java source code. The bytecode is converted into statements and idioms to make it easier to recognize and recover the building blocks of the original Java code. Listing 5-7 demonstrates this.

Listing 5-7. Simple if Statement Java Source

```
public class simpleIf {
    public static void main(String[] args) {

        int a = 12;
        int b = 13;
        if (a!=b) {
                a=b;
```

---

15. D. E. Knuth. "Structured programming with go to statements." *Computing Surveys*, pages 261–302, Dec 1974.

```
            }
        }
    }
```

The main method in Listing 5-7 has the bytecode in Listing 5-8.

Listing 5-8. Simple if Statement in Bytecode

```
 0  bipush 12
 2  istore_1
 3  bipush 13
 5  istore_2
 6  iload_1
 7  iload_2
 8  if_icmpeq 13
11  iload_2
12  istore_1
13  return
```

This is then converted into Java in a series of steps; each step adds more and more information until the entire class file can be assembled into source. You then create a series of tokens in your parser that would produce the output shown in Listing 5-9.

Listing 5-9. Simple if Class—First Pass

```
PushVMI          [0]  bipush 12
StoreVMI         [2]  istore_1
PushVMI          [3]  bipush 13
StoreVMI         [5]  istore_2
LoadVMI          [6]  iload_1
LoadVMI          [7]  iload_2
BranchVMI        [8]  if_icmple 13
LoadVMI          [11] iload_2
StoreVMI         [12] istore_1
ControlVMI       [13] return
```

Although you didn't have any real reductions in the first pass, it soon becomes apparent where you're going at the end of the second pass (see Listing 5-10), because the number of lines is halved.

Listing 5-10. Simple if Class—Second Pass

```
AssignStatement            [0-2]    a = 12;
AssignStatement            [2-4]    b = 13;
IfStatement                [6-10]   Goto 13 if: (a!=b)
AssignStatement            [11-12]  a = b;
ControlVMI         1->     [13]     return
```

The tokens generated in the first pass are used to create the building blocks in the second pass. Note the introduction of the 1-> tag, which tells the next pass where the if branch ends. In the next and final pass (see Listing 5-11), the code can now be easily resolved into something resembling your original Java code in Listing 5-7.

Jive does decompile more complicated structures than your if statement using the same approach of breaking the bytecode into statements, but it uses a lots more passes to do so. To date, I have not been able to track down the original Jive decompiler.

Single Pass Parser

Stack machines, virtual or otherwise, directly mimic the operation of a parser. The parser's constant shifts and reductions are analogous to a stack machine's pop and push actions. This leads us nicely to the fourth and final strategy.

You know it's possible to create a scanner that can handle every possible bytecode instruction. However, you may not have realized that is it possible to code the parser to cover every eventuality that it could possibly come across. The parser grammar would not need to handle nonreducible bytecode—that is such a rare occurrence that you can safely ignore—but it would still need to be at least as good as Mocha.

The main problem here is not how the parser handles simple lines of code such as initializations or assignments. The real difficulty would be how a single-pass parser could handle control flow. It would, by default, not be a general solution and you will have to throw a test suite of Java classfiles at it to make sure it can handle most eventualities.

Strategy Conclusion

You've briefly looked at four strategies for recovering source code from bytecodes in a classfile. The first option was to take Dr. Cifuentes design and reuse the existing code, as described in her thesis. Although dcc is primarily used to recover C source from DOS executables, Dr. Cifuentes thesis describes a more general approach of using it to decompile any binary to a higher-level language. It would be conceivable to use Dr. Cifuentes' UDM for your purposes. It might be tempting

to use a Babel Fish decompiler for all computer languages, how
your task is so much simpler than other decompilation problems,
really be over-engineering a solution.

Alternatively, you can take Lyle Ramshaw's approach and re
statements into a series of repeat- and endloop-like conditions. (
the Jive approach and code the decompiler in a series of passes/
phases.

The final option is to use JLex and Yacc to create a single-pass dec
I deliberately didn't go into this in too much detail, because this option—the simplest option—is the one that you're going to take. In the "Parser Design" section,
I'll explain how to use the single-pass solution to decompile a simple Hello World
example. In the Chapter 6, you're going to see how you can extend the CUP grammar to handle a much more complicated suite of examples.

Parser Design

Human and computer languages share a lot of common elements, namely keywords and a grammar or a sequence of rules. Different languages use completely
different sets of keywords and rules and sometimes even a different alphabet.
Subconsciously your mind processes these keywords or tokens and applies them
to your version of the English language. My version of the rules of the English
language will be slightly different from your version, unless you grew up in the
same area of Dublin, Ireland. Somehow, I doubt if anyone will ever read this in
any other language than English (oh, the humility). But if you are reading this in
French or German then someone must have translated the original syntax into
yet another set of keywords and grammar rules, namely your language or native
tongue.

The main difference between understanding a conversation and a compiler
generating machine code is that the compiler requires a lot fewer keywords and
rules to produce output that the computer can understand—what is called its
native format. If compiling a computer program is a smaller subset of understanding a human language, then decompiling Java is a smaller subset yet again. Let's
take a look at Listing 5-11 and Listing 5-12 to demonstrate.

Listing 5-11. Hello.java

```
public class Hello
{
    public static void main(String args[])
    {
        System.out.println("Hello, World");
    }
}
```

The number of keywords and the limited number of grammar rules allow you to easily tokenize the input and subsequently parse the tokens into Java phrases. Turning this back into code requires some further analysis, but I'll get to that a little later. What you need to do is turn the input data stream into tokens, as shown in Listing 5-12.

Listing 5-12. Hello.class Bytecode Using javap

```
Compiled from Hello.java
public class Hello extends java.lang.Object {
    public Hello();
    public static void main(java.lang.String[]);
}

Method Hello()
    0 aload_0
    1 invokespecial #6 <Method java.lang.Object()>
    4 return

Method void main(java.lang.String[])
    0 getstatic #7 <Field java.io.PrintStream out>
    3 ldc #1 <String "Hello, World">
    5 invokevirtual #8 <Method void println(java.lang.String)>
    8 return
```

Ultimately, you'll be using the XML output from ClassToXML as the input file for your parser. But for the moment, you're going to use the output of javap to get started. Looking at main method in Listing 5-12, which javap generated from Listing 5-11, you can see that tokens can be split into the following types.

- identifiers

- integers

- keywords

- whitespace

Bytecode identifiers are typically constant pool references that take the following form:

```
1 invokespecial #3
```

Integers are usually the data or numbers that follow the opcode to make up a complete bytecode statement. Good examples are numbers that get placed on the stack or labels for a goto statement.

Keywords are the 200 or so opcodes that make up the bytecode language—you'll be looking at these and their constructs in the next chapter.

Finally we need to account for whitespace, which of course includes tabs, blank spaces, new lines, and carriage returns if you're using DOS or Windows. Most decompilers would not be encountering a lot of whitespace in a real classfile, but you need to deal with it in your javap and ClassToXML output.

All these tokens are crucial in order for the parser to be able to do its job and to try to match them with the predefined grammatical rules. You could write your own tokenizer and parser by hand, which would search for the different tokens within the bytecode; however, there are plenty of tools to help you along, so why not take advantage of them? A handcrafted parser would be quicker,[16] but you're looking for ease of use rather than an optimized production quality application.

JLex is the first part of your decompilation process. JLex reads or scans input from a data stream and turns it into valid tokens that are passed on to the CUP parser, which interprets the tokens. The generated yylex program scans each incoming characters of the input bytecode using regular expressions that break the input into strings and tokens. The scanner's primary function is to keep track of the current position in the input stream and generate the tokens for the parser. Listing 5-13 shows some sample bytecode input using the classfile compiled from Listing 5-11.

Listing 5-13. Main Method Bytecode

```
0 getstatic #7 <Field java.io.PrintStream out>
3 ldc #1 <String "Hello World">
5 invokevirtual #8 <Method void println(java.lang.String)>
8 return
```

So without much further ado, let's create a scanner to tokenize the main method in Listing 5-13. First, you'll isolate the javap bytecode so that you're only dealing with the information in Listing 5-14.

Listing 5-14. Decompiler.lex

```
// create a package for the Decompiler
package Decompiler;

// import the CUP classes
import java_cup.runtime.Symbol;
```

---

16. This may not be 100 percent true because the performance section in the JLex manual mentions a lexical analyzer or scanner that soundly outperformed a handwritten scanner.

```
%%
%cup                        // CUP declaration
%%

"getstatic"                 { return new Symbol(sym.GETSTATIC, yytext()); }
"ldc"                       { return new Symbol(sym.LDC, yytext()); }
"invokevirtual"             { return new Symbol(sym.INVOKEVIRTUAL, yytext()); }
"Method"                    { return new Symbol(sym.METHOD, yytext()); }
"return"                    { return new Symbol(sym.RETURN, yytext()); }
\"[a-zA-Z ]+\"              { return new Symbol(sym.BRSTRING, yytext()); }
[a-zA-Z\.]+                 { return new Symbol(sym.BRSTRING, yytext()); }
\<                          { return new Symbol(sym.LABR, yytext()); }
\>                          { return new Symbol(sym.RABR, yytext()); }
\(                          { return new Symbol(sym.LBR, yytext()); }
\)                          { return new Symbol(sym.RBR, yytext()); }
\#[0-9]+|[0-9]+             { return new Symbol(sym.NUMBER, yytext());}
[ \t\r\n\f]                 { /* ignore white space. */ }
.              { System.err.println("Illegal character: "+yytext()); }
```

As yet, this is only a very simple lexical analyzer because it is only a partial speci-fication of the possible opcodes, but it should point you in the right direction.

Gradually, as each character is read, it becomes obvious which regular expres-sion is going to be satisfied and what token will be generated. This assumes that your specification is complete, which at this stage, it most certainly is not, but it will work for this simple example. Tokens are defined by regular expressions in the scanner and the set of these lexical tokens defines the elements of the bytecode language. If there is a syntax error in the input stream or, in other words, if the input isn't syntactically correct, then the scanner will jam. You should also make sure that your regular expressions are not ambiguous, because only the first match will be chosen when two conditions are satisfied, and as a result, the wrong token may be generated.

JLex, and indeed all Lex programs, convert these regular expressions (regexp) into two types of finite automata. First, the regexp are converted to nondetermin-istic finite automata (NFA) where it is still possible to match any condition in more than one way. The aim is to turn the regexps ultimately into deterministic finite automata (DFA) where all transitions from one state to another are singularly defined by, amongst other things, removing all redundant transitions. Or, in other words, all tokens can only be generated in one particular way. A DFA is essentially the set of regular expressions mapped onto a large sparse matrix. It has the disadvantage of being slower to generate, but the significant advantage of being a much quicker simulator.

Ultimately what we are trying to do is create a parse tree using CUP. JLex will generate tokens for the longest sequence of characters from the starting position to the current position that matches a specific regular expression. The parser requests a token from the scanner and then tries to construct a parse tree using a series of shift and reduce operations. Let's take a look at what your first attempt at the CUP parser looks like, in Listing 5-15. You won't define any actions just yet; you just want to make sure it parses.

Listing 5-15. Decompiler.cup

```
package Decompiler;

import java_cup.runtime.*;
import java.util.*;

parser code {:
        . public static void main(String args[]) throws Exception {
                new parser(new Yylex(System.in)).parse();
        }:}

terminal GETSTATIC, NUMBER, LDC, INVOKEVIRTUAL, RETURN, LBR, RBR, LABR; terminal
RABR, BRSTRING, METHOD;

non terminal expr_list, expr_part, expr, vstack, number;

expr_list ::= expr_list expr | expr;
expr      ::= expr_part:e1 expr_part:e2 expr_part:e3
            | number RETURN
              ;

expr_part ::= number:n1 GETSTATIC:s number:n2 vstack
            | number:n1 LDC:s number:n2 vstack
            | number:n1 INVOKEVIRTUAL:s number:n2 vstack
              ;

vstack  ::= LABR BRSTRING:s1 BRSTRING:s2 RABR
            | LABR BRSTRING:s1 BRSTRING:s2 BRSTRING:s3 RABR
            | LABR METHOD BRSTRING:s1 BRSTRING:s2 LBR BRSTRING:s3 RBR RABR
          . ;

number ::= NUMBER:n
              ;
```

You can now compile `decompiler.lex` and `decompiler.cup` as follows:

```
java JLex.Main decompiler.lex
mv decompiler.lex.java Yylex.java
java java_cup.Main decompiler.cup
javac -d . parser.java sym.java Yylex.java
```

It's nothing to write home about just yet, but it does scan and parse each line from the main method.

Take the second line:

```
3 ldc #1 <String "Hello World">
```

This scanner breaks the line into tokens, where LABR is a left angle bracket:

```
NUMBER LDC NUMBER LABR BRSTRING BRSTRING RABR
```

This is then reduced into the non-terminals as follows:

```
LABR BRSTRING BRSTRING RABR -> vstack
NUMBER -> number
NUMBER -> number
number LDC number vstack -> expr_part
```

You need all three lines if you're going to reduce all the way back to `expr_list`. It might also help if you add the actions to see how you get back to the original code. To do this, you'll first need to add some action code so that you can have a variable stack and a type stack for some temporary storage space while you're decompiling the code.

The complete parser for your very simple example is in Listing 5-16.

Listing 5-16. Decompiler.cup—Complete Version

```
package Decompiler;

import java_cup.runtime.*;
import java.util.*;
```

```
parser code {:
        public static void main(String args[]) throws Exception {
                new parser(new Yylex(System.in)).parse();
        }

:}

action code {:

        Stack tStack = new Stack();
        Stack vStack = new Stack();

:}

terminal GETSTATIC, NUMBER, LDC, INVOKEVIRTUAL, RETURN;
terminal LBR, RBR, LABR, RABR, BRSTRING, METHOD;

non terminal expr_list, expr_part, expr, vstack, number;

expr_list ::= expr_list expr | expr;
expr      ::= expr_part:e1 expr_part:e2 expr_part:e3
                {:
                   System.out.println(e1 + "." + e3 + "(" + e2 + ");" );
                :}
              | number RETURN
                {:
                   System.out.println("return;");
                :}

                ;


expr_part ::= number:n1 GETSTATIC:s number:n2 vstack
                {:
                        RESULT=(vStack.pop());
                :}
              | number:n1 LDC:s number:n2 vstack
                {:
                        RESULT=(vStack.pop());
                :}
              | number:n1 INVOKEVIRTUAL:s number:n2 vstack
                {:
                        RESULT=(vStack.pop());
                :}
                ;
```

```
vstack           ::= LABR BRSTRING:s1 BRSTRING:s2 RABR
                 {:
                         tStack.push(s1);
                         vStack.push(s2);
                 :}
              |  LABR BRSTRING:s1 BRSTRING:s2 BRSTRING:s3 RABR
                 {:
                         tStack.push(s2);
                         vStack.push("System." + s3);
                 :}
              |  LABR METHOD BRSTRING:s1 BRSTRING:s2 LBR BRSTRING:s3 RBR RABR
                 {:
                         tStack.push(s1);
                         vStack.push(s2);
                 :}
                 ;


number     ::= NUMBER:n
               {:
                  RESULT=n;
               :}
               ;
```

If you run the code now, the information that you need to extract out of the bytecode is stored on the *vStack* and you pop off the information when the complete expression has been recovered. If you now compile and run the decompiler, you'll get the following output:

```
System.out.println("Hello, World");
return;
```

If you're paying attention, you'll notice that System wasn't exactly derived from the bytecode. However because this snippet of bytecode doesn't have any access to the constant pool, you'd have to add this little kludge to get your little example to work.

In the Chapter 6, you'll be pulling whatever information you need from wherever you need it in the classfile. You first need to preprocess the classfile by converting it to XML using ClassToXML. Next you'll load the XML and decompile each of the individual methods, resolving the constant pool references as you go.

Conclusion

So far I've talked about the tools you can use to create a small working decompiler. You've looked at the different strategies that you might or might not employ, and finally, I created a toy example to show you how your single-pass decompiler will function.

By the end of Chapter 6, you'll have a working decompiler that will be able to handle the majority of Java classes. Chapter 6 will also look at the different internal structures and gradually create a more effective decompiler that can handle a lot more than the "Hello World" example.

Decompiler Implementation

WE ARE NOW at the point where you will learn to actually deal with the individual bytecodes, decompile the opcodes into partial statements and expressions and, ultimately (well that's the plan anyway), back into complete blocks of source code.

If I'm gauging my audience correctly, this chapter, and possibly Chapter 5, will appeal to a significant cross section of readers. We're now at the nub of the problem of how to implement a decompiler using using Java versions of Lex and Yacc, namely JLex and CUP.

To keep this as practical as possible, I'll use a test suite of ten simple programs, each with a different language construct. For each program, I'll reconstruct the original source gradually, building the decompiler as I go. Each program is first compiled, then disassembled and converted into XML using ClassToXML. I'll then look at the Java source and the corresponding method bytecode and create a CUP specification for each example to convert the byte-code back into source.

I'm taking an easy, yet powerful, approach to dealing with the classfile: by having the decompiler pretend to be the Java Virtual Machine (JVM). The decompiler will simulate stack operations as the assembly directs, but it will be working with variable names rather than actual data.

And because the classfile is more than method bytecode, I'll also need to be able to incorporate the remaining information in the classfile to recover import statements, package names, and variable names from the constant pool. So to begin with, I'll take a look at the format of the ClassToXML output, that is, the input for our decompiler that does not deal with recovering the actual code from the bytecodes. This is the supporting cast for the code recovery section. Then I'll expand the section that deals with recovering the expressions and code structure while looking at the test suite.

ClassToXML Output: An Overview

You have seen the ClassToXML format in earlier chapters, where we used it to create a simple obfuscator. It is now going to be used as input for the decompiler. To parse ClassToXML, I first create a JLex specification and then, using the terminal symbols, I create a skeleton CUP file for the classfile grammar.

From the point of view of the decompiler, every ClassToXML output file has the same format:

- A *start token*, (`<root>`), to allow initialization of variables.

- The contents of the *constant pool*, which contain all the metadata for the class.

- *Divider tokens* (`<Fields>`, `<Methods>`, etc.), to separate data and to allow processing between individual sections of the ClassToXML file.

- The *class data*, which includes properties and the constant pool index, followed by a divider token.

- The *field data*, which includes properties and constant pool indices, followed by a divider token. If no fields are used within the class, this may be blank.

- The *method data*, which includes properties, constant pool indices, and assembly code. Methods are separated by semicolons, which can be thought of as *subdivider tokens*.

- An *end token* (`</root>`).

Let's take a look at each section of ClassToXML listed above in more detail.

Constant Pool Overview

Constant pool entries consist of the following:

- Index

- Type (which can be `Integer`, `Long`, `Float`, `Double`, `UTF-8`, `String`, `Class`, `NameAndType`, `FieldRef`, `MethodRef`, or `InterfaceMethodRef`)

- Data (which can be either a constant value or an index—or a pair of indices—to another constant pool entry)

For example, a `MethodRef` type to the `println` function links to its `Class` and `NameAndType` entries, which each link to strings, as shown in Listing 6-1.

Listing 6-1. ClassToXML Output for the Constant Pool

```
<Tag>
  <ConstantPool_Index>12</ConstantPool_Index>
  <Type>CONSTANT_Methodref</Type>
  <Value>43,44</Value>
</Tag>
...
<Tag>
  <ConstantPool_Index>43</ConstantPool_Index>
  <Type>CONSTANT_Class</Type>
  <Value>57</Value>
 </Tag>
 <Tag>
  <ConstantPool_Index>44</ConstantPool_Index>
  <Type>CONSTANT_NameAndType</Type>
  <Value>58,59</Value>
 </Tag>
...
 <Tag>
  <ConstantPool_Index>57</ConstantPool_Index>
  <Type>CONSTANT_Utf8</Type>
  <Value>CONSTVALjava/io/PrintStream</Value>
 </Tag>
 <Tag>
  <ConstantPool_Index>58</ConstantPool_Index>
  <Type>CONSTANT_Utf8</Type>
  <Value>CONSTVALprintln</Value>
 </Tag>
 <Tag>
  <ConstantPool_Index>59</ConstantPool_Index>
  <Type>CONSTANT_Utf8</Type>
  <Value>CONSTVAL(Ljava/lang/String;)V</Value>
 </Tag>
```

Obviously, you'll have to load the constant pool into memory and resolve cross-references between elements in order to create any sort of a useful decompiler. Otherwise, you'll have code without any of the original names of variables and methods.

Class Data Overview

The second section of ClassToXML is the class data. In this limited decompiler, the class data you use consists of merely the class's access flags and ThisClass. You just parse and discard SuperClass and the interface data. The class data for a Hello World program might consist of the following:

```
<AccessFlags>public</AccessFlags>
<ThisClass>15</ThisClass>
<SuperClass>16</SuperClass>
```

Field Data Overview

The third section of ClassToXML is the field data. Field entries consist of the following:

- Access information (public, private, etc.) and properties (static, volatile, etc.)

- Constant pool index of Name

- Constant pool index of Description

- Attribute count

- Attributes

Again, for this decompiler, you need to assume that no attributes belong to any fields. For example, you can see the ClassToXML field data for Listing 6-2 in Listing 6-3.

Listing 6-2. Original arr Field

```
public static int[] arr = {1, 8, 27, 64, 125, 216, 343, 512,
                                                 729, 1000};
public int a = 5;
```

Listing 6-3. arr Field Data and Constant Pool Output

```
<Field>
  <AccessFlags>public static</AccessFlags>
  <Name_Index>17</Name_Index>
  <Description_Index>18</Description_Index>
  <Attribute_Count>0</Attribute_Count>
```

```
    <Attributes />
  </Field>

  . . .

  <Field>
    <AccessFlags>public</AccessFlags>
    <Name_Index>19</Name_Index>
    <Description_Index>20</Description_Index>
    <Attribute_Count>0</Attribute_Count>
    <Attributes />
  </Field>
  <Tag>
    <ConstantPool_Index>17</ConstantPool_Index>
    <Type>CONSTANT_Utf8</Type>
    <Value>CONSTVALarr</Value>
  </Tag>
  <Tag>
    <ConstantPool_Index>18</ConstantPool_Index>
    <Type>CONSTANT_Utf8</Type>
    <Value>CONSTVAL[I</Value>
  </Tag>
  <Tag>
    <ConstantPool_Index>19</ConstantPool_Index>
    <Type>CONSTANT_Utf8</Type>
    <Value>CONSTVALa</Value>
    </Tag>
  <Tag>
    <ConstantPool_Index>20</ConstantPool_Index>
    <Type>CONSTANT_Utf8</Type>
    <Value>CONSTVALI</Value>
  </Tag>
```

Method Data Overview

The method data is the fourth section of ClassToXML. Method data entries of ClassToXML consist of the following:

- Access information (e.g., whether it's public or not) and properties (e.g., whether it's static or volatile)

- Constant pool index of Name

- Constant pool index of Parameters

All other data included in the XML file is discarded.

For example, method data XML for the recurse method shown in Listing 6-4 can be seen in Listing 6-5.

Listing 6-4. recurse Method

```
public static String recurse(int num)
{
   if (num!=0)
      return "crap! " + recurse(num-1);
   else
      return "dammit!";
}
```

Listing 6-5. ClassToXML Method Data Output for recurse

```
<Method>
  <AccessFlags>public static</AccessFlags>
  <Name_Index>17</Name_Index>
  <Description_Index>18</Description_Index>
  <Attribute_Count>1</Attribute_Count>
  <Attributes>
     <Attribute>
     <Attribute_Type>Code</Attribute_Type>
     <Attribute_Length>40</Attribute_Length>
     <Max_Stack>2</Max_Stack>
     <Min_Stack>1</Min_Stack>
     <Code_Length>12</Code_Length>
     <Code>
        <Line>000: getstatic 2</Line>
        <Line>003: bipush 25</Line>
        <Line>005: invokestatic 3</Line>
        <Line>008: invokevirtual 4</Line>
        <Line>011: return</Line>
     </Code>
     <ExceptionTable_Length>0</ExceptionTable_Length>
     <ExceptionTable />
     <CodeAttribute_Count>1</CodeAttribute_Count>
     <CodeAttribute_Name_Index>16</CodeAttribute_Name_Index>
     <CodeAttribute_Length>10</CodeAttribute_Length>
     <LineNumTable_Count>2</LineNumTable_Count>
     <LineNumTable>
```

```
        <LineNumMapping>
            <StartPC>0</StartPC>
            <LineNum>4</LineNum>
        </LineNumMapping>
        <LineNumMapping>
            <StartPC>11</StartPC>
            <LineNum>5</LineNum>
        </LineNumMapping>
      </LineNumTable>
      </Attribute>
      </Attributes>
    </Method>
```

The constant pool entries shown in Listing 6-6 provide the necessary information.

Listing 6-6. ClassToXML Constant Pool Output for recurse

```
<Tag>
  <ConstantPool_Index>19</ConstantPool_Index>
  <Type>CONSTANT_Utf8</Type>
  <Value>CONSTVALrecurse</Value>
</Tag>
<Tag>
  <ConstantPool_Index>20</ConstantPool_Index>
  <Type>CONSTANT_Utf8</Type>
  <Value>CONSTVAL(I)Ljava/lang/String;</Value>
</Tag>
```

The parameter description `<ConstantPool_Index>20</ConstantPool_Index>` is the most important thing here, and I will cover it in greater detail later (see the discussion in the "CUP Specification" section). The type codes inside parentheses, for example `(I)` within the `<Value></Value>` node in Listing 6-6, are the types of data passed into the method, while those outside are the return types of the method.

JLex Specification

To begin the decompiler discussion, I should probably show you the complete lexical specification for breaking down the bytecode into tokens because that will be unchanged from start to finish.

In Listing 6-7, each of the 200 or so bytecodes is broken down into a token along with all the classfile's associated labels and numbers. As I've already mentioned, I'm using the output from the disassembler, ClassToXML, as the input for the JLex scanner.

Listing 6-7. JLex Specification

```
package XMLToSource;
import java_cup.runtime.Symbol;


%%
%cup
%%


"<?xml version=\""|"?>"        { /* ignore */ }

"<root>"                    { return new Symbol(sym.ROOT,yytext());      }
"</root>"                   { return new Symbol(sym.XROOT,yytext());     }
"<MagicNumber>"             { return new Symbol(sym.MAGICNUM,yytext());  }
"</MagicNumber>"            { return new Symbol(sym.XMAGICNUM,yytext()); }
"<MajorVersion>"            { return new Symbol(sym.MAJORVER,yytext());  }
"</MajorVersion>"           { return new Symbol(sym.XMAJORVER,yytext()); }
"<MinorVersion>"            { return new Symbol(sym.MINORVER,yytext());  }
"</MinorVersion>"           { return new Symbol(sym.XMINORVER,yytext());}
"<ConstantPool_Count>"      { return new Symbol(sym.CPCOUNT,yytext());   }
"</ConstantPool_Count>"     { return new Symbol(sym.XCPCOUNT,yytext());  }
"<ConstantPool>"            { return new Symbol(sym.CONSTPOOL,yytext()); }
"</ConstantPool>"           { return new Symbol(sym.XCONSTPOOL,yytext());}
"<Tag>"                     { return new Symbol(sym.CPTAG,yytext());     }
"</Tag>"                    { return new Symbol(sym.XCPTAG,yytext());    }
"<ConstantPool_Index>"      { return new Symbol(sym.CPINDEX,yytext());   }
"</ConstantPool_Index>"     { return new Symbol(sym.XCPINDEX,yytext());  }
"<Type>"                    { return new Symbol(sym.TYPETAG,yytext());   }
"</Type>"                   { return new Symbol(sym.XTYPETAG,yytext());  }
"<AccessFlags>"             { return new Symbol(sym.ACCFLAGS,yytext());  }
"</AccessFlags>"            { return new Symbol(sym.XACCFLAGS,yytext()); }
"<Class_Index>"             { return new Symbol(sym.NT_INDEX,yytext());  }
"</Class_Index>"            { return new Symbol(sym.XNT_INDEX,yytext()); }
"<NameType_Index>"          { return new Symbol(sym.NT_INDEX,yytext());  }
"</NameType_Index>"         { return new Symbol(sym.XNT_INDEX,yytext()); }
"<Name_Index>"              { return new Symbol(sym.NAMEINDEX,yytext()); }
"</Name_Index>"             { return new Symbol(sym.XNAMEINDEX,yytext());}
"<Description_Index>"       { return new Symbol(sym.DESCINDEX,yytext()); }
"</Description_Index>"      { return new Symbol(sym.XDESCINDEX,yytext());}
"<Value>"                   { return new Symbol(sym.VALTAG,yytext());    }
```

```
"</Value>"                    { return new Symbol(sym.XVALTAG,yytext());    }
"<ThisClass>"                 { return new Symbol(sym.THISCL,yytext());     }
"</ThisClass>"                { return new Symbol(sym.XTHISCL,yytext());    }
"<SuperClass>"                { return new Symbol(sym.SUPERCL,yytext());    }
"</SuperClass>"               { return new Symbol(sym.XSUPERCL,yytext());   }
"<Interface_Count>"           { return new Symbol(sym.INTCNT,yytext());     }
"</Interface_Count>"          { return new Symbol(sym.XINTCNT,yytext());    }
"<Interfaces>"                { return new Symbol(sym.INTERFACES,yytext());  }
"</Interfaces>"               { return new Symbol(sym.XINTERFACES,yytext()); }
"<Field_Count>"               { return new Symbol(sym.FIELDCNT,yytext());   }
"</Field_Count>"              { return new Symbol(sym.XFIELDCNT,yytext());  }
"<Fields>"                    { return new Symbol(sym.FIELDS,yytext());     }
"</Fields>"                   { return new Symbol(sym.XFIELDS,yytext());    }
"<Field>"                     { return new Symbol(sym.FIELD,yytext());      }
"</Field>"                    { return new Symbol(sym.XFIELD,yytext());     }
"<Method_Count>"              { return new Symbol(sym.METHCNT,yytext());    }
"</Method_Count>"             { return new Symbol(sym.XMETHCNT,yytext());   }
"<Methods>"                   { return new Symbol(sym.METHODS,yytext());    }
"</Methods>"                  { return new Symbol(sym.XMETHODS,yytext());   }
"<Method>"                    { return new Symbol(sym.METHOD,yytext());     }
"</Method>"                   { return new Symbol(sym.XMETHOD,yytext());    }
"<Attribute_Count>"           { return new Symbol(sym.ATTCNT,yytext());     }
"</Attribute_Count>"          { return new Symbol(sym.XATTCNT,yytext());    }
"<Attributes>"                { return new Symbol(sym.ATTRIBS,yytext());    }
"</Attributes>"               { return new Symbol(sym.XATTRIBS,yytext());   }
"<Attribute>"                 { return new Symbol(sym.ATTRIB,yytext());     }
"</Attribute>"                { return new Symbol(sym.XATTRIB,yytext());    }
"<Attribute_Type>"            { return new Symbol(sym.ATTTYPE,yytext());    }
"</Attribute_Type>"           { return new Symbol(sym.XATTTYPE,yytext());   }
"<Attribute_Length>"          { return new Symbol(sym.ATTLENGTH,yytext()); }
"</Attribute_Length>"         { return new Symbol(sym.XATTLENGTH,yytext());}
"<Max_Stack>"                 { return new Symbol(sym.MAXSTACK,yytext());   }
"</Max_Stack>"                { return new Symbol(sym.XMAXSTACK,yytext());  }
"<Min_Stack>"                 { return new Symbol(sym.MINSTACK,yytext());   }
"</Min_Stack>"                { return new Symbol(sym.XMINSTACK,yytext());  }
"<Code_Length>"               { return new Symbol(sym.CODELEN,yytext());    }
"</Code_Length>"              { return new Symbol(sym.XCODELEN,yytext());   }
"<Code>"                      { return new Symbol(sym.CODETAG,yytext());    }
"</Code>"                     { return new Symbol(sym.XCODETAG,yytext());   }
"<Line>"                      { return new Symbol(sym.LINETAG,yytext());    }
"</Line>"                     { return new Symbol(sym.XLINETAG,yytext());   }
"<ExceptionTable_Length>"     { return new Symbol(sym.EXCLEN,yytext());     }
"</ExceptionTable_Length>"    { return new Symbol(sym.XEXCLEN,yytext());    }
"<ExceptionTable>"            { return new Symbol(sym.EXCTABLE,yytext());   }
```

```
"</ExceptionTable>"              { return new Symbol(sym.XEXCTABLE,yytext()); }
"<CodeAttribute_Count>"          { return new Symbol(sym.CODEATTCNT,yytext());  }
"</CodeAttribute_Count>"         { return new Symbol(sym.XCODEATTCNT,yytext()); }
"<CodeAttribute_Name_Index>"     { return new Symbol(sym.CODEATTNAME,yytext()); }
"</CodeAttribute_Name_Index>"    { return new Symbol(sym.XCODEATTNAME,yytext());}
"<CodeAttribute_Length>"         { return new Symbol(sym.CODEATTLEN,yytext());  }
"</CodeAttribute_Length>"        { return new Symbol(sym.XCODEATTLEN,yytext()); }
"<LineNumTable_Count>"           { return new Symbol(sym.LNTABLECNT,yytext());  }
"</LineNumTable_Count>"          { return new Symbol(sym.XLNTABLECNT,yytext()); }
"<LineNumTable>"                 { return new Symbol(sym.LINENUMTABLE,yytext()); }
"</LineNumTable>"                { return new Symbol(sym.XLINENUMTABLE,yytext());}
"<LineNum>"                      { return new Symbol(sym.LINENUM,yytext());     }
"</LineNum>"                     { return new Symbol(sym.XLINENUM,yytext());    }
"<LineNumMapping>"               { return new Symbol(sym.LNMAP,yytext());       }
"</LineNumMapping>"              { return new Symbol(sym.XLNMAP,yytext());      }
"<StartPC>"                      { return new Symbol(sym.STARTPC,yytext());     }
"</StartPC>"                     { return new Symbol(sym.XSTARTPC,yytext());    }
"<EndPC>"                        { return new Symbol(sym.ENDPC,yytext());       }
"</EndPC>"                       { return new Symbol(sym.XENDPC,yytext());      }
"<HandlerPC>"                    { return new Symbol(sym.HANDLER,yytext());     }
"</HandlerPC>"                   { return new Symbol(sym.XHANDLER,yytext());    }
"<CatchType>"                    { return new Symbol(sym.CATCHTYPE,yytext());   }
"</CatchType>"                   { return new Symbol(sym.XCATCHTYPE,yytext());  }
"SourceFile"|"ConstantValue"|"Code"|"Exceptions"|"InnerClasses"|"Synthetic"|
            "LineNumberTable"|"LocalVariableTable"|"Deprecated"
                                 { return new Symbol(sym.ATTRIBNAME,yytext());  }
"public"|"private"|"protected"   { return new Symbol(sym.ACCESS,yytext());     }
"static"|"final"|"volatile"|"interface"|"abstract"
                                 { return new Symbol(sym.PROPERTY,yytext());    }
"CONSTVAL"+[_A-Za-z0-9!?<>/\\$&\[\]=().,;"\\ "]+
                                 { return new Symbol(sym.CONSTNAME,yytext());   }
"CONSTANT_"                      { return new Symbol(sym.CONSTANT,yytext());    }
"Utf8"                           { return new Symbol(sym.CHARRAY,yytext());     }
"Integer"                        { return new Symbol(sym.INTEGER,yytext());     }
"Float"                          { return new Symbol(sym.FLOAT,yytext());       }
"Long"                           { return new Symbol(sym.LONG,yytext());        }
"Double"                         { return new Symbol(sym.DOUBLE,yytext());      }
"String"                         { return new Symbol(sym.STRING,yytext());      }
"Class"                          { return new Symbol(sym.CLASSREF,yytext());    }
"Fieldref"                       { return new Symbol(sym.FIELDREF,yytext());    }
"Methodref"                      { return new Symbol(sym.METHODREF,yytext());   }
"InterfaceMethodref"             { return new Symbol(sym.INTERFACEREF,yytext());}
"NameAndType"                    { return new Symbol(sym.NAMEANDTYPE,yytext()); }
```

```
"."                      { return new Symbol(sym.DECIMALPT,yytext()); }
","                      { return new Symbol(sym.COMMA,yytext());     }
"-"                      { return new Symbol(sym.NEGATIVE,yytext());  }
[0-9]+                   { return new Symbol(sym.NUMBER, new
                           Integer(yytext())); }
"0x"+[0-9a-f]+           { return new Symbol(sym.HEXNUM,yytext());    }
":"                      { /* ignore */ }
[ \t\r\n]+               { /* ignore white space */ }
"nop"                    { return new Symbol(sym.NOP,yytext());          }
"m1"                     { return new Symbol(sym.M1,yytext());           }
"cmp"+[lg]               { return new Symbol(sym.CMP,yytext());          }
[bcifld]+"2"             { return new Symbol(sym.I2L,yytext());
                         /* This is actually [bcifld]+"2"+[bcifld] */   }
"bipush"|"sipush"        { return new Symbol(sym.BIPUSH,yytext());    }
"ldc"+("2"|"2_w")?       { return new Symbol(sym.LDC,yytext());       }
[abcsilfd]               { return new Symbol(sym.TYPE,yytext());      }
"null"                   { return new Symbol(sym.NULL,yytext());      }
"const"+"_"?             { return new Symbol(sym.CONST,yytext());     }
[bciflda]+"aload"        { return new Symbol(sym.ALOAD,yytext());     }
"load"+"_"?              { return new Symbol(sym.LOAD,yytext());      }
[bciflda]+"astore"       { return new Symbol(sym.ASTORE,yytext());    }
"store"+"_"?             { return new Symbol(sym.STORE,yytext());     }
"pop"+("2")?             { return new Symbol(sym.POP,yytext());       }
"dup"+("2")?             { return new Symbol(sym.DUP,yytext());       }
"dup"+("_x1"|"_x2"|"2_x1"|"2_x2")  { return new Symbol(sym.DUPX,yytext());      }
"swap"                   { return new Symbol(sym.SWAP,yytext());      }
"neg"                    { return new Symbol(sym.NEG,yytext());       }
"add"                    { return new Symbol(sym.ADD,yytext());       }
"sub"                    { return new Symbol(sym.SUB,yytext());       }
"mul"                    { return new Symbol(sym.MUL,yytext());       }
"div"                    { return new Symbol(sym.DIV,yytext());       }
"rem"                    { return new Symbol(sym.REM,yytext());       }
"shr"                    { return new Symbol(sym.SHR,yytext());       }
"shl"                    { return new Symbol(sym.SHL,yytext());       }
"and"                    { return new Symbol(sym.AND,yytext());       }
"or"                     { return new Symbol(sym.OR,yytext());        }
"xor"                    { return new Symbol(sym.XOR,yytext());       }
"iinc"                   { return new Symbol(sym.IINC,yytext());      }
"if_icmp"+("eq"|"lt"|"le"|"ne"|"gt"|"ge")
                         { return new Symbol(sym.IF_ICMP,yytext ());  }
"if"+("eq"|"lt"|"le"|"ne"|"gt"|"ge"|"null"|"nonnull")
                         { return new Symbol(sym.IF,yytext());        }
"goto"+("_w")?           { return new Symbol(sym.GOTO,yytext());      }
"jsr"+("_w")?            { return new Symbol(sym.JSR,yytext());       }
"ret"                    { return new Symbol(sym.RET,yytext());       }
```

```
"tableswitch"                          { return new Symbol(sym.TABLESWITCH,yytext()); }
"lookupswitch"                         { return new Symbol(sym.LOOKUPSWITCH,yytext());}
"return"                               { return new Symbol(sym.RETURN,yytext();    }
"getstatic"                            { return new Symbol(sym.GETSTATIC,yytext()); }
"getfield"                             { return new Symbol(sym.GETFIELD,yytext());  }
"putstatic"                            { return new Symbol(sym.PUTSTATIC,yytext()); }
"putfield"                             { return new Symbol(sym.PUTFIELD,yytext());  }
"invoke"+("special"|"virtual"|"static")
                                       { return new Symbol(sym.INVOKE,yytext());   }
"new"                                  { return new Symbol(sym.NEW,yytext());       }
"newarray"                             { return new Symbol(sym.NEWARRAY,yytext());  }
"arraylength"                          { return new Symbol(sym.ARRAYLENGTH,yytext()); }
"athrow"                               { return new Symbol(sym.ATHROW,yytext());    }
"checkcast"                            { return new Symbol(sym.CHECKCAST,yytext()); }
"instanceof"                           { return new Symbol(sym.INSTANCEOF,yytext()); }
"monitorenter"                         { return new Symbol(sym.MONITORENTER,yytext()); }
"monitorexit"                          { return new Symbol(sym.MONITOREXIT,yytext()); }
"wide"                                 { return new Symbol(sym.WIDE,yytext());      }
"multianewarray"
                                       { return new Symbol(sym.MULTIANEWARRAY,yytext()); }
  .                                    {    /*System.out.print(yytext());*/         }
```

The JLex specification tokenizes or scans the input. But every scanner needs a corresponding parser. The next stage in the deompiler is to create a CUP specification to turn these tokens back into the original source.

CUP Specification

Listing 6-8 is the beginning of our CUP specification. The aim of this chapter is to turn our CUP specification into a full-blown decompiler, but for now, I'll just show the skeleton of the decompiler specification (Listing 6-8) so that we have something that can be compiled together with our JLex scanner.

Although the decompiler isn't nearly complete at this stage, I have included much of the action code in the following listings that is crucial for creating our application—to resolve the constant pool references, for instance.

Listing 6-8. Skeleton CUP Specification

```
package XMLToSource;

import java_cup.runtime.*;
import java.util.*;
import java.lang.*;
```

```
parser code {:
   public static void main(String args[]) throws Exception {
      new parser(new Yylex(System.in)).parse();
   }
:}


action code {:
        boolean forOrWhile, newArray=false, skipFinish = false;
        BitSet varsInUse = new BitSet(0xFF); //FF variables possible
        int level, lowest_num=9999, staticAdjustment=0, lastLine;
        int arrayCounter, arrayElements;
        Object temp;
        String finalMethods="";
        String type, ClassName, MethodName, MethodParam, MethodProperties="",
                space="", outstandingType="";

        ArrayList ConstantType=new ArrayList();
        ArrayList ConstantVal=new ArrayList();
        ArrayList FieldType=new ArrayList();
        ArrayList FieldName=new ArrayList();

        int lineNum=0;

        Stack oStack = new Stack(); //analogous to the operand stack
        Stack ifStack = new Stack(); //keeps track of where an if statement ends
        Stack gotoStack = new Stack(); //keeps track of goto statements branching
        Stack fieldStack = new Stack(); //stores parsed assembly
        Stack finalStack = new Stack(); //eventually stores code
```

resolveConstant recursively resolves the constant pool entry associated with constantPoolIndex and returns it as a string, as shown in Listing 6-9.

Listing 6-9. The resolveConstant Method

```
   public String resolveConstant (int constantPoolIndex)
     {
       String constType, constVal, tempString="";
       int temp1, temp2;
       constType = ConstantType.get(constantPoolIndex).toString();
       constVal = ConstantVal.get(constantPoolIndex).toString();

       if (constType.equals("Integer"))
          tempString = constVal;
       else if (constType.equals("Long"))
          tempString = constVal;
```

```java
            else if (constType.equals("Float"))
               tempString = constVal;
            else if (constType.equals("Double"))
               tempString = constVal;
            else if (constType.equals("String"))
            {
               tempString = "\""+
                  ConstantVal.get(Integer.parseInt(constVal))
                      .toString ()+"\"";
               type = "String";
            }
            else if (constType.equals("Class"))
               tempString = ConstantVal.get(Integer.parseInt(constVal)).toString();
            else if (constType.equals("NameAndType"))
          {
               temp1 = Integer.parseInt(constVal.substring(0, constVal.indexOf(",")));
               temp2 = Integer.parseInt(constVal.substring(constVal.indexOf(",")+1));
               tempString = ConstantVal.get(temp1).toString() +
                              ConstantVal.get(temp2).toString();
             }
            else if (constType.equals("Fieldref"))
             {
               temp1 = Integer.parseInt(constVal.substring(0, constVal.indexOf(",")));
               temp2 = Integer.parseInt(constVal.substring(constVal.indexOf(",")+1));
               if (!resolveConstant(temp1).toString().equals(ClassName))
               {
                  tempString = resolveConstant(temp1) + ".";
               }
               else
               {
               tempString = "";
               tempString += resolveConstant(temp2);
               tempString = tempString.substring(0,tempString.length()-1);
               if (tempString.indexOf("[")!=-1)
                  tempString = tempString.substring(0,tempString.length()-1);
             }
            else if (constType.equals("Methodref") ||
                        constType.equals("InterfaceMethodref"))
             {
               temp1 = Integer.parseInt(constVal.substring(0, constVal.indexOf(",")));
               temp2 = Integer.parseInt(constVal.substring(constVal.indexOf(",")+1));
```

```
        tempString = resolveConstant(temp1) + ".";
        tempString += resolveConstant(temp2);
    }
    else
        tempString = "Error";

    return tempString;
}
```

We use a number of stacks to help resolve the constant pool; oStackDebug and finalStackDebug dump the contents of each of those stacks for ease of debugging, as shown in Listing 6-10.

Listing 6-10. oStackDebug and finalStackDebug

```
    public void oStackDebug(String calledFrom)
    {
     Stack tempStack = new Stack();
     while (!oStack.empty())
         tempStack.push(oStack.pop());
     System.out.println("oStackDebug called from " + calledFrom +
                                    ".");
     for(int i=1; !tempStack.empty(); i++)
     {
       System.out.println("oStack" + i + ": " +
                             tempStack.peek().toString());
       oStack.push(tempStack.pop());
     }
    }
    public void finalStackDebug(String calledFrom)
    {
     Stack tempStack = new Stack();
     while (!finalStack.empty())
         tempStack.push(finalStack.pop());
     System.out.println("finalStackDebug called from " +
                                    calledFrom + ".");
     for(int i=1; !tempStack.empty(); i++)
     {
       System.out.println("finalStack" + i + ": " +
                             tempStack.peek().toString());
       finalStack.push(tempStack.pop());
     }
    }
      :}
```

Next, let us look at the terminal and non-terminal symbol declarations. The terminals are the same as the tokens coming in from scanner and the non-terminals are what we resolve the terminals into, to gradually turn the tokens or terminals into source code. First are the XML tag terminals, which you can see Listing 6-11. There's nothing surprising here; refer to the JLex specification (Listing 6-7) to match the terminal name to the tag.

Listing 6-11. ClassToXML Terminals

```
terminal ROOT, MAGICNUM, MAJORVER, MINORVER, CPCOUNT;
terminal CONSTPOOL, CPTAG, CPINDEX, TYPETAG, ACCFLAGS;
terminal XROOT, XMAGICNUM, XMAJORVER, XMINORVER;
terminal XCPCOUNT, XCONSTPOOL, XCPTAG, XCPINDEX, XTYPETAG;
terminal XACCFLAGS, NT_INDEX, NAMEINDEX, DESCINDEX, VALTAG;
terminal THISCL, SUPERCL, INTCNT, INTERFACES, FIELDCNT;
terminal FIELDS, FIELD, XNT_INDEX, XNAMEINDEX, XDESCINDEX;
terminal XVALTAG, XTHISCL, XSUPERCL, XINTCNT, XINTERFACES;
terminal XFIELDCNT, XFIELDS, XFIELD, METHCNT, METHODS,;
terminal METHOD, ATTCNT, ATTRIBS, ATTRIB, ATTTYPE;
terminal ATTLENGTH, MAXSTACK, MINSTACK;
terminal XMETHCNT, XMETHODS, XMETHOD, XATTCNT, XATTRIBS;
terminal XATTRIB, XATTTYPE, XATTLENGTH, XMAXSTACK, XMINSTACK;
terminal CODELEN, CODETAG, LINETAG, EXCLEN, EXCTABLE;
terminal CODEATTCNT, CODEATTNAME, CODEATTLEN;
terminal LNTABLECNT, LINENUMTABLE;
terminal XCODELEN, XCODETAG, XLINETAG, XEXCLEN, XEXCTABLE;
terminal XCODEATTCNT, XCODEATTNAME, XCODEATTLEN;
terminal XLNTABLECNT, XLINENUMTABLE, LINENUM, LNMAP;
terminal STARTPC, ENDPC, HANDLER, CATCHTYPE, XLINENUM;
terminal XLNMAP, XSTARTPC, XENDPC, XHANDLER, XCATCHTYPE;
```

Next Listing 6-12 shows the terminals for the each of the individual opcodes:

Listing 6-12. Opcode Terminals

```
terminal ACCESS, PROPERTY, CONSTNAME, CONSTANT, DECIMALPT;
terminal COMMA ,CHARRAY, INTEGER, FLOAT, LONG, DOUBLE, STRING, CLASSREF;
terminal FIELDREF, METHODREF, INTERFACEREF, NAMEANDTYPE;
terminal NULL, M1, NEGATIVE, HEXNUM, NUMBER, TYPE, ATTRIBNAME;
terminal NOP, CONST, BIPUSH, LDC, LOAD, STORE, POP, POP2, DUP, DUPX;
terminal NEW, ASTORE, ALOAD, NEWARRAY, ARRAYLENGTH;
terminal SWAP, NEG, ADD, SUB, MUL, DIV, REM, SHL, SHR, AND, OR, XOR, IINC;
terminal I2L, CMP, IF, IF_ICMP, GOTO, JSR, RET, RETURN;
```

```
terminal TABLESWITCH, LOOKUPSWITCH, GETSTATIC, GETFIELD, PUTSTATIC;
terminal PUTFIELD, INVOKE, ATHROW, CHECKCAST, INSTANCEOF;
terminal MONITORENTER, MONITOREXIT, WIDE, MULTIANEWARRAY, IFNULL;
```

Finally, the non-terminals are shown in Listing 6-13. These break up the XML file into bite-sized pieces so that they can be dealt with more easily and can be ultimately converted into code. In CUP and Yacc grammars, general terminals always resolve into non-terminals as part of the parsing process.

Listing 6-13. Listing of All the Non-Terminals

```
non terminal startfile, file, constantpool, constantelement;
non-terminal classname, interfaces, fields, field, methods, method;
non-terminal definitionparts, stmts, expr_part, other;
non terminal property, properties, number, type, access, return, invoke;
non terminal load, bipush, iinc, const, stackops, cmp, if_icmp, if, store;
non-terminal goto, arith, conv, object, arrayops, astore, aload, newarray;
non-terminal arraylength, codeattribs, endcodeattribs, linenumtable;
non-termnal linenummapping, exceptiontable;
```

I'll now look at each non-terminal in a little more detail. In all CUP parsers, well all Yacc parsers to be exact, we convert the scanned tokens or terminals into the final output by converting terminals and non-terminals into other non-terminals until we reach the final non-terminal and the parser exists.

CUP is not unlike the JVM itself, acting like a simple stack machine where each terminal and non-terminal is popped onto a stack. Then when a rule in the parser (specified by the non-terminal) is satisfied, the terminals and non-terminals are popped off the stack and replaced with the new non-terminal. The parser ultimately exists when there are no more terminals to parse and the final rule has been resolved, which in our case, is the file non-terminal, and then the source code is output.

The file Non-Terminal

Select the file non-terminal as the start symbol:

```
start with file;
```

The file non-terminal definition describes the entire higher-level schema of the ClassToXML output, as just described. Because you're parsing most of the "useless" class information (such as field and method counts) in file, the non-terminal definition is very unwieldy, as you can see in Listing 6-14.

Remember, the code following these definitions is executed only once the symbol has been parsed. Once the whole class is decompiled, you will output the final parenthesis as using a simple `System.out.println`.

> **NOTE** *From here on, until we get to the test suite, that is, I will only show the terminals and not the code that manages the terminals. You can find and download the remaining code from the Apress web site (*http://www.apress.com*).*

Listing 6-14. file Non-Terminal

```
file ::= startfile CPCOUNT number XCPCOUNT CONSTPOOL
            constantpool XCONSTPOOL classname interfaces FIELDCNT number
            XFIELDCNT FIELDS XFIELDS METHCNT number XMETHCNT
            METHODS  methods XMETHODS  ATTCNT number XATTCNT
            ATTRIBS ATTRIB  ATTTYPE ATTRIBNAME XATTTYPE XATTRIB
            XATTRIBS  XROOT
          | startfile CPCOUNT number XCPCOUNT CONSTPOOL constantpool
            XCONSTPOOL classname interfaces FIELDCNT number XFIELDCNT
            FIELDS fields XFIELDS METHCNT number XMETHCNT METHODS
            methods XMETHODS ATTCNT  number XATTCNT  ATTRIBS ATTRIB
            ATTTYPE ATTRIBNAME XATTTYPE XATTRIB XATTRIBS  XROOT
          ;
```

The startfile Non-Terminal

In Listing 6-15, you use the `startfile` symbol so that you can set up the constant pool arrays before parsing begins. Null is added at the start of the arrays to match the 1-based indexing used in the bytecode.

Listing 6-15. startfile Non-Terminal

```
startfile ::= number DECIMALPT number ROOT MAGICNUM
          HEXNUM XMAGICNUM MAJORVER number XMAJORVER
          MINORVER number XMINORVER
          ;
```

The constantpool Non-Terminal

Now you can actually read in the constant pool. First set up the superstructure for parsing—the `constantpool` non-terminal, as shown in Listing 6-16. As you saw earlier, this allows the parser to read in every constant pool element.

Listing 6-16. constantpool Non-Terminal

```
constantpool ::=  constantpool CPTAG constantelement XCPTAG
             | CPTAG constantelement XCPTAG
             ;
```

The constantelement Non-Terminal

The `constantelement` non-terminal is the key to the problem. You just have to break it down into the various types of constant element, as shown in Listing 6-17.

Listing 6-17. constantelement Non-Terminal

```
constantelement ::=  CPINDEX number:n XCPINDEX TYPETAG CONSTANT
                CHARRAY:t XTYPETAG VALTAG CONSTNAME:s XVALTAG
             | CPINDEX number:n XCPINDEX TYPETAG CONSTANT INTEGER:t
                XTYPETAG VALTAG number:intVal XVALTAG
             | CPINDEX number:n XCPINDEX TYPETAG CONSTANT INTEGER:t XTYPETAG
             VALTAG NEGATIVE number:intVal XVALTAG
             | CPINDEX number:n XCPINDEX TYPETAG CONSTANT LONG:t XTYPETAG
             VALTAG number:longVal
             | CPINDEX number:n XCPINDEX TYPETAG CONSTANT LONG:t XTYPETAG
             VALTAG NEGATIVE number:longVal XVALTAG
             | CPINDEX number:n XCPINDEX TYPETAG CONSTANT FLOAT:t XTYPETAG
             VALTAG number:f1 DECIMALPT number:f2 XVALTAG
             | CPINDEX number:n XCPINDEX TYPETAG CONSTANT FLOAT:t XTYPETAG
             VALTAG NEGATIVE number:f1 DECIMALPT number:f2 XVALTAG
             | CPINDEX number:n XCPINDEX TYPETAG CONSTANT DOUBLE:t XTYPETAG
             VALTAG number:d1 DECIMALPT number:d2 XVALTAG
             | CPINDEX number:n XCPINDEX TYPETAG CONSTANT DOUBLE:t XTYPETAG
                 VALTAG NEGATIVE number:d1 DECIMALPT number:d2 XVALTAG
             | CPINDEX number:n XCPINDEX TYPETAG CONSTANT
                STRING:t XTYPETAG VALTAG number:index XVALTAG
             | CPINDEX number:n XCPINDEX TYPETAG CONSTANT CLASSREF:t
                XTYPETAG VALTAG number:index XVALTAG
             | CPINDEX number:n XCPINDEX TYPETAG CONSTANT FIELDREF:t
                 XTYPETAG VALTAG number:classindex COMMA number:NaTindex XVALTAG
             | CPINDEX number:n XCPINDEX TYPETAG CONSTANT METHODREF:t
                XTYPETAG VALTAG number:classindex COMMA number:NaTindex XVALTAG
             | CPINDEX number:n XCPINDEX TYPETAG CONSTANT INTERFACEREF:t
```

```
                    XTYPETAG VALTAG number:classindex COMMA number:NaTindex XVALTAG
                  | CPINDEX number:n XCPINDEX TYPETAG CONSTANT NAMEANDTYPE:t
                    XTYPETAG VALTAG number:nameindex COMMA number:typeindex XVALTAG
                  | error
        ;
```

First, you will need to read in the primitive types: the UTF-8 char array, int, long, float, and double. The eight-byte constants (double and long) require *two* constant pool entries, but you have already dealt with this in ClassToXML by merely filling both entries with the whole eight-byte constant value. Negative numbers must include the NEGATIVE terminal. You need to do some tricky string manipulation to correctly read in spaces with their escape characters and to replace < and >, the XML codes for < and >.

Next, you have the more complex constant data types: String, Class, NameAndType, Field, Methodref, and InterfaceMethodref. These types consist of index values to other elements in the constant pool. Once we deal with the constant data types, the constant pool will be ready to use. Decompiling the bytecode without using the constant pool information will not make the source code very readable.

The classname Non-Terminal

Now you need to prepare the class structure by reading in the access properties and the constant pool index of the class name and also by parsing the super-class constant pool index. But, since you don't resolve the superclass, you can discard it.

```
classname ::= ACCFLAGS access:a XACCFLAGS THISCL number:classnum
              XTHISCL SUPERCL number XSUPERCL
         ;
```

The interfaces Non-Terminal

Now read in the (empty) headers for the interfaces. As stated earlier, I am assuming that there are no interfaces in the test suite.

```
interfaces ::=  INTCNT number XINTCNT INTERFACES XINTERFACES
         ;
```

The fields Non-Terminal

Next, you must read in the fields. In Listing 6-18, I am using the fields non-terminal to collect them all. The parameter symbols given in the constant pool

(I, B, L, J, etc.) are outlined by the Java specification. J, for instance, is used for long variables because L is already reserved for class references.

Listing 6-18. fields Non-Terminal

```
fields ::=  fields FIELD field XFIELD | FIELD field XFIELD
       ;
field ::= ACCFLAGS access:a definitionparts:params ATTCNT
          number XATTCNT ATTRIBS XATTRIBS
     ;
```

The methods Non-Terminal

Next read in the methods using the methods non-terminal to collect them all.

```
methods ::=  methods METHOD method XMETHOD
       | METHOD method XMETHOD
       ;
```

For your purposes, each method consists of an access flag (public, private, protected, etc.), an indefinite number of properties (static, volatile, etc.), and constant pool indices for the name and passed/returned parameter types. However, reading in the relevant data requires reading in a lot of data you do not use first, which leads to extremely long non-terminal declarations. To minimize this, you'll need to break the method non-terminal into pieces. In Listing 6-19, the codeattribs non-terminal will precede stmts, which is the assembly code for the method; endcodeattribs will follow it.

Listing 6-19. codeattribs Non-Terminal

```
codeattribs ::= ATTCNT number XATTCNT ATTRIBS ATTRIB ATTTYPE
            ATTRIBNAME XATTTYPE ATTLENGTH number XATTLENGTH
            MAXSTACK number XMAXSTACK MINSTACK number XMINSTACK
            CODELEN number XCODELEN CODETAG
          ;
endcodeattribs ::= XCODETAG EXCLEN number XEXCLEN EXCTABLE exceptiontable
            XEXCTABLE CODEATTCNT number XCODEATTCNT CODEATTNAME number
            XCODEATTNAME CODEATTLEN number XCODEATTLEN LNTABLECNT number
            XLNTABLECNT LINENUMTABLE linenumtable XLINENUMTABLE XATTRIB
            XATTRIBS
          ;
```

The line number table is an often-present attribute of methods; it matches pieces of the bytecode to assembly code line numbers. Again, you just parse and forget it. By doing so, you accumulate an unknown number of line-number mappings with the linenumtable non-terminal and individual mappings with linenummapping, as shown in Listing 6-20.

Listing 6-20. linenumtable and linenummapping Non-Terminal

```
linenumtable ::= linenumtable LNMAP linenummapping XLNMAP
               | LNMAP linenummapping XLNMAP
               ;
linenummapping ::= | STARTPC number XSTARTPC LINENUM number XLINENUM
                 ;
```

And, finally, it's time to deal with the exception table (see Listing 6-21). You need to consider that the exception table may be empty, and so you'll need to add a blank definition. I've included this for completeness's sake because I don't implement the try/catch/finally decompilation in this version, which is the primary use of the exception table.

Listing 6-21. exceptiontable Non-Terminal

```
exceptiontable ::=
                 | STARTPC number XSTARTPC ENDPC number XENDPC HANDLER
                   number XHANDLER CATCHTYPE number XCATCHTYPE
                 ;
```

You then get the method data (access flags, definition parts, and code attributes) using the method non-terminal. The program code is then picked up iteratively using the stmts non-terminal as shown in Listing 6-22. Note that the return type and parameter types are resolved in this non-terminal:

Listing 6-22. method Non-Terminal

```
method ::= ACCFLAGS access:a definitionparts:desc codeattribs
                   stmts endcodeattribs
```

In non-static methods, the local variable 0 is used to hold the this reference; you need to use a global variable, staticAdjustment, to correct for static methods. I also use the level variable to denote the number of conditional statement levels. We won't be addressing conditional statements for some time, however.

Because all the decompiled code is in finalStack backwards, you need to pop objects and add them to the front of outString. Finally, you should add the method information you collected at the start of this function and output it. Note that I skip the <init> and <clinit> methods, because they only exist to initialize field objects; they are dealt with separately.

definitionparts, see Listing 6-23, is the non-terminal you use to set the field and method properties (static, final, etc.), name, and parameters. You must separate it from the `field` and `method` non-terminals so that you know the current object's name while you are analyzing the assembly code.

Listing 6-23. definitionparts Non-Terminal

```
definitionparts::= properties XACCFLAGS NAMEINDEX number:name
            XNAMEINDEX DESCINDEX number:params XDESCINDEX
        ;
```

stmts, shown in Listing 6-24, is the accumulating non-terminal for assembly code. If a new line of code is being added to a preexisting stack, you need to check to see whether any conditional statements end at that point in the program. Conditional resolution is one of the most difficult parts of the program.

Listing 6-24. stmts Non-Terminal

```
stmts ::= stmts LINETAG expr_part XLINETAG
        | LINETAG expr_part XLINETAG
        ;
```

Miscellaneous Non-Terminals

At this point, I'm not yet adding instructions, so I'll just define the built-in `error` non-terminal as the only member of expr_part.

```
expr_part ::= error ;
```

Here is the `number` non-terminal, a very simple non-terminal that is used repeatedly.

```
number ::= NUMBER:n  ;
```

access is similarly simple, but some methods do not have access flags. To provide for these, you must include a "blank" definition.

```
access ::=  | ACCESS:a ;
```

properties is similarly primitive. This is where you set the `staticAdjustment` variable if necessary.

```
properties ::=   properties property | property ;
property ::= | PROPERTY:p ;
```

Finally, the type non-terminal provides type strings to the various instructions that need them.

```
type    ::= TYPE:t ;
```

Test Suite

To complete the remainder of the decompiler code, in particular to build up the expr_part non-terminal, I use a test suite of programs. There are ten programs in the test suite, each demonstrating a different language construct.

- HelloWorld.java

- Basics.java

- MathOps.java

- DoWhile.java and IfTest.java

- Recurses.java

- WhileLoop.java

- ForLoop.java

- ArrayTest.java

- ArrayInit.java

For each of the programs, I begin with the original source and then show the important sections of ClassToXML—that is, the decompiler input. I then discuss the high-level grammar changes we need to make to accommodate this new construct. Next, I show the complete code for those of you who are interested in the details. Finally, I display the decompiler output.

HelloWorld.java

It's now time to start looking at the decompiler XMLToSource in earnest. There is no better place to begin than with a simple HelloWorld example (Listing 6-25). In this program, you'll see several important basic operations including constant loading, method invocation and return, and most importantly, resolution of constant pool elements.

Listing 6-25. HelloWorld.java

```java
public class HelloWorld {
    public static void main(String[] args)
    {
        System.out.println("Hello World");
        return;
    }
}
```

Input

The decompiler currently recognizes the ClassToXML output; it will read in the constant pool and the class information as shown in the previous section. The additional input consists of two generated methods in the classfile separately: a dummy constructor (Listing 6-26) and the main method (Listing 6-27).

Listing 6-26. Dummy Method

```
<AccessFlags>public</AccessFlags>
<Name_Index>9</Name_Index>
<Description_Index>10</Description_Index>
...
<Code>
<Line>000: aload_0</Line>          // pushes this onto the stack
<Line>001: invokespecial 1</Line>     // instantiate an object
<Line>004: return</Line>              // return function
</Code>
```

The second method (Listing 6-27) is our main function.

Listing 6-27. Annotated main Method

```
<AccessFlags>public static</AccessFlags>
<Name_Index>11</Name_Index>
<Description_Index>12</Description_Index>
...
<Code>
<Line>000: getstatic 2</Line>            // get constant pool entry 2, System.out
<Line>003: ldc 3</Line>                  // load "Hello World" onto stack
<Line>005: invokevirtual 4</Line> // call println(Ljava/lang/PrintStream)V,
<Line>008: return</Line>                 // return function
</Code>
```

No local variables are used in this method although local0 is reserved as a reference to the String array of arguments Java requires of main functions. In this case, local0 resolves to public static void main(String[] args).

Grammar

The grammar is as follows:

```
expr_part -> error | return | store | load  | invoke | object ;
return  -> number RETURN  | number type RETURN;
store   -> number type STORE  number;
load    -> number type LOAD number  | number LDC number ;
invoke -> number INVOKE number;
object   -> number NEW number | number GETSTATIC number
type -> TYPE;
```

The return Non-Terminal

There are two return productions: line number and RETURN terminal; and line number, type of value to return, and RETURN terminal.

The return non-terminal is fairly simple. It has two possible variations in the assembly: return is used to return void, whereas ireturn, dreturn, and so on, push a value onto the oStack and then return to the calling method. Note that non-terminal definitions must include the line number of the instruction so that you have immediate access to it.

The store Non-Terminal

The store production consists of the line number, the local variable type, the STORE terminal, and the index of the local variable being used.

The store non-terminal is more complex. Every variable declaration creates a store instruction: primitives in their primitive type, higher-level objects as pointers (astore). To correctly parse an instruction, you have to check its type, verify whether the local variable it references has already been declared, and then store the top element of the oStack in the appropriate local variable.

As with return, different primitive types are identified by a single-character prefix to the store instruction. It's very easy to identify the int, long, float, and double primitives, but what of the class variables stored using astore (that is, stored by address)?

This implementation of the type non-terminal loads the primitive types into a global string type, but ignores the "a" type. The higher-level objects must be addressed differently: the type can be set to String when a string constant is loaded from the constant pool. For other classes, you can use the new instruction to get the variable type.

The load Non-Terminal

The load non-terminal contains two productions: one for the load instruction, which consists of the line number, the local variable type, the LOAD terminal, and the index of the local variable being loaded; and one for ldc, the "load constant" instruction, which consists of the line number, the LDC terminal, and the constant pool index of the constant being loaded.

The ldc instruction is easy to deal with: it gets the constant pool element specified by the index and pushes it onto the oStack. The definition for the load instruction is nearly as simple. First check to see whether the local variable whose value is being pushed onto the oStack has been used before. If it hasn't, it is a parameter of the method and you set the corresponding bit in varsInUse.

```
if (!varsInUse.get(new Integer(n.toString()).intValue()))
        varsInUse.set(new Integer(n.toString()).intValue());
```

Since it's being loaded onto the oStack, the type of the variable doesn't matter and "local"+index (that is, localN) can be pushed onto the oStack.

The invoke Non-Terminal

The invoke production is deceptively simple, consisting of only the line number, the INVOKE terminal, and the constant pool index of the MethodRef for the method being invoked.

The invoke non-terminal is the meatiest you'll encounter in this example: it is the trickiest, the most basic, and the most important. When dealing with invocations, you must be concerned with whether the method being invoked is static (since it will not affect the current reference), virtual, or "special"—although you don't need to worry too much about the last, as it rarely comes up.

The code first resolves the method reference (given by constant pool index), then isolates the number of passed parameters and pops that number of elements from the oStack.

Once the constant pool data for the method has been loaded, the oStack must be checked. If the top element on the oStack is an invocation containing the typeCheck type, the method being invoked belongs to that reference and can be attached to it—for instance, a string concatenation, (StringBuffer.append()), may be attached to another if multiple strings are appended to a StringBuffer.

Next, the decompiler must check whether the method being called is <init>. If it is, this instantiates an object. If the object constructor takes a parameter, you must add it in. Then you need to check to see if the class method being invoked belongs to is the current reference. If it is, you must attach the previous chain of invocations (i.e., tempString.substring(0, tempString.indexOf(".")).You use the outstandingType global string for this. You must check three things: whether outstandingType has been initialized, whether typeCheck (the class to which the method being invoked belongs) starts with it, and whether the oStack is empty. You'll use this in successive cases, too.

The next condition is a special case, the case of appending strings. If the method being invoked is .append("somevalue"), and the top element of the oStack begins with new StringBuffer().append, you can insert + "somevalue" into the argument of append. This returns you to a familiar and efficient style of string concatenation—for example ("value1" + value1 + ".").

If none of these criteria apply, you need to check those same three criteria discussed above: outstandingType, typeCheck, and whether the oStack is empty. If the method returns void, you can push it to the finalStack; otherwise, you must push it to the oStack.

If the outstandingType check fails, you check the return type.

The object Non-Terminal

At present, there are two productions for object; more will be added later. The first, for the new instruction, consists of the line number, the NEW terminal, and the constant pool index of the object being instantiated. The second, for the getstatic instruction, consists of the line number, the GETSTATIC terminal, and the constant pool index of the ClassRef being loaded.

The object non-terminal is the last remaining, and it is fairly simple. The related opcodes putstatic, getfield, and putfield will not become important for some time. The new instruction just gets the class name from the constant pool, stores it in the global outstandingType string, and pushes the new instance of the class onto the oStack. The getstatic instruction is no more difficult: again, just resolve the constant pool reference and push it onto the oStack.

Code

The complete code to handle HelloWorld.java is shown in Listing 6-28.

Listing 6-28. Decompiler Code for HelloWorld.java

```
expr_part  ::= error
               | return
               | store
               | load
               | invoke
               | object
             ;
```

```
return   ::= number:l RETURN:c
                        {:
                            finalStack.push(space + "return; //"+l.toString());
                        :}
              | number:l type:t RETURN:c
                        {:
                            if (!oStack.empty())
                                finalStack.push(space + "return " +
                                oStack.pop().toString()  + "; //"+l.toString ());
                        :}
              ;
store ::= number:l type:t STORE:s number:n
          {:
              if (!oStack.empty())
              {
                  if (varsInUse.get(new Integer(n.toString()).intValue()))
                      finalStack.push(space + "local" + n + "="
                                              +oStack.pop()+"; //" + l);
                  else
                  {
                      finalStack.push(space + type + " local" + n + "="
                                              +oStack.pop()+"; //" + l);
                      varsInUse.set(new Integer(n.toString()).intValue());
                  }
              }
          :}
        ;


load ::= number:l type:t LOAD:i number:n
            {:
                if (!varsInUse.get(new Integer(n.toString()).intValue()))
                        varsInUse.set(new
Integer(n.toString()).intValue());
                if (t.toString().equals("a"))
                        oStack.push("local"+n.toString());
                else
                        oStack.push("local"+n.toString());
            :}
        | number:l LDC:ld number:n
            {:
                oStack.push(resolveConstant(Integer.parseInt(n.toString())));
            :}
        ;
```

```
invoke  ::= number:l INVOKE:s number:n
          {:
            int varCount;
            String tempString, variables="", tempVarTypes, typeCheck="";
            String tempString = resolveConstant (Integer.parseInt(n.toString ()));
            tempVarTypes = tempString.substring(
                            tempString.indexOf("("),tempString.indexOf(")")+1);
            while (tempVarTypes.indexOf("L") != -1 &&
                            tempVarTypes.indexOf(";") != -1)
                tempVarTypes =
                  tempVarTypes.substring(0,tempVarTypes.indexOf("L")+1) +
                      tempVarTypes.substring(tempVarTypes.indexOf(";")+1,
                          tempVarTypes.length ());
            varCount = tempVarTypes.indexOf(")") - tempVarTypes.indexOf("(")-1;
            while (varCount > 0) {
                variables = oStack.pop() + ", " + variables;
                varCount--;
            }
            if (variables.length() > 0)
                variables = variables.substring(0,variables.length()-2);
            typeCheck = tempString;

            if (s.toString().equals("invokevirtual") && typeCheck.indexOf(".")!=-1)
                outstandingType=typeCheck.substring(0,typeCheck.indexOf("."));
            while (typeCheck.indexOf(")L")!=-1)
                typeCheck = typeCheck.substring(typeCheck.indexOf(")L")+1);
            if (!oStack.empty() && oStack.peek().toString().indexOf(typeCheck)!=-1)
            {
                String StackTemp = oStack.pop().toString();
                oStack.push(StackTemp.substring(0,StackTemp.indexOf("L")) + "."
                    + tempString.substring(0,tempString.indexOf("."))+
                    "("+variables+")");
            }
            else if (tempString.substring(tempString.indexOf(".")+1,
                tempString.indexOf("(")).equals("<init>"))
            {
                if (outstandingType != "" && typeCheck.indexOf(outstandingType)!=-1
                    && !oStack.empty())
                    oStack.push(oStack.pop() + "("+variables+")");
                else
                    oStack.push(tempString.substring(0,tempString.indexOf("."))+
                        "("+variables+")");
            }
            else if (tempString.substring(tempString.indexOf(".")+1,
```

```
                tempString.indexOf("(")).equals("toString") &&
                oStack.peek().toString().startsWith("new StringBuffer().append ("))
          {
              tempString = oStack.pop().toString();
              tempString = tempString.substring(25);
              while (tempString.indexOf(").append(") != -1)
                      tempString = tempString.replaceAll(".append"," + ");
              oStack.push(tempString);
          }
          else if (outstandingType != "" &&
                        typeCheck.indexOf(outstandingType)!=-1
                          && !oStack.empty())
          {
              String temp2 = oStack.pop().toString();
              if (temp2.indexOf("Ljava")!=-1)
                      temp2 = temp2.substring(0,temp2.indexOf("Ljava"));
              while (temp2.indexOf("/")!=-1)
                      temp2 = temp2.substring(temp2.indexOf("/")+1);
              if (tempString.endsWith("V"))
                      finalStack.push(space + temp2 + "." +
                       tempString.substring (tempString.indexOf(".")+1,
                       tempString.indexOf("("))+"("+variables+"); //"+l);
              else
                  oStack.push(temp2 + "." +
                     tempString.substring(tempString.indexOf(".")+1,
                       tempString.indexOf("("))+"("+variables+")");
          }
          else if (tempString.endsWith("V"))
                  finalStack.push(space +
                          tempString.substring(tempString.indexOf(".")+1,
                            tempString.indexOf("("))+"("+variables+"); //"+l);
          else
              oStack.push(tempString.substring(tempString.indexOf(".")+1,
                  tempString.indexOf("("))+"("+variables+")");
        :}
            ;
object    ::= number:l NEW:s number:n
          {:
              String tempString =
                          resolveConstant (Integer.parseInt(n.toString ()));
              outstandingType=tempString;
              while (tempString.indexOf("/")!=-1)
                  tempString =
```

```
tempString.substring(tempString.indexOf("/")+1);
                type = tempString;
                oStack.push("new "+tempString);
        :}
    | number:l GETSTATIC:s number:n
        {:
            String tempString =
                        resolveConstant(Integer.parseInt(n.toString ()));
            oStack.push(tempString);
        :}
    ;
```

Output

Once you recompile the CUP and JLex files and run the decompiler, the results
you get are indistinguishable from the original (see Listing 6-29).

Listing 6-29. Decompiled Method

```java
public class HelloWorld {
  public static void main(String[] local0)
    {
    System.out.println("Hello World. ");
    return;
    }
}
```

Basics.java

In this example, the decompiler is extended slightly to support a few more common operations. In this program, you'll see several important basic operations:
primitive type assignation, recasting, initialization of variables, and non-void
returns. We begin with the original code, shown in Listing 6-30.

Listing 6-30. Basics.java

```java
public class Basics
{
  void main(String [] local1)
    {
    int local2=12;
```

```
      double local3=convertToDouble(local2);
      return;
    }
  public double convertToDouble(int local1)
    {
    return (double) local1;
    }
}
```

Input

The first method in ClassToXML's output will of course be the constructor, which can be disregarded. The second is the main function (shown in Listing 6-31).

Listing 6-31. Annotated main Method

```
<AccessFlags />
<Name_Index>9</Name_Index>
<Description_Index>10</Description_Index>
...
<Line>000: bipush 12</Line>            //push 12
<Line>002: istore_2</Line>            //pop and store in local2
<Line>003: aload_0</Line>             //push this
<Line>004: iload_2</Line>                 //push int value of local2
<Line>005: invokevirtual 2</Line>         //call type conversion function
<Line>008: dstore_3</Line>                //store result in local3
<Line>009: return</Line>               //return
```

There is an interesting and important difference between static and non-static methods within the bytecode. Since the main function is a non-static method, local0 is used to store this. Change both functions to public static, recompile the program, and disassemble it with ClassToXML, and you will see that the assembly of the main function is quite different (Listing 6-32).

Listing 6-32. Static main Method

```
<AccessFlags>public static</AccessFlags>
...
<Line>000: bipush 12</Line>
<Line>002: istore_1</Line>
<Line>003: iload_1</Line>
<Line>004: invokestatic 2</Line>
<Line>007: dstore_2</Line>
<Line>008: return</Line>
```

No longer is this loaded before the type conversion method is invoked. Instead, only the contents of local1 (formerly local2) are loaded and the method is invoked.

Last is the tiny type conversion method (Listing 6-33). Little is done within it, as type conversion between primitives requires only a single opcode.

Listing 6-33. Annotated Type Conversion Method

```
<AccessFlags>public</AccessFlags>
<Name_Index>11</Name_Index>
<Description_Index>12</Description_Index>
...
<Line>000: iload_1</Line>              //load passed integer
<Line>001: i2d</Line>            //convert integer to double
<Line>002: dreturn</Line>            //return double value
```

Also note that the type of the return opcode reflects the return type of the method—this helps the JVM ensure security. Though there can be multiple return statements in a method, they all must return the same type.

Grammar

The grammar is as follows:

```
expr_part -> error | return | store | load  | invoke | object |

                          const | ipush | conv;
ipush -> number IPUSH number;
const   -> number type CONST number | number type CONST M1
                | number type CONST NULL;
conv-> number type T2T type;
```

The ipush Non-Terminal

The ipush production consists of the line number, the IPUSH terminal, and the byte or short value to convert to load to the oStack.

Both bipush and sipush sign-extend a byte or a short, respectively, to int, then push it to the oStack. With the abstracted approach the decompiler uses, this is very easy to deal with: it just pushes the number.

The Const Non-Terminal

The const production consists of the line number, the type of constant to load, the CONST terminal, and the constant value to load.

Compared to `ipush`, `const` has a wider range of data types but a smaller range of values. `Const` can push data of type `int`, `long`, `float`, and `double`. `iconst` can push integers 0–5, as well as –1 (`iconst_m1`), onto the oStack; `lconst` longs 0 and 1; `fconst` float 0.0, 1.0, and 2.0; and `dconst` double 0.0 and 1.0. There is also an `aconst` instruction that can push a null object reference. Again, this is easy to parse, requiring only that `M1` and `NULL` terminals be defined.

The conv Non-Terminal

The `conv` production consists of the line number, the type of the value to be converted, the `T2T` terminal, and the type to which it's being converted.

There's one more immensely useful little instruction to address: type-to-type conversion (`t2t`). `T2T` has various forms (`i2l`, `f2d`) can convert most primitives to one another. This will take care of recasting values. You don't need to worry about what type a piece of data is being converted *from*, just what it will be converted *to*. This and the way types are processed make things very simple:

```
oStack.push("(" + type + ") " + oStack.pop());
```

Code

The complete code to handle `Basics.java` is shown in Listing 6-34.

Listing 6-34. Decompiler Code for Basics.java

```
bipush      ::= number:l BIPUSH:p number:n
                    {:   oStack.push(n);   :}
            ;
const       ::= number:l type:t CONST:c number:n
                    {:
                        if (type == "double" || type == "float")
                            oStack.push(n+".0");
                        else
                            oStack.push(n);
                    :}
            | number:l type:t CONST:c M1:m
                    {:   /* iconst_m1 */
                        if (type == "double" || type == "float")
                            oStack.push("-1.0");
                        else
                            oStack.push("-1");
                    :}
```

```
        | number:l type:t CONST:c NULL:n
                    {:    /* aconst_null */
                            oStack.push(n);
                    :}


conv   ::= number:l I2L:i type:t
                {:
                            oStack.push("(" + type + ") " + oStack.pop ());
                    :}
            ;
```

Output

Once the CUP specification is updated and recompiled, the decompiler produces exactly the result we want (Listing 6-35), although I must admit it's very
unlikely that you'd choose local1, local2, and local3 for your variable names.

Listing 6-35. Decompiler Results

```
public class Basics
{
   void main(String[] local1)
     {
     int local2=12;
     double local3=convertToDouble(local2);
     return;
     }
  public double convertToDouble(int local1)
     {
     return (double) local1;
     }
}
```

MathOps.java

The next step is to have programs that change the data in the oStack—to start
with, a simple arithmetic program. You will see that all the arithmetic operations (add, sub, mul, div, and rem) work the same way. Only the iinc increment
instruction needs to be handled differently. The original code is shown in
Listing 6-36.

Listing 6-36. MathOps.java

```
public class MathOps
{
    public static void main(String[] args)
      {
      double finalval = 0.0;
      int test = 12;
      test += 1;
      test -= 4;
      test *= 5;
      test /= 3;
      finalval = (double) test + finalval;
      }
}
```

Input

The main function from ClassToXML is shown in Listing 6-37. The JVM is completely stack-based, so the arithmetic operations work with the top two pieces of data on the oStack. For example, lines 19–23 of the assembly are equivalent to `local1 += (double) local3;`

Listing 6-37. Annotated main Method

```
<AccessFlags>public static</AccessFlags>
<Name_Index>8</Name_Index>
<Description_Index>9</Description_Index>
...
  <Line>000: dconst_0</Line>              //load constant double 0.0
  <Line>001: dstore_1</Line>             //store it in local1
  <Line>002: bipush 12</Line>            //load int 12
  <Line>004: istore_3</Line>             //store it in local3
  <Line>005: iinc 3 1</Line>             //increment local3 by 1
  <Line>008: iinc 3 -4</Line>            //decrement local3 by 4
  <Line>011: iload_3</Line>              //push value of local3 onto stack
  <Line>012: iconst_5</Line>             //push int 5 onto stack
  <Line>013: imul</Line>                 //multiply the two together
  <Line>014: istore_3</Line>             //store product in local3
  <Line>015: iload_3</Line>              //push value of local3 onto stack
  <Line>016: iconst_3</Line>             //push int 3 onto stack
```

```
<Line>017: idiv</Line>                        //INTEGER divide local3 by 3
<Line>018: istore_3</Line>                      //store quotient in local3
<Line>019: iload_3</Line>                        //push value of local3 onto stack
<Line>020: i2d</Line>                      //convert it from integer to double
<Line>021: dload_1</Line>                    //load local1 onto stack
<Line>022: dadd</Line>                   //add local1 to (double) local3
<Line>023: dstore_1</Line>                  //store sum in local1
<Line>024: return</Line>                  //and return
```

Grammar

The grammar is as follows:

```
expr_part -> error | return | store | load  | invoke | object | const | bipush |
                              conv | arith | iinc;
arith -> number type NEG | number type REM | number type ADD
                        | number type SUB | number type MUL | number type DIV;
iinc    -> number IINC number number
                | number IINC number NEGATIVE number;
```

The arith Non-Terminal

Each of the arith productions consists of the line number, the type of the operand(s), and the appropriate opcode name (ADD, SUB, MUL, DIV, REM, or NEG).

Parsing the arithmetic expressions is not difficult: just pop the top two values in the oStack and perform the appropriate arithmetic function; then push the combined instruction back onto the oStack. For lack of a better place to put it, the NEG opcode is also included in arith; this pops the top item on the oStack, switches the sign (whether it's a signed value or an arithmetic expression), and pushes it back.

Unfortunately, arithmetic is a bit more complicated than it looks. If expressions are chained, parentheses are necessary to ensure proper results. Addition and subtraction do not depend on the order of operations, while multiplication and subtraction do. Thus, the multiplication and division non-terminals must check for arithmetic signs as the NEG non-terminal does.

The iinc Non-Terminal

The iinc production consists of the line number, the IINC terminal, the index of the local variable to increment, and the integer increment value (which may be preceded by a negative sign).

Integer increment (iinc) adds or subtracts given values from the value atop the oStack. This requires a new terminal definition, since iinc can take a negative value as the increment. As negative numbers are not defined in the non-terminal expression number, two different productions are used for iinc: an increment and a decrement (IINC number NEGATIVE number). In addition, increment values of one can be caught and the format switched to "i++" from the clunkier "i+=1".

Code

The complete code to handle MathOps.java is shown in Listing 6-38.

Listing 6-38. Decompiler Code for MathOps.java

```
arith       ::= number:l type:t NEG:r
                {:
                    if (oStack.peek().toString().indexOf("+") == -1 &&
                      oStack.peek().toString().indexOf("-") == -1 &&
                        oStack.peek().toString().indexOf("*") == -1 &&
                        oStack.peek().toString().indexOf("/") == -1)
                        oStack.push("-("+oStack.pop().toString()+")");
                      else if (!oStack.peek().toString().trim().startsWith ("-"))
                        oStack.push("-"+oStack.pop().toString());
                      else
                        oStack.push(oStack.pop().toString().trim().substring(1));
                :}
        |   number:l type:t REM:r
                {:
                    temp = oStack.pop();
                    oStack.push(oStack.pop().toString() + "%" +
                                        temp.toString ());
                :}
        |   number:l type:t ADD:m
                {:
                    temp = oStack.pop();
                    oStack.push(oStack.pop().toString() + "+" +
                                        temp.toString ());
                :}
        |   number:l type:t SUB:m
                {:
                    temp = oStack.pop();
                    oStack.push(oStack.pop().toString() + "-" +
                                        temp.toString ());
                :}
```

```
| number:l type:t MUL:m
     {:
         temp = oStack.pop();
         if (temp.toString().indexOf("+") == -1 &&
               temp.toString().indexOf("-") == -1 &&
               temp.toString().indexOf("*") == -1 &&
               temp.toString().indexOf("/") == -1 &&
               oStack.peek().toString().indexOf("+") == -1 &&
               oStack.peek().toString().indexOf("-") == -1 &&
               oStack.peek().toString().indexOf("*") == -1 &&
               oStack.peek().toString().indexOf("/") == -1)
               oStack.push(oStack.pop().toString() + "*" +
                       temp.toString ());
         else if (temp.toString().indexOf("+") == -1 &&
                 temp.toString().indexOf("-") == -1 &&
                 temp.toString().indexOf("*") == -1 &&
                 temp.toString().indexOf("/") == -1)
                 oStack.push("(" + oStack.pop().toString() + ")*" +
                               temp.toString ());
         else if (oStack.peek().toString().indexOf("+") == -1 &&
                     oStack.peek().toString().indexOf("-") == -1 &&
                     oStack.peek().toString().indexOf("*") == -1 &&
                     oStack.peek().toString().indexOf("/") == -1)
                 oStack.push(oStack.pop().toString() + "*(" +
                               temp.toString ()+")");
         else
                 oStack.push("(" + oStack.pop().toString() + ")*(" +
                               temp.toString ()+")");
     :}
| number:l type:t DIV:m
    {:
         temp = oStack.pop();
         if (temp.toString().indexOf("+") == -1 &&
                     temp.toString().indexOf("-") == -1 &&
                     temp.toString().indexOf("*") == -1 &&
                     temp.toString().indexOf("/") == -1 &&
                     oStack.peek().toString().indexOf("+") == -1 &&
                     oStack.peek().toString().indexOf("-") == -1 &&
                     oStack.peek().toString().indexOf("*") == -1 &&
                     oStack.peek().toString().indexOf("/") == -1)
                 oStack.push(oStack.pop().toString() + "/" +
                           temp.toString ());
         else if (temp.toString().indexOf("+") == -1 &&
                         temp.toString().indexOf("-") == -1 &&
```

```
                            temp.toString().indexOf("*") == -1 &&
                            temp.toString().indexOf("/") == -1)
                  oStack.push("(" + oStack.pop().toString() + ")/" +
                            temp.toString ());
              else if (oStack.peek().toString().indexOf("+") == -1 &&
                        oStack.peek().toString().indexOf("-") == -1 &&
                        oStack.peek().toString().indexOf("*") == -1 &&
                        oStack.peek().toString().indexOf("/") == -1)
                        oStack.push(oStack.pop().toString() + "/(" +
                            temp.toString ()+")");
           else
                    oStack.push("(" + oStack.pop().toString() +
                            ")/(" + temp.toString ()+")");
              :}
         ;
iinc      ::= number:l IINC:p number:n1 number:n2
          {:
            if (!n2.toString().equals("1"))
                  finalStack.push(space + "local" + n1 + "+=" +n2+"; //" + l);
            else
                  finalStack.push(space + "local" + n1 + "++; //" + l);
           :}
          | number:l IINC:p number:n1 NEGATIVE number:n2
          {:
            if (!n2.toString().equals("1"))
                  finalStack.push(space + "local" + n1 + "-="+n2+"; //" + l);
            else
                  finalStack.push(space + "local" + n1 + "--; //" + l);
           :}
           ;
```

Output

Adding these into the CUP specification produces nice-looking results (see Listing 6-39).

Listing 6-39. Decompiler Results

```java
public class MathOps
{
  public static void main(String[] local0)
    {
      double local1=0.0;
      int local3=12;
```

```
        local3++;
        local3-=4;
        local3=local3*5;
        local3=local3/3;
        local1=(double) local3 + local1;
        return;
        }
}
```

DoWhile.java and IfTest.java

The next extension of the decompiler allows it to handle conditional statements. Two types of conditional statements do not require the goto opcode by nature— the do-while loop (Listing 6-40) and the if statement (Listing 6-41)—so it is logical to start with them. This small change requires the addition of several new opcodes, the most complicated covered so far.

Listing 6-40. DoWhile.java

```
public class DoWhile
{
        public static void main(String[] args)
        {
                double finalval = 0.0;
                int test = 12;
                do{    test += 1;
                        test -= 4;
                        test *= 5;
                        test /= 3;
                } while (test<=100);
                finalval += (double) test;
                return;
        }
}
```

Listing 6-41. IfTest.java

```
public class IfTest
{
        public static void main(String[] args)
        {
                double test = -3.14159;
                if (test > 100.0 && test < 200.0)
```

```
        test=test - 100.0;
    return;
  }
}
```

Both main functions have only a single control-flow statement to deal with. Their organizations are exactly as you would expect. In the do-while loop, all statements are executed until the conditional test is reached. If it is true, the program branches back to near the beginning; if not, it continues. In the if statement, the conditional is checked and the program branches or continues accordingly.

Be careful here—you need to make sure the decompiler checks whether the line number to which the conditional branches falls before or after the current line. If it falls before the current line, the conditional is a do-while; if it falls after, it is either an if statement or a while or for loop. The opcodes if and cmp always go together; if_icmp is a more efficient combination of the two operations that is used exclusively for integer comparisons. The two can be decompiled the same way, however.

Input

The main function of DoWhile.java is shown in Listing 6-42.

> **NOTE** *From now on, the* <Line> *and* </Line> *tags are omitted for brevity.*

Listing 6-42. Annotated main Method of DoWhile.java

```
000:  dconst_0        //see the assembly from MathOps.java, as this part is
001:  dstore_1         // very similar
002:  bipush 12
004:  istore_3
005:  iinc 3 1
008:  iinc 3 -4
011:  iload_3
012:  iconst_5
013:  imul
014:  istore_3
015:  iload_3
016:  iconst_3
017:  idiv
```

```
018:  istore_3
019:  iload_3        //load local3 onto the stack
020:  bipush 100     //load 100 onto the stack
022:  if_icmple 5    //if local3 <= 100, branch back to 5
025:  dload_1            //otherwise continue
026:  iload_3
027:  i2d
028:  dadd
029:  dstore_1
030:  return
```

The main function of IfTest.java is shown in Listing 6-43. As the bytecode of the main function shows (lines 8–17), the double conditional becomes two nested comparison statements.

Listing 6-43. Annotated main Method of IfTest.java

```
000:  ldc2_w 2       //load double 3.14159265 from the constant pool
003:  dstore_1        //store it in local1
004:  dload_1         //load local 1
005:  ldc2_w 4       //load double 100.0 from the constant pool
008:  dcmpl          //compare local1 to 100.0
009:  ifle 26         //if local1 < 100.0, goto 26
012:  dload_1         //else load local1
013:  ldc2_w 6       //load double 200.0 from the constant pool
016:  dcmpg          //compare local1 to 200.0
017:  ifge 26         //if local1 > 200.0, goto 26
020:  dload_1      //load local1
021:  ldc2_w 4     //load 100.0
024:  dsub           //subtract the two
025:  dstore_1     //store the difference in local1
026:  return        //return
```

Grammar

The grammar is as follows:

```
expr_part -> error | return | store | load  | invoke | object | const
                  | bipush | conv| arith | iinc | if | cmp | if_icmp;
if_icmp -> number IF_ICMP number;
if ->  number IF number;
cmp  -> number type CMP;
```

The if_icmp Non-Terminal

Each of the new productions look simple and if_icmp is no exception. It consists only of the line number, the IF_ICMP terminal, and the branch location.

The first condition to test is whether the branch location is less than or greater than the current line number. If it's less, the loop is a do-while and the end of the loop has been reached. Now the decompiler must move back through the finalStack (popping and pushing lines onto the tempStack) until the branch location is greater than or equal to the current line number.

At this point, it injects "do {" into the finalStack, restores the contents of the finalStack, and outputs the actual while statement. Then the top two items on the oStack are compared. The first item on the oStack, also the rightmost in the while statement, is popped first and stored in a temporary variable. The second is then popped and the while statement is pushed onto the finalStack.

```
finalStack.push(space + "} while (" + oStack.pop().toString() + ">="
                                      + temp.toString () +");");
```

If the branch location is greater than the current line number, however, the decompiler will assume an if statement and push it to the oStack. The goto production, which will be covered later on, determines if that assumption is correct.

The if Non-Terminal

The if production consists of the line number, the IF terminal, and the branch location.

Resolution of the if opcode is similar, but the difference is important: if_icmp compares the top two oStack elements, while if merely compares the top element against zero. It is often used in conjunction with cmp to compare two values. Because cmp can only do less-than and greater-than comparisons, it is not sufficient to set up the if statement conditionals. As a result, the decompiler ignores the comparison type (g or l) of the cmp statement and merely preserves the names of the compared values.

As you see in Listing 6-44, the conditional type is resolved in opposite ways in a do-while loop and in an if statement (or forward-branching loop). For example, if_icmpge becomes >= in a do-while loop but < in an if statement. The reason for this lies in the different constructions of do-while statements and if statements. In a do-while statement, the JVM branches back to the beginning if the conditional statement is true. In an if statement, it doesn't branch if the statement is true—only if the statement is false. Therefore the actual conditions being tested in each case are opposite, and so are the comparison signs.

The cmp Non-Terminal

The `cmp` production consists of the line number, the type of the values being compared, and the `CMP` terminal (which can be either `cmpg` or `cmpl`).

The non-terminal for `cmp` is self-explanatory: the decompiler checks whether the comparison is greater-than or less-than and pushes the comparison onto the oStack.

Code

The complete code to handle `IfTest.java` is shown in Listing 6-44.

Listing 6-44. Decompiler Code for IfTest.java

```
if_icmp ::= number:l IF_ICMP:c number:n
 {:
        Integer nint=new Integer(n.toString());
        Integer lint=new Integer(l.toString());
        Stack tempStack=new Stack();
        int linenum;

        // Is it a for/while or a do-while loop?
        if (nint.intValue()<lint.intValue())
          {
            //Does it surround other loops?
            if (nint.intValue() < lowest_num)
            {
                lowest_num=nint.intValue();
               //If so, set the lowest number to this
                if (!finalStack.empty())
                {
                  linenum=finalStack.peek().toString().indexOf("//");
                  if (linenum != -1)
                      lint = new Integer
                          (finalStack.peek().toString().substring(linenum+2));
                  while (nint.intValue()<=lint.intValue())
                    {
                        tempStack.push(finalStack.pop());
                        linenum=finalStack.peek().toString().indexOf("//");
                        if (linenum != -1)
                          lint = new Integer
                              (finalStack.peek().toString().substring(linenum+2));
                }
            }
```

```
            finalStack.push("do {");
        while (!tempStack.empty())
              finalStack.push("   " + tempStack.pop());
        temp = oStack.pop();


        if (c.equals("if_icmpge"))
              finalStack.push(space + "} while (" +
                  oStack.pop().toString () + ">=" +
                    temp.toString() +");" + " //" + 1);
        else if (c.equals("if_icmple"))
              finalStack.push(space + "} while (" +
                  oStack.pop().toString() + "<=" +
                      temp.toString() +");" + " //" + 1);
        else if (c.equals("if_icmpgt"))
              finalStack.push(space + "} while (" +
                      oStack.pop().toString() + ">" +
                          temp.toString() +");" + " //" + 1);
        else if (c.equals("if_icmplt"))
              finalStack.push(space + "} while (" +
                      oStack.pop().toString() + "<" +
                          temp.toString() +");" + " //" + 1);
        else if (c.equals("if_icmpeq"))
              finalStack.push(space + "} while (" +
                      oStack.pop().toString() + "==" +
                          temp.toString() +");" + " //" + 1);
        else if (c.equals("if_icmpne"))
              finalStack.push(space + "} while (" +
                      oStack.pop().toString() + "!=" +
                          temp.toString() +");" + " //" + 1);
        else
              finalStack.push(space + "} while (" +
                      oStack.pop().toString() + "!!" +
                          temp.toString() +");" + " //" + 1);
        }
    }
    else
    {
        ifStack.push(n);
          temp = oStack.pop();
        if (c.equals("if_icmpge"))
          finalStack.push(space + "if (" + oStack.pop().toString() +
                "<" + temp.toString() +")" + " //" + 1);
        else if (c.equals("if_icmple"))
          finalStack.push(space + "if (" + oStack.pop().toString() +
```

```
                              ">" + temp.toString() +")" + " //" + 1);
                else if (c.equals("if_icmpgt"))
                    finalStack.push(space + "if (" + oStack.pop().toString() +
                          "<=" + temp.toString() +")" + " //" + 1);
                else if (c.equals("if_icmplt"))
                    finalStack.push(space + "if (" + oStack.pop().toString() +
                          ">=" + temp.toString() +")" + " //" + 1);
                else if (c.equals("if_icmpne"))
                    finalStack.push(space + "if (" + oStack.pop().toString() +
                          "==" + temp.toString() +")" + " //" + 1);
                else if (c.equals("if_icmpeq"))
                    finalStack.push(space + "if (" + oStack.pop().toString() +
                       "!=" + temp.toString() +")" + " //" + 1);
                else
                    finalStack.push(space + "if (" + oStack.pop().toString() +
                          "!!" + temp.toString() +")" + " //" + 1);
                    finalStack.push(space + " {");
                    level++;
                    space = space + "    ";
                }
            :}
        ;
    if ::= number:l IF:c number:n
            {:
                int nint = Integer.parseInt(n.toString());
                int lint = Integer.parseInt(l.toString());
                Stack tempStack=new Stack();
                int linenum;
                String condString;
                int trimpoint=-1;

                if (oStack.peek().toString().indexOf("<") != -1)
                    trimpoint = oStack.peek().toString().indexOf("<");
                if (oStack.peek().toString().indexOf(">") != -1)
                    trimpoint = oStack.peek().toString().indexOf(">");

                if (nint<lint)
                {
                    if (trimpoint != -1)
                    {
                        String operand1 =
                          oStack.peek().toString().substring(0,trimpoint);
                        String operand2 =
                          oStack.pop().toString().substring(trimpoint + 1);
```

```
    if (c.equals("ifge"))
        condString = (operand1 + " >= " + operand2);
    else if (c.equals("ifle") )
        condString = (operand1 + " <= " + operand2);
    else if (c.equals("ifgt"))
        condString = (operand1 + " > " + operand2);
    else if (c.equals("iflt"))
        condString = (operand1 + " < " + operand2);
    else if (c.equals("ifeq"))
        condString = (operand1 + " == " + operand2);
    else if (c.equals("ifne"))
        condString = (operand1 + " != " + operand2);
    else
        condString = (operand1 + " !! " + operand2);
    }
    else
    {
    if (c.equals("ifge"))
        condString = (oStack.pop().toString() + " < 0" );
    else if (c.equals("ifle"))
        condString = (oStack.pop().toString() + " > 0" );
    else if (c.equals("ifgt"))
        condString = (oStack.pop().toString() + " <= 0" );
    else if (c.equals("iflt"))
        condString = (oStack.pop().toString() + " >= 0" );
    else if (c.equals("ifnull"))
        condString = (oStack.pop().toString() + " != null" );
    else if (c.equals("ifnonnull"))
        condString = (oStack.pop().toString() + " == null" );
    else if (c.equals("ifeq"))
        condString = (oStack.pop().toString() + " != 0");
    else if (c.equals("ifne"))
        condString = (oStack.pop().toString() + " == 0");
    else
        condString = (oStack.pop().toString() + " == 0)");
}

if (nint < lowest_num)
{
    lowest_num=nint;
    if (!finalStack.empty())
    {
        linenum=finalStack.peek().toString().indexOf ("//");
```

```
                              if (linenum != -1)
                                  lint = Integer.parseInt(finalStack.peek().
                                               toString().substring(linenum+2));
                        while (nint<=lint)
                        {
                          tempStack.push(finalStack.pop());
                          linenum=finalStack.peek().toString().indexOf ("//");
                          if (linenum != -1)
                              lint = Integer.parseInt(finalStack.peek().
                                  toString().substring(linenum+2));
                        }
                  }
             finalStack.push("do {");
             while (!tempStack.empty())
               finalStack.push("    " + tempStack.pop());
               finalStack.push(space + "} while (" + condString +");" + " //" + 1);
           }
        }
        else
        {
            if (trimpoint != -1)
            {
               String operand1 =
                      oStack.peek().toString().substring(0,trimpoint);
               String operand2 =
                      oStack.pop().toString().substring(trimpoint + 1);
               if (c.equals("ifge"))
                      condString = (operand1 + " < " + operand2);
                else if (c.equals("ifle") )
                      condString = (operand1 + " > " + operand2);
               else if (c.equals("ifgt"))
                      condString = (operand1 + " <= " + operand2);
               else if (c.equals("iflt"))
                      condString = (operand1 + " >= " + operand2);
               else if (c.equals("ifeq"))
                      condString = (operand1 + " == " + operand2);
               else if (c.equals("ifne"))
                      condString = (operand1 + " != " + operand2);
                else
                      condString = (operand1 + " !! " + operand2);
            }
            else
            {
```

```
                    if (c.equals("ifge"))
                        condString = (oStack.pop().toString() + " < 0" );
                    else if (c.equals("ifle"))
                        condString = (oStack.pop().toString() + " > 0" );
                    else if (c.equals("ifgt"))
                        condString = (oStack.pop().toString() + " <= 0" );
                    else if (c.equals("iflt"))
                        condString = (oStack.pop().toString() + " >= 0" );
                    else if (c.equals("ifnull"))
                        condString = (oStack.pop().toString() + " != null" );
                     else if (c.equals("ifnonnull"))
                        condString = (oStack.pop().toString() + " == null" );
                     else if (c.equals("ifeq"))
                        condString = (oStack.pop().toString() + " != 0");
                     else if (c.equals("ifne"))
                        condString = (oStack.pop().toString() + " == 0");
                     else
                        condString = (oStack.pop().toString() + " == 0)");
                  }

                finalStack.push(space + "if (" + condString.trim() + ")" +
                                        " //" + l);
                finalStack.push(space + "  {");
                level++;
                space = space + "    ";

                ifStack.push(n);
                lastLine = Integer.parseInt(l.toString());
                }
        :}
        ;


cmp   ::= number:l type:t CMP:c
        {:
                    temp = oStack.pop();
                    System.out.println(c.toString());
                    if (c.toString().trim().equals("cmpg"))
                        oStack.push(space + oStack.pop().toString() + ">"
                                        + temp.toString ());
                    else
                        oStack.push(space + oStack.pop().toString() + "<"
                                        + temp.toString ());
        :}
          ;
```

Output

By recompiling our specifications and running DoWhile and IfTest through them, we obtain exactly what we'd like, as shown in Listings 6-45 and 6-46.

Listing 6-45. Decompiler Results for DoWhile

```
public class DoWhile
{
  public static void main(String[] local0)
    {
      double local1=0.0;
      int local3=12;
      do {
         local3++;
         local3-=4;
         local3=local3*5;
         local3=local3/3;
      } while (local3<=100);
      local1=local1+(double) local3;
      return;
      }
}
```

Listing 6-46. Decompiler Results for IfTest

```
public  class IfTest
{
  public static void main(String[] local0)
    {
      double local1=3.14159;
      if (local1 > 100.0)
        {
         if (local1 < 200.0)
           {
             local1=local1-100.0;
           }
        }
      return;
      }
}
```

Recurses.java

Now that if statements are implemented, the decompiler can process a simple example of recursion, Recurses.java. Although this program (see Listing 6-47) does not introduce any new non-terminals, it demonstrates the difference between invocation of static methods and virtual methods and how if-else statements work.

Listing 6-47. Recurses.java

```
public class Recurses
{
      public static void main(String[] args)
      {
            System.out.println(recurse(25));
            return;
      }
      public static String recurse(int num)
      {
            if (num!=0)
                return "crap! " + recurse(num-1);
            else
                return "dammit!";
      }
}
```

Input

Static invocations, by their nature, can't be chained with any other functions and don't require any references to external classes. If you check the chain of conditionals in the invoke non-terminal, you will see that the invocation on line 5 (Listing 6-48) fails every one and is pushed onto the oStack with its argument by the final else.

Listing 6-48. Annotated main Method of Recurses.java

```
000: getstatic 2              //load System.out
003: bipush 25                //load int 25
005: invokestatic 3        //invoke recurse(int)String
008: invokevirtual 4     //invoke System.out.println(string)
011: return                  //return
```

The major point of interest in the recursion function is the conditional statement in line 1, see Listing 6-49. Because the comparison is against zero, cmp is not required. Since the whole body of the function consists of the two cases (if and else), the else is optional and the decompiler omits it.

Listing 6-49. Annotated Recurse Method:

```
000: iload_0              //load local0, the passed value
001: ifeq 29               //if  local0 ==0, load
004: new 5                //new String
007: dup                   //duplicate the reference
008: invokespecial 6       //create new StringBuffer
011: ldc 7                   //load "crap! "
013: invokevirtual 8       //append it to the StringBuffer
016: iload_0              //load the passed value
017: iconst_1            //load int 1
018: isub                  //decrement local0 by 1
019: invokestatic 3          //call recurse(int)
022: invokevirtual 8       //append the returned value to the StringBuffer
025: invokevirtual 9       //convert StringBuffer to String
028: areturn             //return String
029: ldc 10               //load "dammit! "
031: areturn             //return String
```

Grammar

The grammar is unchanged from the IfTest.java test.

Code

No new code is required.

Output

As we'd hope, the decompiler produces correct results as shown in Listing 6-50.

Listing 6-50. Decompiler Results for Recurses.java

```
public  class Recurses
{
  public static void main(String[] local0)
    {
      System.out.println(recurse(25));
      return;
    }
  public static String recurse(int local0)
    {
      if (local0 != 0)
        {
          return ("crap! ") + (recurse(local0-1));
        }
      return "dammit!";
    }
}
```

WhileLoop.java

The next step is to build on the conditional statement resolution to resolve normal while and for loops. This means introducing the goto opcode, which makes resolving the more complex conditionals possible, though resolving it *correctly* remains difficult. We'll be looking at a "simple" loop in Listing 6-51—a standard while loop.

Listing 6-51. WhileLoop.java

```
public class WhileLoop
{
      public static void main(String[] args)
      {
              String output = "outoutoutput";
              while (output.indexOf("out")!=-1)
              {
                      output = output.substring(3);
                      System.out.println(output);
                }
              return;
      }
}
```

Input

The main function of WhileLoop.java is shown in Listing 6-52.

Listing 6-52. Annotated main Method of WhileLoop.java

```
000: ldc 2                //load "outoutoutput" from the constant pool
002: astore_1              //store a reference to it in local1
003: aload_1               //load a reference to it
004: ldc 3                 //load "out"
006: invokevirtual 4       //invoke output.indexOf(string)
009: iconst_m1          //load -1
010: if_icmpeq 29          //if output.indexOf("out")==1, branch to 29
013: aload_1               //load a reference to local1
014: iconst_3              //load int 3
015: invokevirtual 5       //invoke output.substring(3)
018: astore_1              //store a reference in local1
019: getstatic 6        //load System.out
022: aload_1               //load a reference to local1
023: invokevirtual 7       //call System.out.println(local1)
026: goto 3                //goto 3
029: return                //return
```

Grammar

The grammar is as follows:

```
expr_part -> error | return | store | load  | invoke | object | const |
                  bipush | conv | arith | iinc | if | cmp | if_icmp | goto;

goto -> number GOTO number;
```

The goto Non-Terminal

The goto production consists only of the line number, the GOTO terminal, and the branch location.

The goto non-terminal is somewhat formidable. It serves two major purposes: it can be used in conditional loops, or it can be used in if - else if - else statements. In order to check which context it's being executed in, the decompiler needs to check the current line number and compare it to the branch address. If the branch line number is greater than the current line number, the expression is an if - else if - else sort statement and the branch line number is pushed to the gotoStack (much the same way the branch location was treated in the forward-branching cases of the if and if_icmp statements). If it is less than the current line number, it is a conditional statement of some sort. This is the important context for the time being.

The decompiler then pops finalStack items and pushes them onto the new tempStack, as it did for do-while statements, until it finds a line number less than or equal to the branch address. It then checks to see if the line it has found is the if statement that matches the goto statement. If it is not, it pushes items from the tempStack back onto the finalStack until it is located, then it pops the if statement, trims off everything except for the conditional expression, and stores the conditional statement in a String variable.

Once the loop is done, the decompiler decrements the conditional depth counter, shortens the spacing, pushes the final lines of code onto the finalStack, and pops the now-resolved branch address from the ifStack.

Code

The complete code to handle WhileLoop.java is shown in Listing 6-53.

Listing 6-53. Decompiler Code for WhileLoop.java

```
goto    ::= number:l GOTO:c number:n
            {:
                int nint = Integer.parseInt(n.toString());
                int lint = Integer.parseInt(l.toString());
                int lastint=0;
                temp = "";

                //finalStackDebug("goto");
                Stack tempStack=new Stack();
                int linenum, condStringLineNum=0, tempCounter=0;
                String condString="0", tempString="0";

                if (nint<lint)
                {
                    tempString="//"+l.toString().trim();
                    if (!finalStack.empty())
                    {
                        linenum=finalStack.peek().toString().indexOf("//");
                        if (linenum != -1)
                            lint = Integer.parseInt(finalStack.peek().
                                            toString().substring(linenum+2));
                        while (nint<lint)
```

```
                    {
                        tempStack.push(finalStack.pop());
                        linenum=finalStack.peek().toString().indexOf("//");
                        lastint = lint;
                        if (linenum != -1)
                        lint = Integer.parseInt(finalStack.peek().
                            toString().substring (linenum+2));
                      }
                      linenum=tempStack.peek().toString().indexOf("if");
                    while (linenum == -1)
                    {
                        finalStack.push(tempStack.pop());
                        linenum=tempStack.peek().toString().indexOf("if");
                    }

                        condStringLineNum =
                            tempStack.peek().toString().trim().indexOf (") //");
                        condString=tempStack.pop().toString().trim().
                            substring(4, condStringLineNum);
                }
                  level--;
                  if (space.length()>3)
                    space = space.substring(3);
                  else
                    space = "";

                  int tempcounter = 0;
                      finalStack.push(space +
                        "while (" + condString + ") //" + condStringLineNum);

                  while (!tempStack.empty())
                            finalStack.push(tempStack.pop());
                  finalStack.push(space + "   } ");// + tempString);
                  ifStack.pop();
                  skipFinish = true;
                }
                  else
                {
                    gotoStack.push(n);
                }
            :}
            ;
```

Output

The decompiler now produces the expected results, as shown in Listing 6-54.

Listing 6-54. Decompiler Results for WhileLoop

```
public class WhileLoop
{
  public static void main(String[] local0)
    {
      String local1="outoutoutput";
      while (local1.indexOf("out")!=-1)
        {
          local1=local1.substring(3);
          System.out.println(local1);
        }
      return;
    }
}
```

ForLoop.java

In the beginning there was the while loop, and then a language designer said, "Hey, let's incorporate this initialize-and-increment stuff into a new conditional! Hell, let's call it a for loop!" And he looked and he saw it was good.

The next problem is extending the implementation of the while loop in WhileLoop.java to cover for loops. This is done very easily, as you can see in Listing 6-55.

Listing 6-55. ForLoop.java

```
public class ForLoop {
      public static void main(String[] args)
      {
              String output = "outoutoutput";
              while (output.indexOf("out")!=-1)
              {
                      System.out.println(output.substring(3));
                      output = output.substring(3);
              }
              return;
      }
}
```

This may look the same as WhileLoop.java, and, in fact, it is. However, it meets the criteria for a for loop:

- The line before the while statement assigns a variable within the while loop.

- The last line inside the while loop reassigns or modifies the value of a variable.

That said, it's now obvious that the program can be decompiled to the following:

```
for  (String output = "outoutoutput"; output.indexOf("out")!=-1;
                    output = output.substring(3))
          System.out.println(output.substring(3));
```

Input

The main function of ForLoop.java is shown earlier in Listing 6-52.

Grammar

The grammar remains unchanged from WhileLoop.java.

The goto Non-Terminal, Redux

The goto non-terminal is the only one that needs modification. At the beginning of the first case, the decompiler must test for an assignment, an increment, or a decrement in the top finalStack item. If any of these are true, it assumes a for loop, pops that top item, and stores it in a temporary variable.

The next necessary change is near the end. Where the decompiler once could get away with pushing a while statement and restoring the finalStack, it must now test the forOrWhile boolean and proceed accordingly, then test to ensure the element before the conditional statement is an assignment. If it is not an assignment, it cancels the for loop treatment, pushes a while loop as before, and restores the temp variable to the finalStack. If it is, it must be trimmed and used as the assignment portion of the for loop. Then the decompiler can push the for statement and the body of the loop to the finalStack.

Code

The complete code to handle ForLoop.java is shown in Listing 6-56.

Listing 6-56. Decompiler Code for ForLoop.java

```
goto    ::= number:l GOTO:c number:n
                {:
            int nint = Integer.parseInt(n.toString());
            int lint = Integer.parseInt(l.toString());
            int lastint=0;
            temp = "";

            Stack tempStack=new Stack();
            int linenum, condStringLineNum=0, tempCounter=0;
            String condString="0", tempString="0";
            if (nint<lint)
            {   /* First set of modifications start here */
                if (finalStack.peek().toString().trim().indexOf("=")!=-1
                    || finalStack.peek().toString().trim().indexOf("++")!=-1
                    || finalStack.peek().toString().trim().indexOf("--")!=-1)
                    {
                        forOrWhile = true; //can be rendered as a for loop
                        linenum=finalStack.peek().toString().indexOf("; //");
                        tempString=
                        finalStack.peek().toString().substring(linenum+2).trim ();
                        temp = finalStack.pop().toString();
                     }
                    else
                    {
                        forOrWhile = false;
                        tempString="//"+l.toString().trim();
                    }
                    /* First set of modifications end here */
                    if (!finalStack.empty())
                    {
                        linenum=finalStack.peek().toString().indexOf("//");
                        if (linenum != -1)
                            lint = Integer.parseInt(
                                finalStack.peek().toString().substring(linenum+2));
                        while (nint<lint)
                        {
                            tempStack.push(finalStack.pop());
                            linenum=finalStack.peek().toString().indexOf("//");
                            lastint = lint;
                            if (linenum != -1)
                                lint = Integer.parseInt(finalStack.peek().
```

```
                            toString().substring (linenum+2));
            }
            linenum=tempStack.peek().toString().indexOf("if");
            while (linenum == -1)
            {
               finalStack.push(tempStack.pop());
               linenum=tempStack.peek().toString().indexOf("if");
            }

            condStringLineNum = tempStack.peek().toString().
                            trim().indexOf (") //");
            condString=tempStack.pop().toString().trim().
                            substring(4, condStringLineNum);
            }
            level--;
            if (space.length()>3)
              space = space.substring(3);
            else
              space = "";

          int tempcounter = 0;
          /* Second set of modifications start here*/
          if (forOrWhile)
          {
               linenum=finalStack.peek().
                                   toString().indexOf ("//");
              while (linenum == -1)
               {
                  tempcounter++;
                  tempStack.push(finalStack.pop());
                  linenum=finalStack.peek().
                            toString().indexOf ("//");
               }
              if (finalStack.peek().toString().indexOf("=")!=-1 &&
          (finalStack.peek().toString().startsWith("local") ||
          finalStack.peek().toString().indexOf(" local") != -1))
              {
                  tempStack.push(finalStack.peek().toString().
                            substring(0, linenum));
                  while (tempcounter > 0)
                  {
                       finalStack.push(tempStack.pop());
                       tempcounter--;
```

```
            }
            finalStack.push(space + "for (" +
tempStack.pop().toString().trim() + " " +
condString.trim() + "; " +
temp.toString().substring(0,
temp.toString().indexOf(";")).trim() + ") " +
finalStack.pop().toString().substring(linenum));
            temp = "";
        }
        else
        {
            //executed if prior line not an assignment
            while (tempcounter > 0)
            {
                finalStack.push(tempStack.pop());
                tempcounter--;
            }
            finalStack.push(space +
                "while (" + condString.trim () + ") //"
                +condStringLineNum);
        }
        }
        else  //while statement from earlier example
            finalStack.push(space + "while (" +
                condString + ") //" + condStringLineNum);
            /* Second set of modifications end here */
    while (!tempStack.empty())
            finalStack.push(tempStack.pop ());
    if (!temp.equals(""))
            finalStack.push(temp);
    finalStack.push(space + "  } ");// + tempString);
    ifStack.pop();
        skipFinish = true; //clean-up part of stmts
        }

    while (!tempStack.empty())
            finalStack.push(tempStack.pop());
    finalStack.push(space + "  } ");// + tempString);
    ifStack.pop();
    skipFinish = true;
    }
    else
```

```
                                           {
                                              gotoStack.push(n);
                                           }
                          :}
                        ;
```

Output

Decompiling ForLoop now gives the expected for loop version (see Listing 6-57).

Listing 6-57. Decompiler Results for ForLoop

```java
public  class ForLoop
{
  public static void main(String[] local0)
    {
      for (String local1="outoutoutput";
                      local1.indexOf("out")!=-1; local1=local1.substring(3))
        {
          System.out.println(local1.substring(3));
        }
      return;
    }
}
```

ArrayTest.java

And now for something completely different. After the long, hard slog of conditionals, arrays are easy. The initial sample program, see Listing 6-58 will use a for loop to load a three-element string array with the cubes of the array indexes. This requires three new array operations: array loading, array storing, and array initialization.

Listing 6-58. ArrayTest.java

```java
public class ArrayTest
{
    public static void main(String args[])
    {
        String arr[] = new String[3];
        for (int i = 0; i <= 2; i++)
            arr[i] = "Result = " +i * i * i;
    }
}
```

Input

The ClassToXML input for the ArrayTest.java is shown in Listing 6-59.

Listing 6-59. Annotated main Method for ArrayTest.java

```
000: iconst_3            //load int 3
001: anewarray 2         //initialize new three-element array of type String
004: astore_1            //store ref to array in local1
005: iconst_0            //load int 0
006: istore_2            //store in local2
007: iload_2             //load local2
008: iconst_2            //load int 2
009: if_icmpgt 44        //if local2 > 2, branch to 44
012: aload_1             //load ref to local1[]
013: iload_2             //load local2
014: new 3               //new String
017: dup                 //duplicate it
018: invokespecial 4     //initiate StringBuffer
021: ldc 5               //load "Result = "
023: invokevirtual 6     //append to StringBuffer
026: iload_2             //load local2
027: iload_2             //load local2
028: imul                //square local2
029: iload_2             //load local2
030: imul                //cube local2
031: invokevirtual 7     //append to StringBuffer
034: invokevirtual 8     //convert to string
037: aastore             //store in local1[local2]
038: iinc 2 1            //increment local2 by 1
041: goto 7              //branch to 7
044: return              //return
```

Grammar

The grammar is as follows:

```
expr_part -> error | return | store | load  | invoke | object | const | bipush
             | conv | arith | iinc | if | cmp | if_icmp | goto | arrayops;

arrayops  -> aload | astore | newarray;
aload -> number ALOAD;
astore ->  number ASTORE;
newarray  -> number NEWARRAY number;
```

The aload Non-Terminal

The aload production consists only of the line number and the ALOAD terminal. Because no argument is required, you might guess that everything is done using the oStack. You'd be right; the JVM loads the data at the index given by the top oStack element from the array given by the next-to-top oStack element. If this seems confusing, see the code below, see Listing 6-60.

The astore Non-Terminal

The astore production consists only of the line number and the ASTORE terminal. Again, no argument is required. The top element on the oStack is stored at the index given by the next-to-top oStack element in the array given by the second-to-top oStack element.

The newarray Non-Terminal

The newarray production consists of the line number, the NEWARRAY terminal, and the type of the new array. There are two forms of this opcode: newarray and anewarray. The newarray opcode is used to initialize primitive-typed arrays. Its argument, which ranges from 4 to 11, specifies the primitive type. The anewarray opcode is used for higher-level arrays; its argument is, as you'd expect, a constant pool reference to the name of the class or interface the array is composed of. It can also be used with multianewarray to create a multidimensional array, but this decompiler does not implement that.

Code

The complete code to handle ArrayTest.java is shown in Listing 6-60.

Listing 6-60. Decompiler code for ArrayTest.java

```
arrayops ::= aload
                | astore
                | newarray
                ;
aload ::= number:l ALOAD:s
            {:
                String tempString=oStack.pop().toString();
                oStack.push(oStack.pop() + "[" + tempString + "]");
            :}
            ;
```

```
astore ::= number:l ASTORE:s
              {:
                  String tempString=oStack.pop().toString();
                  tempString = "[" + oStack.pop().toString() +
"]="+tempString+";";
                  finalStack.push(space + oStack.pop() + tempString);
              :}
              ;
newarray ::= number:l NEWARRAY:s number:n
        {:
            int testType=Integer.parseInt(n.toString());
            String tempString;

            newArray = true;
            arrayElements = Integer.parseInt(oStack.peek().toString());

            switch (testType)
            {
              case 4:
                  tempString = "boolean";
                  break;
              case 5:
                  tempString = "char";
                  break;
              case 6:
                  tempString = "float";
                  break;
              case 7:
                  tempString = "double";
                  break;
              case 8:
                  tempString = "byte";
                  break;
              case 9:
                  tempString = "short";
                  break;
              case 10:
                  tempString = "int";
                  break;
              case 11:
                  tempString = "long";
                  break;
              default:
                   tempString = "error";
                   break;
```

```
        }
        type = tempString;
        oStack.push("new " + tempString + "[" + oStack.pop() +"]");
      :}
| number:l type:t NEWARRAY:s number:n
      {:
        type = resolveConstant(Integer.parseInt(n.toString()));
        while (type.indexOf("/")!=-1)
              type = type.substring(type.indexOf("/")+1);
        oStack.push("new " + type + "[" + oStack.pop() +"]");
      :}

           ;
```

Output

Recompiling the CUP spec and running the XML through the decompiler recovers
the original program correctly, as shown in Listing 6-61.

Listing 6-61. Decompiler Results for ArrayTest

```
public  class Arraytest
{
  public static void main(String[] local0)
    {
      String local1[]=new String[3];
      for (int local2=0; local2<=2; local2++)
        {
          local1[local2]=("Result = ") + ((local2*local2)*local2);
        }
      return;
    }
}
```

ArrayInit.java

Finally, the decompiler will be extended to handle initialized arrays. To extend
the decompiler, the remaining three opcodes from the object non-terminal are
needed: putstatic, getfield, and putfield.

This example (see Listing 6-62) is also the first time the field-parsing non-
terminal is used. Initialization of variables stored in static (class) fields is done
using a special initialization method called <clinit>. Initialization of other field
variables is done in the <init> method, which up to now had been ignored.

Listing 6-62. ArrayInit.java

```
public class ArrayInit
{
    public static int[] arr = {1, 8, 27, 64, 125, 216, 343, 512, 729, 1000};
    public int a = 5;
    public static String mork = "from Ork!";

    public static void main(String args[])
    {
        int[] arr2 = {1, 8, 27, 64, 125, 216, 343, 512, 729, 1000};
        for (int i = 0; i < 10; i++)
            System.out.println("arr[" + i + "] = " + arr[i]);
    }
}
```

Input

The introduction of initialized fields has two effects on the code section of the XML file: first, it causes the <init> method, which was previously ignored, to become useful, since it is used to initialize a; second, it creates a new <clinit> method, which is used to fill the arr[] field and the mork variable (see Listing 6-63).

Listing 6-63. Annotated <init> Method for ArrayInit.java

```
000: aload_0              //load this
001: invokespecial 1       //init Object
004: aload_0              //load this
005: iconst_5            //load int 5
006: putfield 2        //store it in field 2 (a)
009: return
```

The initialization of arrays is done in a specific manner, which is shown in lines 5–61 of Listing 6-64. This produces a finalStack that looks like the following:

```
new int[10][0]=1;
new int[10][1]=8;
new int[10][2]=27;
new int[10][3]=64;
new int[10][4]=125;
new int[10][5]=216;
new int[10][6]=343;
```

```
new int[10][7]=512;
new int[10][8]=729;
new int[10][9]=1000;
```

Although the syntax is incorrect, this gives you some idea of how the structure looks in memory.

Listing 6-64. Annotated <clinit> Method for ArrayInit.java

```
000: bipush 10        //load int 10
002: newarray 10       //create ten-element int array
004: dup               //duplicate ref to array
005: iconst_0          //load array index
006: iconst_1          //load int value to store
007: iastore            //store
008: dup                 //duplicate ref to array
009: iconst_1          //load array index
010: bipush 8        //load int value to store
012: iastore            //store
013: dup                  //etc.
014: iconst_2
015: bipush 27
017: iastore
018: dup
019: iconst_3
020: bipush 64
022: iastore
023: dup
024: iconst_4
025: bipush 125
027: iastore
028: dup
029: iconst_5
030: sipush 216
033: iastore
034: dup
035: bipush 6
037: sipush 343
040: iastore
041: dup
042: bipush 7
044: sipush 512
047: iastore
048: dup
```

```
049: bipush 8
051: sipush 729
054: iastore
055: dup
056: bipush 9
058: sipush 1000
061: iastore
062: putstatic 10    //store reference to this array in static field 10 (arr [])
065: ldc 13                  //load "from Ork!" from constant pool
067: putstatic 14    //store the ref to the string in static field 14 (mork)
070: return
```

The main method poses few surprises and does not expose any new concepts, so we'll get straight to the new stuff.

Grammar

The grammar is as follows:

```
object -> number GETSTATIC number | number GETFIELD number | number
                PUTSTATIC number | number PUTFIELD number;
```

The getfield Non-Terminal

The getfield production consists of the line number, the GETFIELD terminal, and the constant pool index of the field to access.

The getfield opcode can be resolved in exactly the same manner as getstatic.

The putfield Non-Terminal

The putfield production consists of the line number, the PUTFIELD terminal, and the constant pool index of the field to access.

To resolve putfield, the decompiler first checks to see whether the top item on the oStack is a new array. If the sum of the indices of [and '] in the top item is greater than six (this eliminates all non-new array elements), it is regarded as an array assignment. The decompiler reads in the array length, pops that number of items from the oStack, trims off everything but the assigned values, and produces a curly-bracketed, comma-delimited result.

If the current method name is <init>, the result must be stored in the fieldStack. The decompiler pops items from the fieldStack and pushes them to a temporary stack until it finds the proper field name. It then inserts the assignment operation and restores the `fieldStack`. If the current method name is not `<init>`, the result can be stored in the `finalStack`.

The putstatic Non-Terminal

The `putstatic` production consists of the line number, the `PUTSTATIC` terminal, and the constant pool index of the field to access.

Resolution of `putstatic` is identical to that of `putfield`, but the current method must be `<clinit>` for the result to be stored in the `fieldStack`.

Code

The complete code to handle `ArrayInit.java` is shown in Listing 6-65.

Listing 6-65. Decompiler Code for ArrayInit.java

```
object ::= number:l GETSTATIC:s number:n
        {:
                String tempString =
                        resolveConstant(Integer.parseInt(n.toString ()));
                oStack.push(tempString);
        :}
| number:l GETFIELD:s number:n
        {:
                String tempString =
                        resolveConstant(Integer.parseInt(n.toString ()));
                oStack.push(tempString);
        :}
| number:l PUTFIELD:s number:n
    {:
        String tempString = oStack.pop().toString();
        if (tempString.startsWith("new") &&
                tempString.indexOf("[")+tempString.indexOf("]")>6)
        {
            int numOfElements =
                Integer.parseInt(tempString.substring(tempString.indexOf("[")+1,
                    tempString.indexOf("]")));
            tempString = "}";
            for (int i = 0; i<numOfElements; i++)
              {
                  String temp1 = finalStack.pop().toString();
                  tempString = temp1.substring(temp1.indexOf("]=")+2,
                      temp1.indexOf (";"))  + tempString;
```

```
                if ((numOfElements - i)>1)
                    tempString=", " + tempString;
              }
            tempString ="{" + tempString;
        }
        if (MethodName.equals("<init>"))
        {
            Stack tempStack = new Stack();
            String tempFieldName =
                resolveConstant(Integer.parseInt(n.toString ()));
            String newBetterType = "";
            if (tempFieldName.indexOf("Ljava")!=-1)
            {
                newBetterType =
                    tempFieldName.substring(tempFieldName.indexOf("Ljava"),
                                        tempFieldName.length());
                tempFieldName = tempFieldName.substring(0,
                                        tempFieldName.indexOf("Ljava"));
                while (newBetterType.indexOf("/")!=-1)
                    newBetterType = newBetterType.substring
                        (newBetterType.indexOf("/")+1);
              }
                while (!fieldStack.peek().toString().endsWith(" " +
                        tempFieldName + ";") && !fieldStack.empty())
                    tempStack.push(fieldStack.pop());
                String temp1 = fieldStack.pop().toString();
                fieldStack.push(space + temp1.substring(0,temp1.length()-1) + " = "
                                        + tempString + ";");
                while (!tempStack.empty())
                    fieldStack.push(tempStack.pop());
              }
            else
                finalStack.push(space +
                    resolveConstant(Integer.parseInt(n.toString ())) +
                        " = "+tempString+"; //" + l.toString());
            :}
| number:l PUTSTATIC:s number:n
{:
      String tempString = oStack.pop().toString();
      if (tempString.startsWith("new") &&
              tempString.indexOf("[")+tempString.indexOf("]")>6)
      {
          int numOfElements =
              Integer.parseInt(tempString.substring(tempString.indexOf("[")+1,
                      tempString.indexOf ("]")));
```

231

```
            tempString = "}";
            for (int i = 0; i<numOfElements; i++)
            {
                String temp1 = finalStack.pop().toString();
                tempString = temp1.substring(temp1.indexOf("]=")+2,
                        temp1.indexOf(";"))  + tempString;
                if ((numOfElements - i)>1)
                        tempString=", " + tempString;
            }
            tempString ="{" + tempString;
    }
    if (MethodName.equals("<clinit>"))
    {
        Stack tempStack = new Stack();
        String tempFieldName =
                resolveConstant(Integer.parseInt(n.toString ()));
        String newBetterType = "";
        if (tempFieldName.indexOf("Ljava")!=-1)
        {
            newBetterType =
                    tempFieldName.substring(tempFieldName.indexOf("Ljava"),
                                    tempFieldName.length());
            tempFieldName = tempFieldName.substring(0,
                                        tempFieldName.indexOf("Ljava"));
            while (newBetterType.indexOf("/")!=-1)
                newBetterType = newBetterType.substring
                    (newBetterType.indexOf("/")+1);
        }
        while (!fieldStack.peek().toString().endsWith(" " + tempFieldName + ";")
                    && !fieldStack.empty())
            tempStack.push(fieldStack.pop());
        String temp1 = fieldStack.pop().toString();
        fieldStack.push(space + temp1.substring(0,temp1.length()-1) + " = "
                                                    + tempString + ";");
        while (!tempStack.empty())
                    fieldStack.push(tempStack.pop());
    }
    else
      finalStack.push(space +
          resolveConstant(Integer.parseInt(n.toString ())) +
                    " = "+tempString+"; //" + l.toString());
    :}
```

Output

Decompiling the class file using this new CUP spec returns the original program, see Listing 6-66. Note that, due to the implementation of the fieldStack, the order of the fields in the decompiled program is reversed. Obviously, this does not affect program execution.

Listing 6-66. Decompiler Results for ArrayInit:

```
public  class ArrayInit
{
  public  String mork = "From ork!";
  public  int a = 5;
  public  int[] arr = {1, 8, 27, 64, 125, 216, 343, 512, 729, 1000};
  public void main(String[] local1)
    {
     int local[]={1, 8, 27, 64, 125, 216, 343, 512, 729, 1000};
     for (int local3=0; local3<10; local3++)
       {
        local0.append(arr[local3]).println(toString());
       }
     return;
    }
}
```

Summarizing Decompiler Implementation

It's now time to take stock, take a step back and see exactly where we are. Read on and we'll explore this more.

What We Have

We now have a method for decompiling Java classes. Our lexical analyzer cuts ClassToXML's output into usable tokens for our parser to digest, and our parser returns something close to the original source of the program. How robust and how complete is our decompiler, though?

What Remains

Unfortunately, our decompiler is not very robust at present. There are opcodes we do not parse and facets of the class file structure that are not dealt with, such as interfaces and the exception tables. Although these are important in a full-scale decompiler, their inclusion here would occupy many, many more pages. We will review the remaining opcodes briefly and I will present hints and tips for decompiling them.

Remaining Opcodes

The first group of remaining opcodes are low-level JVM operations. The first opcode, NOP, is the most useless (literally). Unless you want to do estimates of the JVM's clock speed, you can just dump this command, which causes no operation to be performed.

For our purposes, WIDE can also be discarded. This opcode specifies that the next local variable referenced is 16 bits rather than 8 bits. Obviously, this doesn't affect our particular JVM.

The next pair are also very simple. POP and POP2 merely pop and discard the top word and double word on the oStack, respectively. Implementation is trivial.

SHL and SHR are identical and opposite operations. The top word is popped and shifted left and right by the number of digits specified by the five lower bits of the next word, and the result is pushed back onto the oStack.

Next we have the three logical operators: AND, OR, and XOR. These perform the respective bitwise operations between the top two values on the oStack. Implementation for all three is simple.

Next, we have subroutine commands. JSR jumps to a local subroutine defined within a method; practically speaking, it implements finally. It first pushes the contents of the program counter plus three onto the oStack, then it branches to the program counter value plus an offset provided by the argument of the opcode. This is a trickier command; implementation is similar to that of GOTO.

RET returns from a subroutine. It just loads an address from a specified local variable and stores it in the program counter. Implementation is, again, tricky.

The next group consists of opcodes similar to those we have already implemented. The DUPX instruction is very similar to DUP, but it inserts the top word beneath the next item on the oStack. SWAP is another stack operation, which merely swaps the top two words on the oStack. Implementation is similar to DUP but will require a temporary storage area for stack items.

MULTIANEWARRAY (surprisingly enough) initializes a multidimensional array. The opcode itself takes two arguments: the type and the number of dimensions being created. It then pops the top element of the oStack, which is the number of dimensional sizes stored on the oStack. Then come the dimensional sizes themselves; these specify the number of array elements in each dimension. This multidimensional array is a complicated construction, but it should be tractable if you've gotten this far.

ARRAYLENGTH is a much simpler array command that returns the length of a given array in memory. Resolution is not too difficult.

TABLESWITCH and LOOKUPSWITCH are similar operations that use offset tables, allowing for computed jumps. The former branches to the table entry whose index is given by the object on top of the oStack; the latter actually does a comparison of values to choose the branch location and is thus produced by most switch statements.

ATHROW, as you might expect, throws an exception (see the discussion of exception handling tables momentarily) and checks for a handler. It's a very involved instruction and one you could commonly find in programs that use try/catch/finally statements.

Next, we have some simple procedural operations. CHECKCAST checks whether the top oStack element can be cast to a different type. INSTANCEOF checks whether an object or array is a member of a particular class. Both are fairly simple, in that there's no other way to do what they do. Decompiling them, however, may be involved.

Finally, we have two extremely particular commands: MONITORENTER and MONITOREXIT. These are used in multithreaded programs to lock and to release the thread's access to an object. Multithreaded operations are also beyond the scope of this book.

Exception Handling Tables

ClassToXML ignores the exception-handling tables that belong to each method. These come into use when we use try/catch/finally statements. They are essentially another form of conditional statement, and resolution is very similar. One major catch, however, is that the tables are stored after the method code in the classfile—in order to process them using our parser, we would have to use a much more complicated program or change the order of information within the classfile when outputting it to XML.

Other Problems of Decompilation

A full-featured decompiler would have to deal with the interfaces directly. It would have to apply a robust, unshakeable, and powerful conditional resolution to defeat control-flow obfuscators—this is the weakest point of decompilers from .NET's Anakrino to Java's Mocha. It's much easier to know where a program needs to go and to make it difficult to get there than it is to reverse the changes in the flow of the program.

Many of the remaining things in the classfile that we ignore don't hurt us. The line number table—which is not even present in final builds—is pretty much useless for our purposes. So too are most of the other possible attributes— SourceFile, Synthetic, LocalVariableTable, and Deprecated with the possible exception of InnerClasses.

Conclusion

The complete code for our decompiler, XMLToSource, is available on the Apress website (http://www.apress.com). I plan to add new keywords and constructs over time as the Java language evolves past JDK 1.5. I will also add new constructs occassionally to make the decompiler much more robust and complete. I welcome any reader contributions to help in this effort.

CHAPTER 7

Case Studies

WE ARE NOW almost at the end of our journey. By now you should have a sound understanding of the overall principles of how to decompile, and hopefully, how to make some attempts at protecting your code. Having said that, I've found from clients and colleagues that even if you understand what decompilation and obfuscation really mean, it still doesn't help you figure out what practical measures you can take to protect your code. A little knowledge can often create more questions than answers.

The Competency Centre for Java (JCC) shows an example of this on their deCaf web site FAQ:

> *Is it true that no one will ever be able to decompile my deCaf protected application?*
>
> *NO. deCaf does not make decompilation impossible. It makes it difficult. Making decompilation impossible is impossible.*

So, in this chapter we're going to look at some case studies to try to help you overcome this conundrum. Hopefully one of the cases will closely match your situation and help you come to a conclusion on how to best protect you code. Each of the case studies will have the following format:

- Problem description

- Pros and cons of the different options

- Solution

Case Studies

To help provide you with more practical insights into how to protect your code, we'll now take a look at several case studies. Please note that the names of these companies have been changed to protect the innocent.

Case Study 1: To J2ME or Not to J2ME?

This case study looks at the implications of decompiling mobile Java code.

Problem Description

WAP Corp has the rights to an image rendering application written in C++ that it wants to port to Java so that it can be used on cell phones running the Java 2 Platform, Micro Edition (J2ME). Moving to Java will mean that they can roll out the application to many more phones than before because the Java Virtual Machine (JVM) offers a huge portability advantage over the previous proprietary systems. Multimedia cell phones have a significant market share in the US and an even larger market share elsewhere.

WAP Corp believes that this new application will present a real competitive advantage in speed and views the Java application as a significant part of their future revenue. However, if there's one thing they don't want to do, it is to allow their code to end up in the hands of any of their rivals, which would cause their competitive edge to evaporate.

WAP Corp sees the following as their only possible options:

- Performing obfuscation

- Moving to a server-based application

- Seeking legal protection

- Patenting the algorithm

Pros and Cons

Obfuscation is nowhere near 100 percent secure, but method overloading and code irreducibility are the most effective forms. However, when some form of code irreducibility is used, there is always the fear that the Java application might not pass the Java Verifier and might never get executed. Unfortunately, the application would have to be tested on all cell phones to ensure that it executed correctly after obfuscation, which would destroy the major portability advantage of moving to the Java platform. But if the code doesn't use the strongest obfuscation possible, then it's going to be decompiled with very little effort.

Moving to a server-based application would protect the code. But because of the bandwidth considerations, the information passing between the server and the client cell phone needs to be kept to a minimum. The cell phone needs to render the data. It has the processing power, and the application speed is largely built around a client-server architecture. However, sending the rendered data to the cell phone will eat up the bandwidth and add several hundred milliseconds to the time it takes to display the image.

Legal protections are only good after the fact. WAP Corp doesn't want to engage in a lengthy legal battle, which could bankrupt it before the courts come to any agreement. Some of WAP Corp's competitors have much deeper pockets so they could survive if they won or lost in court and can almost certainly afford better lawyers.

Patenting the algorithm would open it to the competition but would act as an extra revenue source if any competitors wanted to license it.

Solution

WAP Corp decided to employ a dual strategy: they obfuscated the code to provide some basic level of protection, but they also patented the algorithm in the US, Europe, and Japan because obfuscation would only offer "good enough" protection to keep out the casual hacker. The obfuscation had the added benefit of shrinking the deployed classfiles by 20 percent.

Case Study 2: Consultant's Code

In this case study, we explore what happens when a consultant doesn't want the client to have access to his or her code. We're not exploring the reasons why, just how to meet the need to protect the code.

Problem Description

More often than not, a consultant's code belongs to the client. But sometimes it is in the consultant's interest not to give away the code. The consultants at Initiative Consulting are in just such a predicament; they have used the same inventory application code in many deployments. The last thing they want to do is allow the internal IT department at their present engagement to extend their code that has evolved over several engagements. Next year's business plan includes a significant portion of revenue coming from releasing the application as a stand-alone product.

This web-based Struts application has a significant business component and is always deployed at the client site. If the consultants had used a scripting language such as Perl or VBScript, the code would be visible to anyone who has access to the web server's directories. But from previous client's support questions, it had become obvious over the past few months that their Java classfiles are being decompiled and extended.

Initiative Consulting's main objective is to protect their intellectual property. They see their options as follows:

- Employ obfuscation

- Use code generation

- Use an Application Service Provider (ASP) model

Pros and Cons

Obfuscation has some major advantages for Initiative Consulting. This inventory application has only been rolled out to a limited number of clients and is not generally available. Assuming the obfuscator does more than simply rename the methods names, then it is unlikely that their clients would have the time or the expertise to decompile the obfuscated code. More importantly, it is very unlikely that the intellectual property would be compromised by any source code finding its way into the hands of any potential competitors. The one caveat is that the obfuscator would also have to be able to handle any maintenance upgrades for software patches that get applied from time to time.

When protecting intellectual property concerns are an issue, it can help to use code generation to move the code to a higher metadata level. Because this is a Struts application, each part of the front end code—web pages, forms, actions, and beans—could be generated from an XML definition file and converted into Java Server Pages (JSP) and Java. However, the majority of the business logic is in the business layer, which is not so easy to generate.

Moving the code to an ASP model where the client enters their inventory data into remote databases would protect the real intellectual core of the code, but Initiative Consulting would need to move to a different business model to support this new infrastructure. Web services Application Programming Interfaces (APIs) would also need to be developed so that clients could still integrate the code with existing applications. However, it would still be a hard sell for any existing clients.

Solution

Initiative Consulting decided that an obfuscator that could handle maintenance releases would be the best solution for their needs. The risk of a single client decompiling the code was significant, but the risk of a client going to the trouble of trying to unravel obfuscated code was not seen as very significant. Although code generation and an ASP model were interesting to entertain, the cost would have been too prohibitive at this time.

Case Study 3: I Can't Find My Code

Here we investigate how decompilers can help when the source code is inadvertently lost or deleted.

Problem Description

Somewhere in the world just about now, some developer or manager has come to realize that they've lost their code. That sinking feeling is in their stomach as they hear the scraping sound of the hard drive whirr, a sound as unmistakable as a loose fan belt in a car, a sound that tells them that their code is now toast. Even if the developer has good backups, it can take considerable time for their network department to retrieve the appropriate backup tape. And, of course, this always happens close to a deadline or after the original developer who wrote the code has left.

Usually this only happens once or twice and then the developer suddenly becomes very adept at backing up different copies of their code on a floppy, on a USB drive, on a CD, in Visual SourceSafe or CVS,[1] and so on. Those who have been badly hit often make multiple copies just to be sure. For many, this isn't a joke and is a really painful experience that results in missing a very public deadline, or getting overlooked for a job promotion or, worse still, getting fired.

Sometimes, if they're lucky, they've written all the code in Java and have access to recent classfiles, and suddenly, a decompiler becomes their new best friend.

Pros and Cons

Decompilers really do recover the majority of the code. Sure, the comments are gone, but the developer can often use the Javadoc help files for their classes to re-create them. Thankfully, as long as they didn't obfuscate the code, it will be readable and will easily decompile.

Solution

The solution is to use a free decompiler that can be downloaded off the Web to decompile the classes. The only down side is that some of classfiles are apt to be a little out of date, but instead of losing countless hours of development time, if the developer uses such a decompiler, he or she will only loose a couple of days.

The bigger picture solution is to invest in a proper backup solution on the network and make sure that it is backed up and tested at regular intervals.

---

1. I never knew that CVS stood for Concurrent Version Systems until the editor made me look it up.

Case Study 4: See No Evil, Hear No Evil

In this case study, we examine the zero option or what happens if we completely ignore the decompilation and hope it goes away.

Problem Description

For many people, the fear of someone decompiling their Java application or applet is nowhere near the top of the list of things that they should do something about. It ranks way below installing the latest web server security patches. Sure, it's something that they'd like to protect against, but nobody has the time.

There are two simple options in this scenario:

- Use obfuscation to protect the application.

- Ignore the problem because it's not really a problem.

Pros and Cons

Obfuscation does raise the bar and stops most people from recovering your source code. The cost of decompilation is that you are giving away money spent on research and development.

However, there are many reasons to ignore the problem. It's a common belief that if you write good applications, then the source will protect itself. Using upgrades and having good support are much better ways to protect your code than obfuscation or any of the other techniques discussed in this book.

Software development is about how you apply your knowledge, not about getting access to someone else's applications. The original code these days probably came from a design pattern, so nobody cares if it's hacked. And all developers, well the good ones anyway, can always think of a better way of doing something after it's completed, so why worry?

Chances are that if someone is so unimaginative that they have to resort to stealing your code, then they won't be capable of building on the code and turning it into something useful.

Surely the problem is that someone could crack the program, but that can happen on any platform. It's not as if the newspapers are full of reports about people who decompile a product and rebadge it as their own, and we're forever hearing about the latest Microsoft exploit, so it can't be a problem.

Solution

Although I talk about reasons to protect your code throughout this book, it is often worthwhile to take some time to play devil's advocate. The solution for many is to simply ignore the problem using the arguments I just laid out and to assume that it doesn't even exist as a real issue.

Case Study 5: Ice Cream for Escrow[2]

Remember, there are other ways of protecting your code other than simple obfuscation. Here, we take a look at protecting your code legally by housing the code using a third-party company that specializes in escrowing code.

Problem Description

T & C Solutions had a profiling application that they wrote in 100-percent Java to take advantage of Sun's marketing push in the late 1990s for pure Java applications. T & C knew that obfuscation only provided limited protection, so they wanted to explore some alternative options.

The options that they saw open to them were as follows:

- Source code escrow

- Encryption

- Fingerprinting

Pros and Cons

Source code escrow is typically an agreement created as a client safeguard in case the consultant company goes out of business or some disaster occurs that makes it so they can no longer support the code. However, escrow is also a fairly simple legal option that you can use to protect your intellectual copyright. The source code can be mailed to your attorney by registered mail. This dates the source code in case any future litigation arises concerning who first produced the code. Also, several third-party companies such as Iron Mountain[3] will allow you to upload product code in a much more structured web-based environment.

---

2. With apologies to Captain Beefheart.

3. http://www.ironmountain.com

In Chapter 4, I covered why encryption wasn't the best defense against decompilation—sooner or later the classfile has to be unencrypted. With custom classloaders, it is always possible that a hacker can gain access to the bytecode. However, you can use the Digital Millennium Copyright Act (DMCA) as a defense because it makes it a crime to circumvent any anti-piracy or encryption mechanisms. So the very act of classfile encryption makes it a crime under the DMCA. However, be aware that you'll also experience a considerable performance hit if you unencrypt the code at runtime.

It's worth noting that obfuscation could be considered an anti-piracy mechanism; this means that anyone decompiling obfuscated code may be subject to prosecution under the DMCA, but that has yet to be tested in court.

I also covered fingerprinting in Chapter 4, which is where a copyright notice or watermark is applied to the binary code using a fingerprinting tool. This tool encodes the information in a dummy method that never gets executed. The fingerprint can be recovered at a later stage if the code was decompiled and then added to another application. Unfortunately, the hacker can strip the dummy method from your application, thereby removing the fingerprint.

Solution

T & C Solutions decided to escrow the code using a third-party web-based system. This was used in conjunction with a series of fingerprints within the source code so that the code could be matched to the exact source code held in escrow, just in case anyone tried to repurpose the original source.

Conclusion

When the idea for this book was first conceived, it seemed that Java applets were going to take over the Web and march all over web pages as we knew them. But this never happened. The inevitable problems with download speeds and probably most importantly, the look and feel of a Java applet all conspired to turn Java applets into little more than a niche market on the World Wide Web.

Having said that, Java has outgrown its early roots and is very unlikely to disappear any time soon. As a language, Java is quite rightly in the top tier and is used in web-related and network applications and, more increasingly, in standard desktop applications where its object-oriented nature appeals to a different audience than, say, Visual Basic. It seems that Java has found itself a nice fit somewhere between the complexity of C and C++ applications. Applets have given way to applications and servlets, which of course, cannot be easily downloaded and decompiled. But Java classes, inside or outside of a jar file, still need to be distributed whenever Java programs are sold as shrinkwrapped software, and so they are still just as susceptible to decompilation.

The security restrictions on Java applets are, not surprisingly, pretty intense—an applet has to get by the Java bytecode Verifier before it can run within the protected applet sandbox. The class loader and the Java Verifier conspire to make it even harder to obfuscate Java code. Many obfuscators and bytecode manglers fail to get past this stage, and so they are pretty much useless at protecting your applet code (classfile encryptors are particularly prone to this problem). However, now that we've all moved to a more application-centric class model, there is much more scope for protecting your Java code, that is, assuming your code does not have to pass through a Java Verifier.

Having said that, no matter what anyone tells you, although there have been some significant developments in protecting bytecode, as yet, the only secure way of protecting your code is to compile it into an executable. Sun and others will tell you that executables are not exactly safe from decompilation either. But it is several orders of magnitude more difficult to decompile an executable than it is to decompile intermediate bytecode. Unfortunately bypassing bytecode and converting it into native format destroys any portability you might hope to have because it can no longer be used on any other platform or operating system. You may then find yourself asking the question "Well, why on earth did I write it in Java in the first place?"

Will this change in the near future? Well, I may be tempting fate, but I have to feel that the JVM design will be fixed. It has taken a number of years to write this book, and during that time, nothing has changed fundamentally with the design. New keyword and constructs will always have to be added to the decompiler, but the basic architecture of the JVM will remain the same. So, unlike other programming books, I suspect that, because of backward compatibility issues, the Java classfile is always going to be susceptible to decompilation.

The whole premise of this book is to show individual users how to decompile code from Java classes and what protection schemes are available and what they actually mean. In general, people are much more curious than fraudulent, and it is highly unlikely that anyone will use a decompiler to steal a software company's crown jewel. Instead, they just want to take a peek and see how it all fits together—Java decompilers enable the average programmer to look much further into what are normally just black boxes. This book helps the user peek over that edge.

You might wonder where to go next. Things I'd suggest you try from here are using the JLex and CUP code in the downloads area of the Apress web site to try and extend the code if it doesn't decompile your particular classfile. There are also several open-source decompilers available on the Web, such as JODE, which also provide a wealth of information.

I've tried my best to make this book easy to read. I've consciously decided to make it more practical than theoretical while still trying to avoid making it just an introduction to decompilers by including and analyzing a working decompiler. I hope it was worth the effort on my part and yours, and just remember, things change fast around here, so keep an eye on the Apress website[4] for further updates.

---

4. Or http://www.decompilingjava.com

Classfile Grammar

ALTHOUGH THE complete code is on the Apress web site (http://www.apress.com), I have included the complete CUP specification here (see Listing A-1). All the underlying code has been removed, but it does provide an overview of a classfile's bytecode grammar.

Listing A-1. Bytcode Grammar

```
terminal ROOT, MAGICNUM, MAJORVER, MINORVER, CPCOUNT, CONSTPOOL, CPTAG;
terminal CPINDEX, TYPETAG, ACCFLAGS, XROOT, XMAGICNUM, XMAJORVER;
terminal XMINORVER, XCPCOUNT, XCONSTPOOL, XCPTAG, XCPINDEX, XTYPETAG;
terminal XACCFLAGS, NAMEINDEX, DESCINDEX, VALTAG, THISCL, SUPERCL, INTCNT;
terminal INTERFACES, FIELDCNT, FIELDS, FIELD, XNAMEINDEX, XDESCINDEX;
terminal XVALTAG, XTHISCL, XSUPERCL, XINTCNT, XINTERFACES, XFIELDCNT;
terminal XFIELDS, XFIELD, METHCNT, METHODS, METHOD, ATTCNT, ATTRIBS, ATTRIB;
terminal ATTTYPE, ATTTYPEINDEX, ATTLENGTH, MAXSTACK, MINSTACK;
terminal XMETHCNT, XMETHODS, XMETHOD, XATTCNT, XATTRIBS, XATTRIB;
terminal XATTTYPE, XATTTYPEINDEX, XATTLENGTH, XMAXSTACK, XMINSTACK;
terminal CODELEN, CODETAG, LINETAG, EXCLEN, EXCTABLE, CODEATTCNT;
terminal CODEATTNAME, CODEATTLEN, LNTABLECNT, LINENUMTABLE;
terminal XCODELEN, XCODETAG, XLINETAG, XEXCLEN, XEXCTABLE, XCODEATTCNT;
terminal XCODEATTNAME, XCODEATTLEN, XLNTABLECNT, XLINENUMTABLE;
terminal LINENUM, LNMAP, STARTPC, ENDPC, HANDLER, CATCHTYPE, SRCFILE;
terminal CONSTIDX, XLINENUM, XLNMAP, XSTARTPC, XENDPC, XHANDLER;
terminal XCATCHTYPE, XSRCFILE, XCONSTIDX, ACCESS, PROPERTY, CONSTNAME;
terminal CONSTANT, DECIMALPT, COMMA, CHARRAY, INTEGER, FLOAT, LONG;
terminal DOUBLE, STRING, CLASSREF, FIELDREF, METHODREF, INTERFACEREF;
terminal NAMEANDTYPE, NEGATIVE, HEXNUM, NUMBER, TYPE, ATTRIBNAME;
terminal NOP, CONST, BIPUSH, LDC, LOAD, STORE, POP, POP2, DUP, DUPX, NEW;
terminal ASTORE, ALOAD, NEWARRAY, ARRAYLENGTH;
terminal SWAP, NEG, ADD, SUB, MUL, DIV, REM, SHL, SHR, AND, OR, XOR, IINC;
terminal I2L, CMP, IF, IF_ICMP, GOTO, JSR, RET, RETURN;
terminal TABLESWITCH, LOOKUPSWITCH, GETSTATIC, GETFIELD, PUTSTATIC;
terminal PUTFIELD, INVOKE, ATHROW, CHECKCAST, INSTANCEOF;
terminal MONITORENTER, MONITOREXIT, WIDE, MULTIANEWARRAY, M1, NULL;
```

```
non terminal startfile, file, constantpool, constantelement, classname;
non terminal interfaces, fields, field, methods, method, attribs, attrib;
non terminal definitionparts, stmts, expr_part, other, property;
non terminal properties, number, type, access, return, invoke, load;
non terminal bipush, iinc, const, stackops, cmp, if_icmp, if, store, goto, arith;
non terminal conv, object, arrayops, astore, aload, newarray, codeattribs;
non terminal endcodeattribs, linenumtable, linenummapping, exceptiontable;

start with file;

startfile ::= number DECIMALPT number ROOT MAGICNUM HEXNUM XMAGICNUM
MINORVER number XMINORVER MAJORVER number XMAJORVER
            ;

file ::= startfile CPCOUNT number XCPCOUNT CONSTPOOL constantpool XCONSTPOOL
classname interfaces FIELDCNT number XFIELDCNT FIELDS XFIELDS METHCNT number
XMETHCNT METHODS methods XMETHODS ATTCNT number XATTCNT ATTRIBS attribs
XATTRIBS XROOT
      | startfile CPCOUNT number XCPCOUNT CONSTPOOL constantpool XCONSTPOOL
classname interfaces FIELDCNT number XFIELDCNT FIELDS XFIELDS METHCNT number
XMETHCNT METHODS methods XMETHODS ATTCNT number XATTCNT XROOT
      | startfile CPCOUNT number XCPCOUNT CONSTPOOL constantpool XCONSTPOOL
classname interfaces FIELDCNT number XFIELDCNT FIELDS fields XFIELDS METHCNT
number XMETHCNT METHODS methods XMETHODS ATTCNT number XATTCNT ATTRIBS
attribs XATTRIBS XROOT
      | startfile CPCOUNT number XCPCOUNT CONSTPOOL constantpool XCONSTPOOL
classname interfaces FIELDCNT number XFIELDCNT FIELDS fields XFIELDS METHCNT
number XMETHCNT METHODS methods XMETHODS ATTCNT number XATTCNT XROOT
      ;

attribs ::= attribs attrib
      | attrib
      ;

attrib ::= ATTRIB ATTTYPE ATTRIBNAME XATTTYPE ATTTYPEINDEX number
 XATTTYPEINDEX ATTLENGTH number XATTLENGTH SRCFILE number XSRCFILE
XATTRIB
      | ATTRIB ATTTYPE ATTRIBNAME XATTTYPE ATTTYPEINDEX number
XATTTYPEINDEX ATTLENGTH number XATTLENGTH CONSTIDX number XCONSTIDX
XATTRIB
      ;
```

```
constantpool ::=  constantpool CPTAG constantelement XCPTAG
               | CPTAG constantelement XCPTAG
               ;


constantelement ::=  CPINDEX number:n XCPINDEX TYPETAG CONSTANT CHARRAY:t
XTYPETAG VALTAG CONSTNAME:s XVALTAG
               | CPINDEX number:n XCPINDEX TYPETAG CONSTANT INTEGER:t
XTYPETAG VALTAG number:intVal XVALTAG
               | CPINDEX number:n XCPINDEX TYPETAG CONSTANT INTEGER:t
XTYPETAG VALTAG NEGATIVE number:intVal XVALTAG
               | CPINDEX number:n XCPINDEX TYPETAG CONSTANT LONG:t XTYPETAG
 VALTAG number:longVal
               | CPINDEX number:n XCPINDEX TYPETAG CONSTANT LONG:t XTYPETAG
 VALTAG NEGATIVE number:longVal XVALTAG
               | CPINDEX number:n XCPINDEX TYPETAG CONSTANT FLOAT:t XTYPETAG
 VALTAG number:f1 DECIMALPT number:f2 XVALTAG
               | CPINDEX number:n XCPINDEX TYPETAG CONSTANT FLOAT:t XTYPETAG
 VALTAG NEGATIVE number:f1 DECIMALPT number:f2 XVALTAG
               | CPINDEX number:n XCPINDEX TYPETAG CONSTANT DOUBLE:t XTYPETAG
 VALTAG number:d1 DECIMALPT number:d2 XVALTAG
               | CPINDEX number:n XCPINDEX TYPETAG CONSTANT DOUBLE:t XTYPETAG
 VALTAG NEGATIVE number:d1 DECIMALPT number:d2 XVALTAG
               | CPINDEX number:n XCPINDEX TYPETAG CONSTANT STRING:t XTYPETAG
 VALTAG number:index XVALTAG
               | CPINDEX number:n XCPINDEX TYPETAG CONSTANT CLASSREF:t
XTYPETAG VALTAG number:index XVALTAG
               | CPINDEX number:n XCPINDEX TYPETAG CONSTANT FIELDREF:t
XTYPETAG VALTAG number:classindex COMMA number:NaTindex XVALTAG
               | CPINDEX number:n XCPINDEX TYPETAG CONSTANT METHODREF:t
 XTYPETAG VALTAG number:classindex COMMA number:NaTindex XVALTAG
               | CPINDEX number:n XCPINDEX TYPETAG CONSTANT INTERFACEREF:t
 XTYPETAG VALTAG number:classindex COMMA number:NaTindex XVALTAG
               | CPINDEX number:n XCPINDEX TYPETAG CONSTANT NAMEANDTYPE:t
XTYPETAG VALTAG number:nameindex COMMA number:typeindex XVALTAG
               | error
               ;
```

```
classname ::= ACCFLAGS access:a XACCFLAGS THISCL number:classnum XTHISCL
  SUPERCL number XSUPERCL
            ;


interfaces ::=  INTCNT number XINTCNT INTERFACES XINTERFACES
            ;


fields ::= fields FIELD field XFIELD | FIELD field XFIELD
          ;


field ::= ACCFLAGS access:a definitionparts:params ATTCNT number XATTCNT ATTRIBS
  XATTRIBS
          ;


methods ::= methods METHOD method XMETHOD | METHOD method XMETHOD
          ;


codeattribs ::= ATTCNT number XATTCNT ATTRIBS ATTRIB ATTTYPE ATTRIBNAME
  XATTTYPE ATTTYPEINDEX number XATTTYPEINDEX ATTLENGTH number
  XATTLENGTH MAXSTACK number XMAXSTACK MINSTACK number XMINSTACK
  CODELEN number XCODELEN CODETAG
              ;


endcodeattribs ::= XCODETAG EXCLEN number XEXCLEN EXCTABLE exceptiontable
  XEXCTABLE CODEATTCNT number XCODEATTCNT CODEATTNAME number
  XCODEATTNAME CODEATTLEN number XCODEATTLEN LNTABLECNT number
  XLNTABLECNT LINENUMTABLE linenumtable XLINENUMTABLE XATTRIB XATTRIBS
              ;


linenumtable ::= linenumtable LNMAP linenummapping XLNMAP | LNMAP linenummapping
  XLNMAP
              ;


linenummapping ::=
              | STARTPC number XSTARTPC LINENUM number XLINENUM
              ;


exceptiontable ::=
              | STARTPC number XSTARTPC ENDPC number XENDPC HANDLER number
  XHANDLER CATCHTYPE number XCATCHTYPE
              ;


method ::= ACCFLAGS access:a definitionparts:desc codeattribs stmts
endcodeattribs
          ;
```

```
definitionparts ::= properties XACCFLAGS NAMEINDEX number:name XNAMEINDEX
 DESCINDEX number:params XDESCINDEX
                  | XACCFLAGS NAMEINDEX number:name XNAMEINDEX DESCINDEX
 number:params XDESCINDEX
                  ;

stmts ::= stmts LINETAG expr_part XLINETAG
        | LINETAG expr_part XLINETAG
        ;


expr_part ::= store
            | load
            | stackops
            | bipush
            | const
            | cmp
            | if_icmp
            | if
            | iinc
            | arith
            | conv
            | goto
            | number:l other
            | invoke
            | object
            | return
            | arrayops
            ;


return ::= number:l RETURN:c
        | number:l type:t RETURN:c
        ;

store ::= number:l type:t STORE:s number:n
        ;

load ::= number:l type:t LOAD:i number:n
      | number:l LDC:ld number:n
      ;

invoke ::= number:l INVOKE:s number:n
        ;
```

```
object ::= number:l NEW:s number:n
        | number:l PUTFIELD:s number:n
        | number:l PUTSTATIC:s number:n
        | number:l GETSTATIC:s number:n
        | number:l GETFIELD:s number:n
        ;


stackops ::= number:l DUP
          ;


bipush ::= number:l BIPUSH:p number:n
        ;


const ::= number:l type:t CONST:c number:n
        | number:l type:t CONST:c M1:m
        | number:l type:t CONST:c NULL:n
        ;


conv ::= number:l I2L:i type:t
      ;


arith ::= number:l type:t NEG:r
        | number:l type:t REM:r
        | number:l type:t ADD:m
        | number:l type:t SUB:m
        | number:l type:t MUL:m
        | number:l type:t DIV:m
        ;


iinc ::= number:l IINC:p number:n1 number:n2
       | number:l IINC:p number:n1 NEGATIVE number:n2
       ;


cmp ::= number:l type:t CMP:c
      ;


if_icmp ::= number:l IF_ICMP:c number:n
         ;


if ::= number:l IF:c number:n
     ;
```

```
goto ::= number:l GOTO:c number:n
     ;

arrayops ::= aload
          | astore
          | newarray
          ;

aload ::= number:l ALOAD:s
       ;

astore ::= number:l ASTORE:s
        ;

newarray ::= number:l NEWARRAY:s number:n
          | number:l type:t NEWARRAY:s number:n
          ;

number ::= NUMBER:n
        ;

access ::= | ACCESS:a
        ;

properties ::= properties property | property
             ;

property ::= PROPERTY:p
          ;

type ::= TYPE:t
      ;



other ::= NOP
       | POP
       | POP2
       | DUPX
       | SWAP
       | SHL
       | SHR
       | AND
       | OR
```

```
| XOR
| JSR
| RET
| TABLESWITCH
| LOOKUPSWITCH
| ATHROW
| CHECKCAST
| INSTANCEOF
| MONITORENTER
| MONITOREXIT
| WIDE
| MULTIANEWARRAY
| ARRAYLENGTH
;
```

Index

A

access flags
  field information in, 40–41
  for methods, 44
  overview, 35
aggregation obfuscations, 98–102
  clone methods, 100
  defined, 98
  inline and outline methods, 98–99
  interleave methods, 99
  loop transformations, 100
ALGOL, 7
aload non-terminal, 224
ANTLR, 130
applets
  protection mechanism for, 87
  searching for unlicensed, 88
  splitting code in, 106–108, 120
  writing two versions of, 86–89, 120
applications
  simple protection mechanism for, 87
  writing two versions of, 86–89, 120
architecture of JVM, 126
arith non-terminal, 196
arithmetic operations in MathOps.java,
  194–200
ArrayInit.java, 226–233
  <clinit> method, 226, 228–229
  code for decompiler, 230–232
  decompiler results for, 233
  getfield non-terminal, 229
  grammar for, 229–230
  <init> method for, 226, 227–228
  putfield non-terminal, 229–230
  putstatic non-terminal, 230
  sample listing, 227
arrays. See also ArrayInit.java;
  ArrayTest.java
  array transformations, 104
  handling initialized, 226–233
  loading string, 222–226
ArrayTest.java, 222–226
  aload non-terminal, 224
  annotated main method for, 223
  decompiler code for, 224–226
  decompiler results for, 226
  grammar for, 223–224
  newarray non-terminal, 224
  sample listing, 222
astore non-terminal, 224

Atari v. Nintendo, 12
attributes
  classfile method, 45–46
  field, 41
  getLocalHostName() method, 56
  method, 45–46
  paint() method, 58
  SourceFile and InnerClasses, 59–60
attributes count, field, 41

B

Basics.java, 190–194
  code for decompiler, 193–194
  const non-terminal, 192–193
  conv non-terminal, 193
  decompiler results, 194
  grammar for, 192–193
  ipush non-terminal, 192
  main method, 191
  original code, 190–191
  static main method, 191–192
  type conversion method, 192
Boolean split lookup table, 103
building obfuscators, 105–106
bytecodes. *See also* recovering source
  code from bytecode
  breaking into tokens, 165–170
  defined, 122
  mapping to opcodes, 48–55
  recovering source code from,
    141–148
  types of, 127

C

case studies, 237–245
  ignoring problems of decompilation,
    242–243
  J2ME obfuscation strategies, 237–239
  overview, 237, 244–245
  protecting consultant's code, 239–240
  reconstructing lost source code, 241
  source code escrow, 243–244
Casting class, 114
Cifuentes, Christina, 123–124, 141,
  143–144, 148
class data section of ClassToXML, 160,
  162
class fields. *See* fields
class methods. *See* methods

class transformations, 103–104
classfiles, 22–60. *See also* constant
    pools
  access flags, 35
  attributes count for fields, 41
  bytecode grammar for CUP
    specification, 247–254
  bytecode to opcode mapping for
    methods, 48–55
  constant pool, 26–35
  constant pool count, 26
  decompiler design and elements of,
    125–127
  design and function of, 18
  disassembled XML, 25
  fields, 38–41
  interfaces, 36–38
  JavaDump effects on, 71
  magic number, 25–26
  method attributes for, 45–46
  methods, 42–59
  minor and major version numbers,
    26
  parts of, 23–24
  SourceFile and InnerClasses
    attributes, 59–60
  structure of, 24
  This and Super classes, 36
classname non-terminal, 178
ClassNavigator, 67, 69–70
ClassToSource decompiler, 121
ClassToXML output file, 159–165
  ArrayTest.java main method, 223
  Basics.java main method, 191
  class data section of, 162
  constant pool entries for, 160–161,
    162–163, 165
  converting classfiles to XML, 156
  exception handling tables ignored by,
    235
  field data overview of, 162–163
  format of, 160
  MathOps.java main method, 195–196
  method data in, 163–165
  terminals, 174
clone methods for aggregation
  obfuscations, 100
cmp non-terminal, 204
code fingerprinting, 14
codeattribs non-terminal, 179
compilation flags, 81–86, 120
  compiling with -g flags, 81–86
  decompiled version of
    HelloWorld.java, 84–86
  effect on HelloWorld.java bytecode,
    81–82
  removing information in
    HelloWorld.classfile with, 82–84

compiler-compiler tools, 128–130. *See
    also* CUP compiler-compiler tool
compilers, 2–3
computation obfuscation, 94–98. *See
    also* obfuscators
  adding redundant operands, 96–97
  extending loop conditions, 94
  inserting dead or irrelevant code, 94
  parallelizing code, 97–98
  unreducible bytecode control flow,
    94–96
  writing sloppy code, 97
conditional statements. *See also* loops
  DoWhile.java, 200–210
  extending loop conditions for
    obfuscation, 94
  ForLoop.java, 217–222
  IfTest.java, 200–210
  loops and goto statements, 95, 142
  resolving with WhileLoop.java,
    213–217
  WhileLoop.java, 213–217
const non-terminal, 192–193
constant pool count, 26
constant pools, 26–35
  ClassToXML entries for, 160–161,
    162–163, 165
  CONSTANT_Utf8_info structure, 27
  cp_info structure, 26
  Hello.class, 28–33
  JVM field descriptors, 34
  reading, 183
  tags, 27
constantelement non-terminal, 177–178
constantpool non-terminal, 176–177
CONSTANT_Utf8_info structure, 27
control obfuscations, 93–102
  aggregations, 98–102
  computation transformations, 94–98
  ordering transformations, 100–102
  transformations with, 89
conv non-terminal, 193
converting static to procedural data, 103
copyright laws and decompiled code,
  9–12
costs
  defined, 80
  overview of strategy, 120
cp_info structure, 26
Crema, 9, 91–92
CUP compiler-compiler tool. *See also*
    CUP decompiler specification
  debugging output for, 139–140
  declarations in, 136
  derivative of Yacc parser, 135–136
  grammar for, 139–140
  installing, 136
  overview, 129

symbols in, 137–139
user routines, 137
CUP decompiler specification
    bytecode grammar for, 247–254
    classname non-terminal, 178
    codeattribs non-terminal, 179
    constantelement non-terminal,
       177–178
    constantpool non-terminal, 176–177
    Decompiler.CUP decompiler
       specification, 153–156
    definitionparts non-terminal, 181
    exceptionable non-terminal, 180
    fields non-terminal, 178–179
    file non-terminal, 175–176
    interfaces non-terminal, 178
    linenumtable and linenummapping
       non-terminal, 180
    listing of all non-terminals, 175
    methods non-terminal, 179–181
    miscellaneous non-terminals,
       181–182
    opcode terminals for, 174–175
    resolveConstant method, 171–173
    skeleton specification for
       decompiler, 170–171
    startfile non-terminal, 176
    stmts non-terminal, 181
custom class loaders, 108–109

D

data obfuscation, 89, 102–104
    converting static to procedural data,
       103
    storage and encoding methods,
       102–103
    transformation data via aggregation,
       103–104
    transformations with, 89–90
dcc decompiler
    back-end processing, 144
    front-end parser, 143
    origins of, 3
    UDM, 141, 143, 144
dead code, 94
declarations in CUP, 136
decompiler code
    ArrayInit.java, 230–232
    ArrayTest.java, 224–226
    Basics.java, 193–194
    DoWhile.java and IfTest.java, 210
    ForLoop.java, 219–222
    IfTest.java, 204–209
    MathOps.java, 197–200
    Recurses.java, 213
    WhileLoop.java, 215–216
Decompiler.cup, 153–156

Decompiler.lex, 151–152
decompilers, 72–75. *See also*
    ClassToXML output file; designing
       decompilers; implementing
       decompilers
    dcc, 3, 141, 143–144
    about decompiling, 1
    decompiled fingerprinted code,
       115–116
    decompiling exceptions, 56–57
    decompiling interpreters, 124
    development of, 6–9, 122–125
    functions of, 2–3
    ignoring problems of decompilation,
       242–243
    JAD, 74
    Java's vulnerability to, 3–5
    JODE, 74–75
    legal implications of, 9–12
    Mocha, 1, 9, 73
    moral issues of decompiling, 12–13
    overview, 72
    reconstructing lost source code, 241
    skeleton CUP, 170–171
    SourceAgain, 73–74
    virtual machine, 3
    Visual Basic, 8–9
definitionparts non-terminal, 181
design of classfiles, 18
designing decompilers, 121–157
    classfile and JVM elements in,
       125–127
    design of JVM and, 123
    parser design, 149–156
    recovering source code from
       bytecode, 141–148
    tools used, 128–140
    using compiler-compiler tools,
       128–130
DFA (deterministic finite automata), 152
Diettrich, Hans-Peter, 8–9
digital fingerprinting code, 110–117, 120
    Casting class with dummy method,
       114
    Casting target class, 113
    criteria for good, 112
    decompiled fingerprinted code,
       115–116
    examples of, 113–117
    jmark command-line parameters,
       114
    recovering fingerprint, 115
Digital Millennium Copyright Act
    (DMCA), 10
Digital Rights Management (DRM)
    software, 109–110, 120
directives in JLex, 132–133
disassembled XML classfile, 25

disassemblers, 67–72
    ClassNavigator, 67, 69–70
    IceBreaker, 67, 68–69
    JavaDump, 70–72
    overview, 67–68
divider tokens, 160
DMCA (Digital Millennium Copyright
    Act), 10
DOS decompilers, 7
DoWhile.java, 200–210
    annotated main method of, 201–202
    cmp non-terminal, 204
    decompiler results for, 210
    grammar for, 202–204
    if non-terminal, 203
    listing for, 200
DRM (Digital Rights Management)
    software, 109–110, 120
dummy constructors, 183
dummy methods, 111, 112, 114

E

educational uses for Java
    decompilation, 13, 16
encoding, 102
encryption, 108–109, 120
end tokens, 160
*EU Directive on Legal Protection of
    Computer Programs*, 11
European Union (EU) licensing laws, 10,
    11
evaluation copies, 86
evolution of decompilers, 6–9
exceptionable non-terminal, 180
exceptions
    decompiling, 56–57
    exception handling tables, 235

F

fair use laws, 10
fields, 38–41
    attributes count, 41
    defined, 126
    field data section of ClassToXML,
        160, 162–163
    field descriptors for constant pool, 34
    finding human interface's, 39–40
    forcing field attributes in Hello
        localhost, 28
    information in access flags, 40–41
fields non-terminal, 178–179
file non-terminal, 175–176
files. *See also* classfiles
    adding line numbers to JLex, 133–135
    classfiles, 22–25
    divisions of JLex, 131

fingerprinting. *See* digital fingerprinting
    code
flow analysis tools, 128
ForLoop.java, 217–222
    decompiler code for, 219–222
    decompiler results for, 222
    goto non-terminal for, 218
    sample listings, 217–218
fragile super classes, 124

G

-g flags, 81–86
getfield non-terminal, 229
getLocalHostName() method, 48–57
goto non-terminal
    ForLoop.java, 218
    WhileLoop.java, 214–215
goto statements
    breaking out of control loop with, 95
    example of poor, 145–146
    pseudocode replacing, 145
    transforming into loops and breaks,
        142
grammar
    ArrayInit.java, 229–230
    ArrayTest.java, 223–224
    Basics.java, 192–193
    CUP, 139–140, 247–254
    decompiled HelloWorld.java,
        184–186
    DoWhile.java, 202–204
    IfTest.java, 202–204
    MathOps.java, 196–197
    Recurses.java, 212–213
    WhileLoop.java, 214–215

H

HAT (Heap Analysis Tool), 20
heap, 19, 20
Hello.class
    constant pool, 28–33
    hexadecimal dump of, 22–23
    methods, 42–44
Hello.java, 22, 149–150
HelloWorld.classfile, 82–84
HelloWorld.java
    basic decompiler operations with,
        182–190
    compilation flag effects on bytecode
        in, 81–82
    decompiled version of, 84–86
    decompiler code for, 186–190
    dummy and main methods for,
        183–184
    grammar for decompiled, 184–186
    invoke non-terminal in, 185–186

load non-terminal in, 185
object non-terminal in, 186
return non-terminal in, 184
store non-terminal in, 184
HelloWorld thread example, 98
hexadecimal dump of Hello.class, 22–23
hexidecimal editors, 7, 61–64
high-mode obfuscation, 90
HoseMocha, 94
human interfaces for classfile, 36–37

I

IceBreaker, 67, 68–69
if non-terminal, 203
if statements, 146–148
if-else statements, 211
if_icmp non-terminal, 203
IfTest.java, 200–210
   annotated main method of, 202
   cmp non-terminal, 204
   decompiler code for, 204–209
   decompiler results for, 210
   grammar for, 202–204
   if non-terminal, 203
   if_icmp non-terminal, 203
   listing for, 200–201
iinc non-terminal, 196–197
implementing decompilers, 159–236.
   See also test suite programs; *and*
   programs listed by name
   ArrayInit.java in test suite, 226–233
   ArrayTest.java in test suite, 222–226
   Basics.java in test suite, 190–194
   ClassToXML output file, 159–165
   CUP specification, 170–175
   dealing with remaining opcodes,
      234–235
   decompiler code for HelloWorld.java,
      186–190
   DoWhile.java and IfTest.java in test
      suite, 200–210
   dummy and main methods for
      HelloWorld.java, 183–184
   exception handling tables, 235
   ForLoop.java in test suite, 217–222
   HelloWorld.java in test suite, 182–190
   JLex specification, 165–170
   MathOps.java in test suite, 194–200
   overview, 159
   problems of decompilation, 235
   programs in test suite, 182
   Recurses.java in test suite, 211–213
   summary of, 233–236
   tips for decompiling unparsed
      opcodes, 233–235
   WhileLoop.java in test suite,
      213–217

<init> methods
   for ArrayInit.java, 226, 227–228
   unraveling, 47–48
inline and outline aggregation methods,
   98–99
InnerClasses attributes, 59–60
insecure code, 64–67
installing
   CUP, 136
   JLex, 134
interface as classfile element, 36–38, 126
interfaces non-terminal, 178
interleaving aggregation methods, 99
invoke non-terminal, 185–186
IPR (Intellectual Property Rights)
   protection schemes, 14–15,
   109–110, 120
ipush non-terminal, 192
irrelevant code, 94

J

J2ME obfuscation strategies, 237–239
JAD (Java Decompiler), 74
Java
   bytecode to opcode mapping, 48–55
   decompiler design in, 123–125
   decompiling interpreters, 124
   educational uses for decompilation,
      13, 16
   example of source code, 5
   fragile super classes, 124
   software protection for, 13–15
   taking advantage of insecure code,
      64–67
   vulnerability to decompilation, 3–5
Java Decompiler (JAD), 74
Java Native Interface (JNI), 117
Java Tree Builder (JTB), 128
Java Virtual Machine. *See* JVM
JavaDump, 70–72
javap source code output, 5–6
Jive, 142, 146–148
JJTree, 128
JLex
   adding line numbers to files with
      scanner, 133–135
   breaking bytecodes into tokens with,
      165–170
   directives in, 132–133
   file divisions in, 131
   installing, 134
   main method bytecode, 151
   overview, 129, 131–132
   regular expression rules for, 133
   user code in, 132
jmark, 112, 113
JNI (Java Native Interface), 117, 118–119

JOBE, 92–93
JODE, 74–75
JTB (Java Tree Builder), 128
JVM (Java Virtual Machine). *See also*
    classfiles
    architecture of, 126
    classfiles and classfile elements,
        22–25, 125–127
    decompiler design and design of, 123
    decompiling Java with, 1, 3–6
    field descriptors, 34
    heap, 19, 20
    Java's vulnerability to decompilation,
        3–5
    method area, 20, 21
    obfuscators compatible with, 90
    opcodes in, 122, 127–128
    program counter registers, 20, 21
    publications about, 17
    stack and stack processor, 20, 21, 126
    structure of, 19–20

K

Krakatoa decompilation, 142, 144–146,
    149

L

LALR(1) parser, 130
layout obfuscations, 89, 91–93
legal implications of decompilers, 9–12
Lex, 128, 129, 130
licensing software, 86–88
linenumtable and linenummapping
    non-terminal, 180
LL(k) parsers, 130
load non-terminal, 185
loops
    breaking out of control, 95
    extending loop conditions, 94
    goto conditional, 214–215
    implementing while, 217–222
    loop transformations, 100
    reorder, 101–102
    reversing, 102
    transforming for aggregation
        obfuscations, 100
    unrolling, 100
    WhileLoop.java, 213–217

M

magic numbers, 25–26
main method bytecode for JLex, 151
MathOps.java, 194–200
    annotated main method in, 195–196
    arith non-terminal, 196

decompiler code for, 197–199
decompiler results for, 199–200
grammar for, 196–197
iinc non-terminal, 196–197
original code for, 195
merging scalar variables, 103
methods, 42–59
    access flags for, 44
    annotated Recurses.java, 211–212
    ArrayInit.java <clinit>, 226, 228–229
    ArrayInit.java <init>, 226, 227–228
    ArrayTest.java main, 223
    attributes for, 45–46
    Basics.java, 191–192
    code attributes for exceptions, 56–57
    decompiling getLocalHostName(),
        48–57
    DoWhile.java, 201–202
    dummy and main HelloWorld.java,
        183–184
    as element of classfile, 126
    Hello.class, 42–44
    invoking, 182–183
    MathOps.java, 195–196
    method area of JVM, 20, 21
    method data in ClassToXML output
        file, 160, 163–165
    native, 19, 117–119, 120
    paint(), 57–59
    resolveConstant, 171–173
    unraveling <init>, 47–48
    WhileLoop.java main, 214
methods non-terminal, 179–181
Mocha, 1, 9, 73
moral issues of decompiling Java, 12–13

N

Native Method Interface (NMI), 117
native methods, 19, 117–119, 120
newarray non-terminal, 224
NMI (Native Method Interface), 117
non-terminals
    aload, 224
    arith, 196
    astore, 224
    classname, 178
    cmp, 204
    constantelement, 177–178
    constantpool, 176–177
    CUP specification, 175
    definitionparts, 181
    exceptionable, 180
    fields, 178–179
    file, 175–176
    getfield, 229
    goto, 214–215, 218
    if, 203

if_icmp, 203
iinc, 196–197
interfaces, 178
invoke, 185–186
ipush, 192
linenumtable and linenummapping,
   180
load, 185
methods, 179–181
miscellaneous CUP, 181–182
newarray, 224
object, 186
parsing behavior in CUP, 175
putfield, 229–230
putstatic, 230
resolving tokens and terminals into, 174
return, 184
startfile, 176
stmts, 181
store, 184
Num.lex scanner, 133–135

O

obfuscators, 88–106, 120. *See also*
   aggregation obfuscations;
   computation obfuscation; ordering
   obfuscations
   building, 105–106
   case study of J2ME obfuscation
      strategies, 237–239
   control obfuscation, 89, 93–102
   data obfuscation, 89, 102–104
   defeating decompilers with, 235
   high-mode obfuscation, 90
   layout obfuscation, 89, 91–93
   overview, 75–76, 88–90, 104–105
   protecting code with, 14–15
   types of, 89
object non-terminal, 186
opcodes
   dealing with remaining, 234–235
   defined, 122
   in JVM instruction set, 122, 127–128
   mapping bytecodes to, 48–55
   tips for decompiling unparsed, 233–235
ordering obfuscations, 100–102
   reorder loops, 101–102
   reorder statements and expressions,
      100–101
ordering transformations, 104
oStackDebug and finalStackDebug
   sample listings, 173

P

paint() method attributes, 45–46, 57–59
parallelizing code, 97–98

Parser.cup, 138–139
parsers
   dcc front-end, 143
   CUP and Yacc, 135–136
   designing, 149–156
   LALR(1), 130
   LL(k), 130
   Parser.cup sample listing, 138–139
   recovering source code with single
      pass parser, 142, 148
   single pass, 142, 148
   terminals and non-terminals in CUP,
      175
p-code (pseudocode)
   overview, 9
   replacing goto statements, 145
peephole optimization, 142
potency, 80, 120
program counter registers, 20, 21
protecting source code, 79–120. *See also*
   obfuscators
   compilation flags, 81–86, 120
   digital fingerprinting code, 110–117,
      120
   digital rights management software,
      109–110, 120
   encryption, 108–109, 120
   native methods, 117–119, 120
   obfuscation, 88–106, 120
   overview, 79–81
   selling source code, 117, 120
   strategies for, 120
   web services and server-side
      execution, 106–108, 120
   writing two versions of code, 86–89,
      120
pseudocode. *See* p-code
publications about JVM, 17
putfield non-terminal, 229–230
putstatic non-terminal, 230

R

Ramshaw's algorithm, 142, 144–146, 149
recovering source code from bytecode,
   141–148
   Jive, 142, 146–148
   overview, 141–142
   Ramshaw's algorithm, 142, 144–146,
      149
   single pass parser, 142, 148
   universal decompiling machine, 141,
      143–144
recurse method
   annotated methods of Recurses.java,
      211–212
   ClassToXML constant pool output, 165
   ClassToXML data output for, 164–165

Recurses.java, 211–213
  annotated methods of, 211–212
  decompiler results for, 213
  grammar, code, and output for,
    212–213
  sample listing, 211
redundant operands, 96–97
registers and decompiler design, 123
regular expression rules for JLex, 133
reorder loops, 101–102
reorder statements and expressions,
  100–101
resilience, 80, 120
resolveConstant method, 171–173
return non-terminal, 184
reverse engineering, 10, 11

S

sample listings
  annotated ArrayInit.java <clinit>
    method, 228–229
  annotated ArrayInit.java <init>
    method, 227–228
  annotated Basics.java method, 191
  annotated DoWhile.java method,
    201–202
  annotated IfTest.java method, 202
  annotated MathOps.java method,
    195–196
  annotated type conversion method
    for Basics.java, 192
  arr field for ClassToXML, 162–163
  ArrayTest.java, 222
  breaking out of control loop with
    goto statement, 95
  Casting target class, 113
  classfile structure, 24
  ClassToXML constant pool output for
    recurse, 165
  ClassToXML terminals, 174
  codeattribs non-terminal, 179
  compilation flag effects on bytecode,
    81–82
  compilation flags in
    HelloWorld.classfile, 82–84
  const non-terminal for Basics.java,
    192–193
  constant pool entries for
    ClassToXML, 160–161
  constantelement non-terminal in
    CUP, 177–178
  constantpool non-terminal in CUP,
    176–177
  CONSTANT_Utf8_info structure, 27
  conv non-terminal for Basics.java,
    193
  cp_info structure, 26

Crema-protected code, 91–92
CUP non-terminals, 175
CUP specification, 170–171
CUP user routines, 137
custom class loaders, 108–109
debugging output for CUP, 139–140
decompiled fingerprinted code,
  115–116
decompiled HelloWorld.java, 84–86
decompiled output for
  HelloWorld.java, 190
decompiler code for Basics.java,
  193–194
decompiler code for HelloWorld.java,
  186–190
decompiler code for IfTest.java,
  204–209
decompiler code for MathOps.java,
  197–199
Decompiler.cup, 153–156
Decompiler.lex, 151–152
decompiler results for ArrayInit.java,
  233
decompiler results for DoWhile.java
  and IfTest.java, 210
decompiling if statements in Jive,
  146–148
definitionparts non-terminal in CUP,
  181
digital fingerprint, 115
disassembled XML classfile, 25
DoWhile.java, 200
dummy and main methods for
  HelloWorld.java, 183–184
exceptionable non-terminal in CUP,
  180
fields of human interface, 39–40
file non-terminal in CUP, 175–176
Hello.class, 22–23
Hello.class constant pool, 28–33
Hello.class methods, 42–44
Hello.java, 22, 149–150
Hello Localhost with initializers, 38
HelloWorld thread example, 98
hex dump of test class, 63–64
human interfaces for classfile, 36–37
IfTest.java, 200–201
insecure code, 64–66
Java source code, 5
javap source code output, 5–6
jmark command-line parameters,
  114
JNI header file, 118–119
linenumtable and linenummapping
  non-terminal in CUP, 180
loop reversals, 102
loop unrolling, 100
main method bytecode, 151

method non-terminal in CUP, 180
native methods in code, 118
Num.lex scanner, 133–135
obfuscating strings added to
    XMLToClass example, 106
opcode terminals for CUP
    specification, 174–175
original Basics.java code, 190–191
original code for MathOps.java, 195
oStackDebug and finalStackDebug,
    173
paint method attributes, 45–46
Parser.cup, 138–139
pseudocode replacing goto
    statements, 145
recovering fingerprint, 115
recurse method data output in
    ClassToXML, 164–165
Recurses.java, 211
resolveConstant method, 171–173
showBalance and emailInvoice, 99
showBalanceEmailInvoice, 99
simple protection mechanism for
    applications, 87
startfile non-terminal in CUP, 176
stmts non-terminal in CUP, 181
variable obfuscations, 102–103
variable swapping, 101
XML-RPC client method call, 107
XML-RPC response, 108
XMLToClass example, 105–106
SandMark, 113
Sega v. Accolade, 11–12
selling source code, 117, 120
server-side protection of source,
    106–108, 120
single pass parsers, 142, 148
software
    Digital Rights Management, 109–110,
        120
    licensing, 86–88
    protection strategies for Java, 13–15
source code. *See also* protecting source
    code; recovering source code from
    bytecode
    compilation flags in, 81–86, 120
    decompiling to understand JVM, 1
    digital fingerprinting of, 110–117, 120
    digital rights management software
        for, 109–110, 120
    encrypting, 108–109, 120
    example of Java, 5
    native methods and, 117–119, 120
    obfuscation of, 88–106, 120
    protecting consultant's code,
        239–240
    reconstructing lost, 241
    recovering from bytecode, 141–148

selling, 117, 120
source code escrow, 243–244
web services and server-side
    execution of, 106–108, 120
writing two versions of, 86–89, 120
SourceFile attributes, 59–60
stacks
    defined, 20, 21
    operations in goto, 214–215
    resolving CUP constant pool with,
        173
    stack processor in JVM, 126
start tokens, 160
startfile non-terminal, 176
static methods
    Basics.java, 191–192
    invocation of, 211
stmts non-terminal, 181
storage and encoding methods for data
    obfuscation, 102–103
store non-terminal, 184
stretching loops, 145
Super class, 36
symbols in CUP, 137–139

T

tags, constant pool, 27
terminals. *See also* non-terminals
    ClassToXML, 174
    CUP opcode, 174–175
    parsing behavior in CUP, 175
    resolving into non-terminals, 174
test suite programs. *See also programs
    listed by name*
    ArrayInit.java, 226–233
    ArrayTest.java, 222–226
    Basics.java, 190–194
    DoWhile.java, 200–210
    ForLoop.java, 217–222
    HelloWorld.java, 182–190
    IfTest.java, 200–210
    listing of, 182
    MathOps.java, 194–200
    Recurses.java, 211–213
    WhileLoop.java, 213–217
This class, 36
tokens
    breaking bytecodes into, 165–170
    ClassToXML output file, 160
    resolving into non-terminals, 174
tools, 61–77, 128–140
    decompilers, 72–75
    disassemblers, 67–72
    flow analysis, 128
    hexidecimal editors, 61–64
    Lex, 128, 129, 130
    obfuscators, 75–76

used for designing decompilers,
128–140
using compiler-compiler, 128–130
transformations
array, 104
class, 103–104
computation, 94–98
data obfuscation and, 89–90
loop, 100
ordering, 104
threads for confusing hackers,
103–104
TVC (Transient Variable Caching),
101

U

UDM (universal decompiling machine),
141, 143, 144
U.S. Copyright Act, 12
user code in JLex, 132
user routines in CUP, 137

V

Van Vliet, Hanpeter, 7, 9
variables
Basics.java handling of, 190–194
merging scalar, 103
splitting to create obfuscation, 103
variable swapping, 101
version numbers, 26
virtual machine decompilers, 3
virtual methods, 211
Visual Basic decompilers, 8–9

W

web services and server-side execution,
106–108, 120
WhileLoop.java, 213–217
annotated main method of, 214
decompiler code for, 215–216
decompiler results for, 217
goto non-terminal, 214–215
grammar for, 214–215
sample listings, 213

X

XML-RPC
client method call, 107
response, 108
XMLToClass disassembler
obfuscating strings added to, 106
original sample listing, 105–106
XMLToSource decompiler
resolveConstant method in CUP
specification, 171–173
skeleton CUP specification for,
170–171
viewing basic operations in
HelloWorld.java, 182–190

Y

Yacc. *See also* CUP compiler-compiler
tool
CUP as derivative of, 135–136
function of, 135
overview, 128, 129, 130–131